We CAN GET *There* FROM HERE

We CAN GET There FROM HERE

by Christopher Phelan

Simi Valley, CA

Copyright © 2011 by C.M.R. Phelan

Terra Nova Publishing LLC
543 Country Club Drive, #B-301
Simi Valley, CA 93065
www.terranovapublishingllc.com

All rights reserved. No part of this book my be reproduced without written permission from the publisher, except by a reviewer who may quote brief passages or reproduce illustrations in a review, nor may any part of this book be reproduced, stored in a retrieval system, or transmitted in any form or by any means electronic, mechanical, photocopying, recording, or other, without written permission of the publisher.

Printed in the United States of America

ISBN Paperback Version: 978-0-9837786-2-2
ISBN Kindle Version: 978-0-9837786-3-9

First Printing 2011

Cover and Interior Design: Creative Publishing Book Design

Dedication

This book is dedicated to my wife, Carole, who inspired, encouraged and supported me through all the years of growth, preparation and writing with her loving care. That love was deeply returned by the author.

Christopher J. Phelan

Note to the Reader

On July 20, 2004 at 11:40 p.m. my beloved husband left this planet and returned to the Father's House. He left this manuscript behind, asking me to edit it and take steps to have it published. With his help from the 'other side' I have done so, and trust that the reader will find it as rewarding as I found my work on it, which I dedicate with all my love to him.

Carole Mary Phelan

Contents

Acknowledgements	xi
Preface	xiii
Introduction	1
1 Psychic Man Is a Total Entity	5
2 Creation Is Here to Stay	17
3 The Prodigal Son	33
4 Getting Rid of Mistakes	49
5 The Impersonal Life	57
6 Atlantis – The Creation Saga	71
7 Ambassadors of the Spiritual World	83
8 Spirit Teachers and Guides	97
9 The Rise of Aquarian Consciousness	111
10 Karmic Law and Spiritual Ignorance	123
11 Spiritual Growth and Sexual Unfoldment	129
12 Endless Love Here and Now	145

13	Endless Love and the Seven Sacred Planets	155
14	Is Satan for Real?	165
15	Can We Really Know God?	179
16	Invoke – Don't Beg	191
17	Becoming a Whole Person	205
18	Truth Develops Awareness	219
19	Can Consciousness Be Individualized?	231
20	From Individual to Collective Consciousness	239
21	Becoming Universal Mind	249
22	The Mind Is a Broad Avenue	261
23	Living the Spiritual Life	273
24	Creating Our Tomorrow Today	287
25	The Future of Man	301

Acknowledgements

Everyone who has ever written a book, worked as a teacher or managed a business knows that preceding them is a whole retinue of inspiring forebears. The present writer is no exception, and the list of acknowledgements below is a mere short list of those who have inspired the present work.

ALDER, Vera Stanley	KNIGHT, Gareth
BARDO, Franz	KRISHNAMURTI, J.
BEHNER, Joseph S.	KUHN, Alvin Boyd
BLAVATSKY, H.P.	LEADBETTER, C.W.
CAMPBELL, Joseph	LeMESURIER, Paul
CHURCHWARD, James	LETHBRIDGE, Thomas
DE CHARDIN, Pierre Teilhard	LEVI
DONNELLY, Ignatius	MERTENS-STIENON, M.
GAUQUELIN, Michel	MICHEL, John
GIBRAN, Kahlil	NICOL, Maurice
GOLDSMITH, Joel	OUSPENSKY, P.D.
GREENLEES, Duncan	ROBERTSON, John
GREY, William	SAGAN, Carl

HEINDEL, Max
HELENE, Corinne
HIERONYMOUS, Robert
HODSON, Geoffrey
HOLROYD, Stuart
HOUSTON, Jean
JUNG, Carl

SINNETT, A.P.
SPENCE, Lewis
STEINER, Rudolf
TOMPKINS, Peter
UNGER, Merrill F.
VELIKOVSKY, Immanuel
WAITE, A.E.

And the following:
      THE BHAGAVAD GITA
      THE HOLY BIBLE
      THE UPANISHADS

Preface

Anyone who reads this book will find that it is not a book of new ideas, but a work of eternal ideas clothed in different words from those in which they were presented in the past. It is the writer's belief that all ideas have existed in eternality since before time and space began. As spiritual evolution has progressed, and the created universe continues to come into manifestation, humanity has introduced new words to describe its understanding of that which is now in outer existence.

It is true that in presenting these eternal ideas in an altered format or even perhaps in a different sequence, we will see for the first time a whole new dimension of spiritual understanding. I offer these ideas in their present format because I have found them to assist me in my search for an identity and expression of life beyond that most of us experience in the mundane. I now *know* that we can get there from here.

Introduction

This book is an attempt to offer support for those who are already convinced that life has more to offer than they have yet seen. These pages may well provide the map they are seeking, in much the same way it has for myself.

In any serious pursuit of the "better life", we must begin our search with an honest appraisal of our current status. If we lie let us admit it to ourselves, and if we are frequently unhappy let us not pretend to others that we live the life of a saint's serenity. Any journey of self-discovery must start from where we are right now, and not from where we would like to be.

When we look at our life, we see people and things with which we are familiar and with which, for the most part, we feel secure. We have parents, sisters, brothers, relatives, friends, working companions and all sorts of people we encounter at irregular intervals. We also have regularized and acceptable phenomena – sunlight, moonlight, wind, rain and snow. In addition, we have acquired all kinds of personal possessions. All these make up the world that is presented to our senses on a daily basis. This is the Cosmos which is in manifestation in our private lives.

There is, however, another part of the Cosmos with which we are all intimately related – the world of our own 'inner beingness'. It is in the interaction of these two worlds that creation and growth take place. This is where the outer Cosmos, impacting upon our personality, produces either a reaction or a response. When it is a reaction, it stems from the personality; when it is a response it emanates from the inner being and causes us to manifest another step on our long evolutionary journey.

This is the domain of all philosophical, religious and psychological teaching. The twelve great religious scriptures of the world all tell the same creation story: "In the beginning God created the heavens and the earth....". What does this mean in real terms for us in the here and now? It means that the creation process was established at the very beginning of the Cosmos and that there is no evidence of any change in the process since. It is still in operation. It also means that thought, the instrument of consciousness, is the precursor of all material expression by which we are surrounded. And, finally, it means that the process continues to be constantly active.

Although this process has not ceased to function, it is currently widely overlooked, especially in our intimate daily lives. In times of stress, awareness of our 'thought process' almost disappears altogether. However, the impetus of creation continues to function even while awareness of it remains occluded.

When we look a little deeper at this phenomenon of occlusion we find this to be where the majority of mankind resides today. As the creative power or impetus of evolution descends from the state of Chaos (the state of no-thing-ness) through the varying and increasingly denser planes of life, it surrenders its rarefied 'Beingness" to the condition we call solidness. The other name for this condition is effect. Together with the increasing density there is a corresponding increase in occlusion. This occlusion conveys us into the plane of the 'underworld' (hell or earth) with a resulting loss of awareness of our origin.

This means that we, Divine Spirit or Universal Consciousness, have consciously ordained our sojourn of density and occlusion. We are the lost sheep of scripture. As lost sheep we are victims, and remain so as long as we remain dogmatic and adamant on the limitations of our condition. We are much like the drunk in the hypnotist's stage show.

Because we live in the modern world of nuclear physics, we must give attention to our place in this world. This is where the impact point of consciousness is focalized at this time. No amount of wishful thinking will alter this fact. Alteration will not take place in that way. At this time humanity is poised on the threshold of an escape hatch from occlusion and disorientation, and where we are right now in our evolutionary journey is not a bad place to be.

We have already established that the atom, a basic unit of matter, is composed of no-thing-ness, other than a field of positive and negative energy. We have learned how we can rearrange the adjustment within the atom in order to change one element into another. This is the state of Man's science here and now. This is the state of the art of our awareness of the creation process.

In the past the alchemists (forerunners of today's scientists) blended both material and esoteric knowledge in the production of a science intended to speed up the process of evolutionary nature. They worked on the transmutation of matter and the transformation of themselves simultaneously. They worked on capturing the essence of cosmic mechanics to transmute both mineral and mankind. We have now reached the point in our resurrection and ascension where we can pick up the work of the alchemists and actively begin to change ourselves and the material world we have manifested.

How then do you and I move from occlusion and effect to awareness and enlightenment? First and foremost, we must, at the very least, begin to realize that there is a greater power than can be generated by the biology of the human body. The energy of the food chain and the smoke stack will not suffice for atomic man. This power is available to each of us because it is already the very essence of our beingness. In fact, it is our beingness. It is consciousness itself and there is no-one living on this earth, or beyond, who would deny that they are conscious.

We must, if we are to resolve the issues of our daily living, accept the responsibility of our consciousness being the source of all our manifestation. We must accept that consciousness as being the creative consciousness, the *only* consciousness. We cannot be in charge of our lives if we place the causation factor outside our own beingness. If we do that we must have duality or 'strange gods', and "a kingdom divided against itself cannot stand".

We must begin to attune our thoughts to the realization that there is but one source for all the diversity in universal expression. Any mental hedging on this can only result in continued occlusion and material dis-ease and disorder. We cannot be 'creators' as long as we choose to be effect.

Our Saviour and/or Messiah is the vibration or plane of consciousness wherein we recognize our origin and ongoing status of Divinity – "I and my Father are One; all that the Father has is mine; the place whereon I stand is Holy Ground".

With this recognition we enter the world of the inner life of peace, joy and dominion, and an outer life in complete harmony with ourselves and with all the world of Mankind, animal and matter. This is where we can go from here to There, and we can go right now.

CJP

Chapter 1

Psychic Man Is a Total Entity

At first glance the title of this chapter may give an appearance of a discrepancy or a separateness between the word psychic and the word man. In actual fact there is no separateness at all. Then what is this thing we call psychic or psyche? It is after all a word we hear being bandied about quite a bit in our society today, even if many who use it do not really know what it means. The word psyche is a Greek word meaning Soul (the Center of Beingness).

This Soul Center of Beingness is the point of appearance of individual consciousness emerging from Universal Consciousness. It is what is called the 'birth of Venus'. What is being talked about here is the condition where individual Soul expression manifests for the very first time in the Cosmos. This emergence or first manifestation from the condition of Chaos or the state of no-thing-ness, carries with it all the potentialities of the state of humanhood which we see manifested here and now. Man, therefore, is nothing less than the expression of this Soul Center of Beingness. The body of Man is the physical expression of this Soul state we call the psyche. We can therefore say that to live is to be psychic and to be psychic is to live. The implications of this fact are most profound and of fundamental significance to the understanding of the entire field of evolution. The evolution being spoken of here is inclusive of that which we call psychological, biological and spiritual. There is no separation between these; they are part and parcel of the same process. We can say with authority that the body of Man is evolving in complete conformity with the psyche of Man. The body of Man is carrying the manifestation of what the psyche needs to express and is expressing at any time along the line of its development.

The first level of expression we enter into following our 'emergence' is the Monadic or Angelic state of Beingness. Another name for this state is Light Beings. There are also several esoteric names, among which Elohim and Demiurge are two of the most common. This plane is also frequently called the Super-Conscious. One of the chief characteristics and functions of Super-Consciousness or Angelic Beingness is to organize the sub-atomic matter of the Cosmos into forms that we see on earth as physical manifestations. One of the commonest of these forms is the physical body we call Man. This body-form is the outer expression of the individual character of a particular Angelic Being or psyche. In effect this means that each and every human we encounter on this earth is an angel doing their particular 'thing'. All of us, without exception, are exactly individual manifesting angels.

A question often asked is whether there are boy angels and girl angels. The truth is there are neither boy angels nor girl angels, but there are expressions of angels which may be boy or girl expressions. There are also expressions of angels which do not appear in the realm of sexuality at all. These expressions are called such names as caring, compassion, service, love, etc.

In the course of the formulation of physical form and the descent from the exalted plane into the material plane the characteristic of Angelic Beingness or Super-Consciousness is never lost. There is, however, an awareness loss which results in the drawing of a veil over the consciousness of origin. It is the influence of this loss that inspires so many people today to pursue the path of self-development (particularly spiritual self-development) and meditation. In real terms there is no such thing as a separate human, there is only the Angelic Being who is currently and temporarily manifesting their physical presence.

Because there is so much misinformation regarding the qualities of the psychic realm, it is absolutely necessary at this stage that we clear our mind of as much of this misinformation as possible. The first of these mis-beliefs is that there are psychic people who have been specially selected to be elite and have special gifts not given to the rest of humanity. This is totally untrue. The only reason anyone has psychic ability is that they have reached a certain level of expression which all humans reach in the course of their evolutionary track. The second fallacy is that psychic information is automatically more worthy or accurate than that received through normal intellectual channels. Both psychic and intellectual data is frequently inaccurate. Both also have a record of accuracy.

The chief reason for the inaccuracy in the psychic realm of information is that what is received by the psychic is filtered through the veil which obscures origin and source at one and the same time. Because many psychics are not even aware of the origin and source of their information, they are not aware that the data therein may be clouded and warped in the telling.

From what is outlined above we can easily arrive at a simple description of Man in terms that can be easily understood by most people. Man is an amalgam of the biological, mental and spiritual substance of Cosmic Matter. Here it might be as well to point out that Soul and Spirit are not one and the same. The substance of Soul is Spirit, but not all Spirit manifests as Soul. Spirit is the Essence of Cosmic Matter. Another name by which Spirit is known is Fohat. This is the condition of Divine Consciousness that parents the Soul level of Beingness. We might, therefore, say that when Soul Being manifests as Man we are observing the point at which God becomes visible in the physical universe.

The manifested consciousness of God above the vibration of Man is not perceivable on the material plane of consciousness. This is why so many scientific researchers have difficulty in testing and analyzing the behavior pattern of Psi phenomena. Such phenomena only barely touch the material plane of consciousness, and therefore do not reach the lower level of instrumental analysis. The instruments of Psi researchers can only observe and measure the *effects* of Psi activity. As the instrument of analysis is itself a material plane vibration instrument, it cannot of itself zero in on vibrations that are far away and beyond its own plane.

Humanhood is the lowest plane at which the Angelic Consciousness can be seen in physical form. Therefore, what are we saying in stating psychic man is a total entity? We are actually saying that the totality of Man is God Expression. At the same time we are not saying that the totality of Man is the totality of God Expression. As Hamlet said: "There are more things in heaven and earth, dear Horatio, than are dreamt of in your philosophy". This does not mean that the potentialization of what we are does not bring us into the state of being totally aware and totally God-Expressing. That is exactly what Man is destined to become.

There is but One Source and One Energy in the Cosmos. With the recognition and acceptance of this concept the entire grandeur and power of the Cosmos becomes ours to express. For millions of years Man has been proceeding along a preordained path of manifestation. We call it evolution. This is a path of self-assigned spiritual expression. Self-assigned means that no one has sent us here and no one has condemned us to be here. We are in the physical state because we have decided to manifest in the physical vibration. Of all the nine groups of angels, there is only one group which assumed the undertaking of expressing at the physical humanhood level. There are no new members. We are all charter members with paid up subscriptions. *There are no new Souls in the earth plane.*

This material world in which we express our Divinity is and has been maintained through the system of reproduction. The Monadic or Angelic Kingdom first reproduced itself at a slightly lower vibratory rate of consciousness. Below this level comes an even lower one still. This process continues until we reach the level where Angel Soul begins to take on the form of the human structure. Each of these levels is a specific plane of consciousness. For every expression of inner and outer manifestation there is a corresponding plane of consciousness. What is really being expressed is that plane of consciousness. All manifestation throughout the entire Cosmos is an expression of consciousness. In psychology Divinity is usually referred to as conscious mind and/or unconscious mind. When religion speaks of consciousness it calls it Divinity. There is hardly a better word that could be used, for that is what Universal Consciousness actually is at all times. All of Mankind is Divine because we are consciousness in expression. The only difficulty with this is that most people do not want to be Divine, or they refuse to be Divine (but they are) because they do not want the responsibility that goes along with being Divine. For many people it is so much nicer and easier to be able to place the 'blame' on someone else.

The basic or primal rule of manifestation is the law of reproduction. This law is maintained in all aspects of matter, both animate and inanimate. The Mineral Kingdom reproduces itself and does so by an accreting process. The law continues to apply in both the Plant and Animal Kingdoms.

The process that takes place in the Human Kingdom follows the same lines with one fundamental variation. In the case of the human, the system of accretion changes from the spontaneous volition of the animal kingdom to the individual conscious selection and utilization of sub-atomic form patterns. This selection and utilization is performed by a conscious Soul/Being.

The procedure is quite simple. When a couple conceive, the Soul/Being (psychic man) of the personality to be expressed in the physical world assumes sovereignty of the egg being fertilized. From this point onward the entire structuring process is conducted by the Soul/Being in question in total conformity with the spiritual evolutionary needs of that Soul/Being. The parents-to-be are the channel to the environment necessary for Soul growth. At the same time, the needs of the parents for their own growth and development is inherently germane to the whole procedure. From what has gone before, we can begin to see the intimate and finely tuned details of the grand plan of Evolution. No detail is too small to be overlooked.

Together with the law of reproduction, there is another major aspect in the activity of the Soul/Being (psychic man), which is called 'movement and direction'. These two combined produce the most profound characteristic of all life, for which in these pages I will use the word 'change'. All change in evolutionary life results always from a change of consciousness, because life is an expression of consciousness. The first evidence of a changed expression of consciousness at the material level is found in the layers of rock, in the changing forms of plants and animals, and in the changing form of human inhabitants of this planet. The rise and fall of civilizations over the course of history is further evidence of such a change. As an integral part of the creation paradigm – the naming process – we have to find new words to express the ideas and identify the objects that we have brought into manifestation as, for example, in the case of plastic.

As Soul/Beings we are in charge of the creation process. The instrument employed in the application of our sovereignty is our 'power of decision'. There is but one reason why we ever fail to reach and make decisions, which is that we have not accepted the fact that our individual consciousness is Divine Consciousness. As long as we remain in the 'outer courtyard' we will never enjoy the benefits of the 'Holy of Holies'. As long as we keep putting 'Divinity' outside of ourselves and on a pedestal, we remain victims in body and in mind.

At this time, whatever our sex, whatever our age, all of us are the sum total of all we have ever been. We all have within the total of all the potential we will ever manifest in times yet to come. We have never received anything we did not need and we have never been deprived of anything we needed.

The most primordial act of life is the spiritual atom dividing itself and giving birth to another atom of totally similar character. This is the act of God Consciousness sub-dividing itself *without loss of power or quality*. This is the beginning of the process we see in biology and in all aspects of the creative universe. Once fission has begun there is no force anywhere in the universe to arrest its progress or development. This is so because the power being spoken of is the power of the Cosmos itself, and this power is what society calls GOD. We are this power in expression, and to consider ourselves anything other than this power is no more or no less than spiritual arrogance. It is certainly not humility. Anyone saying their power comes from any other source is both ignorant and temporarily severely occluded. In scriptural terms this is what is meant by the sin of pride or dwelling in darkness.

Spiritual pride is the state of consciousness which says "I am a separate entity". When this concept is put forward we are saying we have an alternative source and therefore we believe in duality. There cannot be Omniscient, Omnipresent and Omnipotent God at one and the same time as we have duality in our thinking. As long as we accept duality, we can never function successfully on a spiritual consciousness level in this material world, and this is what is meant when scripture tells us "A house divided against itself cannot stand". Scripture also says "Unless the Lord build the house, they labor in vain that build it". The word Lord in this context means spiritual law.

If we are not consciously using spiritual law in our thoughts, words and deeds we are not doing a very good job at the human-hood level. We are doing the best job a human can do, but that is all. It is for this reason that we so often hear statements such as "Everything was going so well and then suddenly, right out of nowhere, it all fell apart". What happens in such circumstances is that we forget who we are; we remove creative cause from our activity, whereas utilizing spiritual consciousness as part of our daily life is precisely the function of 'psychic' man, and we are here on this planet to do just that.

When we forget to express spiritual consciousness we become merely Bill or Joan doing it, with all the weakness and frailties of occluded consciousness. One of the ways of overcoming this weakness is to stay in touch with the name of spiritual consciousness. Spiritual consciousness is Divine Consciousness and is known as "I AM", hence the first words of the Ten Commandments are "I AM the Lord....".

I stated earlier that "to live is to be psychic, to be psychic is to live". Therefore, if you are living, you *are* psychic, but there are many living people who are not expressing their psychic ability because they have not realized they have the ability or they have impaired it by not realizing its source. As we continue to use such abilities without conscious renewal from source we find that they diminish. This explains why people who test well at the beginning of a Psi experiment often do not do well later in the test. Again scripture tells us "to those who have it shall be given, and from those who have not it shall be taken".

When we make the recognition of our Divinity and use our 'psychic' powers in service without expectation of reward rather than to show off, our ability grows. Whenever we attempt to focus our attention on our psychic ability alone, we sooner or later run into a problem, which arises from the fact that we tend to drain our store of spiritual supply without at the same time renewing it from source. The personality has an unlimited appetite for reward and approval from outside itself. Adulation can be the cancer of psychic and spiritual development.

What we are really seeing when we look at each other in all our physical frailties and all our material difficulties is an unfinished 'act of consciousness'. Life is a two-act drama, and we are now in the final scene of the first act. We live in the Western world in a culture that is Judaic-Christian. Our consciousness is impregnated with the conceptions and misconceptions of that culture, and we live in a framework of a belief system that functions at an almost totally pragmatic level. "You have to protect yourself with life insurance". Can you imagine what would happen if the insurance companies were to discover their clients are "immortal"? For example, in the corporate world we call some acts which are unethical 'the cost of doing business'. In the political world it is called 'influencing the wheels of progress'. The only reason these people are functioning in this way is that they do not know they are operating as the Anti-Christ.

To clearly understand what the Anti-Christ is, we must first come to understand what Christ Consciousness is, namely that consciousness which makes the recognition that the 'I' and the 'me' are one and together they are one with the 'Father'. Therefore the Anti-Christ is that consciousness that does not or has not as yet accepted itself as being the one and same consciousness as Divine Consciousness. There is not and never was a personality on this plane that is uniquely the Anti-Christ. If we fail to recognize that the consciousness of the Anti-Christ is that which believes there is a duality, we burden ourselves with unnecessary concern and worry.

For those of us who wish to make the change from our culturalization to an awareness of our Divinity, the journey can be a joy and a great reward. The first essential step is to recognize how impoverished the 'duality' consciousness really is in its day to day handling of its affairs. It is beset with fear, anger, greed and envy. It has little if any room for enjoying its substance, no matter how large it may be. We need to rise above the law of 'duality', which is a game of chance. Even with economic forecasts people lose their shirts!

Rising above the law does *not* mean breaking the law of society, but rather rising above the *need* to break the law. It means not *using* the 'cost of doing business' syndrome. It means to realize that our good fortune does not come from 'knowing the right people', but from knowing the true source of our well-being. This is what Jesus meant when he said "I am in this world, but not of it". This is accepting our own Divinity in all our daily thoughts, words and actions. This is the process of becoming a total psychic entity. This is the beginning of living the Soul Life in outer expression, re-establishing and re-expressing our angelic consciousness.

Once we have entered into this realm of consciousness we are no longer merely human, but have become exalted humanhood on our way to ever better and greater expression. As in the story of the Prodigal Son, although still dwelling in the 'far country', we have begun the journey home to our Father's House. For this journey we do not need the High Priests of the mind power institutions or the prelates of the 'only way' denominations. We need only recognize and accept that our individual consciousness is Divine Consciousness. It is a private matter. No-one and no organization can give or sell 'salvation'. We cannot give to or share salvation with our family, friends or neighbors, but we can share the results of our spiritual growth with them through concern, compassion, kindness and love. Not only must we not judge – we must not preach or cajole. There is an old rhyme which is totally metaphysical in meaning: "Little Bo-Peep has lost her sheep, and cannot tell where to find them; but leave them alone and they will come home, wagging their tails behind them". It could not be said better.

In order to move from our occlusion, from our ignorance of our Divinity, we have to make a conscious effort to initiate the transmutative process. It is not going to 'just happen'; it requires our decision and application. The easiest way to initiate the change is to select as a trigger something which we do regularly every day. We select one of our daily habits and use it as a reminder that what we are doing at that moment is the action of our Divinity. It can be as simple as brushing our teeth or making our morning coffee. All actions are conducted by Divine Power anyway, whether we know it or not. We do not have to set up a whole new set of habits; we do have to change the recognition of who is doing what is being done. Formerly it was the 'me', but with the new concept it is now the 'I'.

Following this path of development we do not have to interfere with anyone's given life style or privacy. In acting in this manner we 'go in our closet and pray'. In psychological terms we have taken the responsibility away from the personality and given it to the super-consciousness. To round out this process and make it an organic stimulator we also make the verbal statement "I pronounce you good". The 'you' in this instance is the 'action' involved at the time. By this simple process we are taking charge of what we create in our lives. As we continue to use this process we begin to eliminate our impaired thinking and replace it with clear thinking that brings about those things and conditions we want in our life.

In the very first instance in which we do this we have begun to alter the structure of the spiritual atom and, by so doing, change the magnetic field and draw to ourselves that which we need to enhance our evolutionary growth. This change brings about effects in our material and spiritual life at one and the same time. In plain simple language, we have become conscious Soul/Beings and have taken dominion over the 'earth'. We have become psychic beings. It is for this we have come – that we may have life and have it more abundantly.

Chapter 2

Creation Is Here to Stay

Creativity is a commonly used word in our society which has, in fact, become a very misused word. Much of what is called creativity is no more than the repetition of the well-worn and hackneyed. When we engage in any programmed procedural reaction we are not being creative, we are being re-active. As long as we are unconsciously reactive we are not in a position to call upon the creative power of our super or spiritual consciousness. When we engage in procedural reaction we diminish our creative ability and revert to an energy that is already stereotyped. In so doing we do not turn on the faucet of our inner Divine Energy.

We are all acquainted with the well-worn handshake, but few among us have even the faintest idea of why we use this procedure when we meet an acquaintance. Therefore, if the next time we meet that person we were to embrace them it would set up a whole new stream of consciousness, which would not only be new for the recipient but also for the donor. At the very worst we would shock the recipient, but a shock releases a new flow of energy form. Any form that is created by consciousness for the first time, activates the entire realm of creative consciousness.

Creation is a live force and power, but in order to be dynamic it needs the vitalization of a new channel through which to express. If we do not accept the livingness of creativity by allowing it ever fresh channels of expression we diminish into a stereotyped reaction in our mental, emotional and physical activity.

There is no difficulty in keeping the creative consciousness in the active state. The movement of attention to a different or unfamiliar focus is the activator of the creative flow of consciousness. Attention is the main tool of creation and, when linked with desire, consciousness achieves its goals. It is only when attention is splintered or countermanded by limiting instructions that the goals get set aside. The movement of attention brings consciousness into a new area of application, and this initiates a completely new arrangement of outpouring and inpouring stimuli. This process is going on before our very eyes every day, but we are rarely aware that it is happening.

To understand what creation really is it is necessary to recognize and accept that attention is the focal point of the I AM in action. In doing so we have refocused and have expanded our awareness, because we consciously and deliberately focused our attention into a new or alternative concept.

By the power of our own indwelling I AM Consciousness we have refocused *our* attention. This is what is meant by the statement "Out of darkness comes the Light". Through this refocusing action we generated an entirely new episode of spiritual energy flow.

Whenever we let ourselves get into a state of boredom, all we have to do to alleviate it is consciously refocus our attention on an entirely different object or situation, and we will restart the flow of inpouring creative consciousness. How often have we said: "I am so bored. There is nothing to do"? *Right now*, as you read this, make the decision that the next time you feel boredom coming on, you will remember to consciously alter the focus of your attention. By doing this we begin to take control of our attention and thereby control the direction of creative thought processes. It does not matter what we refocus on; it is the refocusing action that triggers the creative flow. Creative spirit is only too happy to get out of the rut! Boredom is a cup that is already filled with a particular experience. This cup needs emptying – refocusing. Our change of attention provides a new cup for creative spirit to flow into.

The creative act is not an act of the past but an act of the here and now. In earthly terms, we are not talking about creating something out of nothingness, about stage magic or miracles. When the average person talks about magic or miracles they are referring to having an object appear or disappear in their presence with a total absence of lapsed time. There is no such state as having something come out of nothing; all things come out of something and that something is *Consciousness*. Things come out of consciousness through the door of attention. We have to take the particles of the essence of things and redirect them to the vicinity of our presence. We have to realize that we have dominion over our creation, that it is ours. The entire creative process works through the process of 'imaging in'. When we learn the truth of this process and are prepared to accept that there is One and only One Consciousness in the Cosmos, we as individuals become co-creators in the grand plan of creation.

The creation process that is referred to here is the same process that is used to create a change of emotional output from anger to passiveness. We can take the energy (spiritual atoms) of anger, hate, jealousy and so on and, by transmuting them ("making all things new"), redirect them into beneficent expression. We do this by *consciously* focusing our attention of the I AM of self while using a channeling tool of the mind. The tool can be an affirmative declaration such as: "I surrender body, emotions, mind and soul here, now and hereafter. Let there not be me and mine, but Thee and Thine alone. Be Thou me". While carrying out this exercise, our dedicated attention *must* be kept fixed on the I AM Consciousness.

In order that there can be no confusion regarding what is being referred to here, a description of mind and of consciousness is in order. The mind is *not* the brain, but *is* an entity of consciousness expression. It has no weight, no mass and no volume. It exists outside the realm of the dimensions of physics. The brain is the motor control system used by the mind to operate the physical body. Consciousness is the essence of the Cosmos. It is that of which the Cosmos is constructed. We might say that 'Consciousness is the Mind of God'. Finally, we can say the consciousness and the mind are not limited to physical earth expression only.

In the time it takes to recite the affirmation energy will have begun to convert towards the condition we are changing. From here we can go forward to make the most beautiful dress, play the most wonderful music, write the most stirring words or even be the most relaxed we have ever been. We are frequently told that we have to get rid of our "stinking thinking" or banish our personality. We do not, in fact, have to banish or get rid of either. What we must do is inaugurate a conscious connection between our personality and our I AM Consciousness. We have to bring the personality under the dominion of that Consciousness. We enhance the personality with spiritual awareness. A great number of people become very confused by this form of approach, many of them feeling they have to give up most of the things they enjoy in life. This is not true at all. The truth is that we begin to enjoy the things already in our lives, together with others that are added, in an enhanced manner. The added aspects are usually an enhanced joy, an uplifted emotional well-being and an expanded awareness.

Bearing this in mind, a question arises as to the 'personality'. Is there a persona and is it automatically good or destined to be bad? There is also much dispute as to what the persona consists of in the first place, and this dispute is most ardently argued in the departments of religion and psychology. The broad body of the religionists tend to see life in terms of solitary introspection, and objects are viewed as shut in upon themselves in a kind of 'imminence'. The mainstream of psychology appears to see objects, conditions and relationships as though they consist entirely of external action in transitory relationships.

The easiest way to ascertain whether or not there is such a thing as a personality is to remember the last time you "saw" yourself do something as if you were merely an observer. As you watched you probably made a judgment of the behavior in question. That which was watching was the I AM self and that which was doing was the personality. This is as close as we can get to an understanding of this condition of consciousness while we are incarnated in a physical body.

There is one other happening, not available at this time to all people, that aids the understanding of the body/persona versus pure consciousness state. I refer to what is called an out-of-body experience, which leaves no doubt in the mind of the beholder of the non-dependence of consciousness upon the body/persona for its existence. Those who have this type of experience say with a great deal of conviction that there is no sense of morality, goodness or badness, connected to the state of awareness existing during the out-of-body state. Also there is no doubt of the sense of 'being'.

No-one has ever gone through this experience and later said: "I was out of my body and I had no sense of awareness".

The best psychological, religious or metaphysical exposition of the story of the 'psyche' (soul/being) and its journey into personality is found in the parable of the Prodigal Son. Here we learn of the journey of the soul/being in all its psychological implications. We learn of the soul/being in its journeying of manifestation through the several planes of consciousness, beginning with the involutionary part of the evolution process. In this part we come to understand that the soul/being, having completed its emergence from Universal Divine Consciousness (leaving the Father's House), continues down through the planes (lowers its vibratory rate), and becoming enmeshed with physical matter, increases the occlusion that accompanies the ensuing density. This occlusion and density *is* the 'Far Country', the state of personality consciousness (see the King James V. Bible – Luke 15:vv11-24). Having arrived in the Far Country with the memory of the place of origin totally occluded, the sense of creative power is now totally dormant. This is the state of 'darkness of understanding' or complete unawareness other than that of bodily sensation. After a sojourn in this state of existence the soul/being awakens – "I will arise and go to my Father's House". From this point onwards consciousness as expressed through the personality becomes devoted to the process of self-discovery, self-development and spiritual enlightenment. This is what being 'reborn' truly means.

What then is the key to this creative process of which we speak? If we are already deeply set in the personality, how can we restart our engine of creation? The first thing to be done is to realize and accept that the consciousness we are expressing is running at low speed – maybe even idling! The second step is to initiate the desire to express ourselves at an ever-increasing level of well-being and awareness, which we initiate by energizing the desire level of our consciousness, and making the decision to improve a specific aspect of our personality. We start by taking a look at someone we know and some aspect about them we do not like, and we will have found the aspect in ourselves with which we can start. We energize the desire level of change by taking on the same intensity of feeling we have for the physical things we want, and using it to achieve the changed condition of personality we desire. Because we are Divine Consciousness it will work. We are already creative; it is only our unawareness of it that has made it seem to not be present.

To make our decision for self-development strong and powerful we must release all our previous condemnations of ourselves. We must come to realize that all we have ever done is what we needed to do in our Soul growth. All forms of self-growth and self-development could be radically improved if those involved in helping and receiving the help were to accept there never was a time in the past when anything that was done could have been otherwise. Any form of speculation as to what might have happened is nothing more than an intellectual pastime. It is of value to know that what happened in the past is what was needed, but is not what has to re-happen in the present or in the future. Once again the words of scripture put this concept most precisely: "Seek ye first the kingdom of heaven, and all others will be added unto you". The heaven here talked about is the state of consciousness from which flows all that we desire in our life expression.

When we successfully change our personality, the new 'self' will bring about those things and relationships with which we wish to surround ourselves. This condition is the 'kingdom of heaven on earth'. This new state of being is what brings forth fruit 'one hundredfold'. It brings the Cadillac, the swimming pool, the better health and all the happiness that 'man is heir to'.

Our psychological term for this state of soul/being is self-actualization. It exists for all of us – there are no specially elect. We can all get there from here.

As we begin to move into our evolutionary creative consciousness, we find ourselves focusing more and more on achieving an awareness of our conscious divinity. At the same time, we also find ourselves focusing less and less on 'things' we want, in the full knowledge that what is required for our well-being will come forth from consciousness in due course. We soon realize that what we lack is the symptom of a low grade consciousness in just the same way that cancer or any other bodily disease is a symptom of a discordant consciousness.

There is a retired Royal Air Force doctor who, for many years now, has been teaching people to heal their own cancer through the practice of a specialized form of meditation. What the good doctor has taught them to do is alter the vibratory rate of their consciousness. When they do this successfully the cancer cells can no longer live in their bodies. In effect, because the 'house' has been renovated, the cancer cells move out and find a home more acceptable to themselves.

At this point a word or two about the commodity called desire seems to be in order. Many of us have been told all our lives that desire is wicked, evil and many other less commendable things. Nothing could be further from the truth – desire is the engine of creation. Desire is the vehicle used by the I AM Consciousness to bring about its plan on earth. We and desire are instruments of that plan always. Even while we are still unaware of our divinity and are out there seeking satisfaction of our human wants, we are fulfilling the Divine plan. To think that we could have a desire that did not stem from the Divine level of consciousness is nothing less than personality pride.

As long as desire lasts in the earth plane it is utilized by the creative process. Beyond a certain stage of consciousness development desire is no longer necessary. We do not have to desire to be unfolded. We do not have to desire to have a higher consciousness or act in a divine manner. Because we do act in a divine manner, we are tender and full of compassion towards others because we recognize that we are all one with the Father. This is the state of at-one-ment.

There are guidelines on some of the steps which aid us in achieving this approach to life. We need to have an ongoing positive response to the doingness of whatever we are doing. We must learn not to re-evaluate an action after we have expressed it in the outer world. What is done is done, but this does not mean that we do not plan differently for future action. Condemnation and ridicule of past activities sever the flow of creative consciousness to present action. Many people spend time berating the job with which they are currently involved, instead of using the obstacle the job is as an opportunity.

The opportunity they are missing is the one that would help them to develop their discernment in the selection of their next job. This lesson is the very least they might learn from the experience of the current job. Once we begin to see the job as an opportunity we also notice that we are not nearly so fatigued by our daily efforts. This is our first clue that we are on the right track. Following this we find that we lose our sense of age in terms of the energy we have available to us for the tasks we undertake, and we do not feel any particular age. This is the first breath of the feeling of immortality, and leads to a fearlessness about life in general.

Metaphysically this condition is known as the fountain of youth, and we have begun to get in touch with the eternality of our consciousness. As a result our body and our actions respond in kind to this fact. Because of the definite change in our consciousness first the causal body changes, then the astral body changes, resulting in changes in the etheric and physical bodies. This happens because all of the energy that is outflowing is now doing so in an optimum and harmonious manner.

There is a fundamental rule that must be observed at all times in this whole developmental procedure, namely that we may command nature as long as and to the extent to which we are prepared to obey it in daily life. Having planted a seed in the soil of consciousness in the early morning we must not go out in the hours of darkness to dig it up and analyze it for results. The seed having been planted, we must allow it to germinate at the divine rate of growth. Many people make the error of trying to impose material earth time on eternal spiritual law. We can never do that successfully. "Please God, give me patience and give it to me right now" has never worked and never will.

In order to become an active creator there are certain things we must put into practice before we can receive our 'merit badge'. The first of these is the *acceptance of Self as a creator*. Although this is obvious, it is overlooked by many in the metaphysical domain. It makes no difference how inept we are at this stage of our creativity. Even if our life is in what might be called a shambles, *it is what we have created*. There is no escape clause in this law. There is no escape because this is a fundamental Cosmic Law. It is never too late to begin to accept ourself as a creator – *now* is and always has been the best time. We can begin by repeating "I am the creator of my own circumstances, and I can change these circumstances by the power of my consciousness". Used for thirty-three days, this affirmation can bring about the most significant change in our well-being.

The second, and no less vital factor is that the recognition of our creator consciousness *must be made in humility*. Here we have to be clear in our mind as to the difference between 'humility' and 'humbleness'. To condemn ourselves for our actions is 'humbleness' – the denial of divinity. "I was not aware what I was doing to you, and I assure you I will not ever do it again" is 'humility'. This is acceptance of our dominion over our own 'lower nature', and the other name for lower nature is the personality. While making our apology to our victim, we must also keep in mind that what has happened needed to happen for us and for the other person involved. *Divine Law is never absent.*

A third factor must be borne in mind and applied constantly in the process of creative action. The "I" of self is the same "I" that is the "I" of all individuals throughout humanity. There is but one power operating in this universe. It is not an accident or a happenstance. This is the power that causes the sun to shine, the tides to ebb and flow. This power operating in the universe is the one and the same power that is operating in our consciousness. The name of this power is *I AM*.

Any two people living their lives in close contact every day have more than enough opportunities to practice creative development. Every time we open our mouth to speak to each other we have an opportunity. It is important to realize that spiritual altitude is gained best in the conditions of abrasion rather than in the comfort of an isolated ashram. The diamond is polished by being pressed against the wheel. We are improved by being pressed against the wheel of life every day. Next time someone jumps all over us, let us pause and not jump all over them in turn. If we pause and make the recognition that they are operating from their divinity, we will have made a leap in our spiritual development. Leaps in development are not made in meditation, but in the opportunities provided later by the stillness achieved in meditation.

Partnerships, whether marriage, co-habiting, family or business groups, are the truest and most rigorous testing ground of creative spiritual growth. Great care must be taken in putting such groups together. The same degree of care and attention must be given to the validity of maintaining or dissolving them. Learning and changing are essential parts of growth, so we must constantly be alert to the need for change when all the lessons have been learned from the association. Even greater care must be exercised in terminating relationships. If the lesson of life in the relationship has not been learned, the cost is very high. We will be compelled to return continuously to the conditions of the same type of relationship until the lesson has been learned. It is best to get it right the first time, but very few of us manage that. After we have learned to recognize and accept ourselves as creators, the lessons are more easily learned, but the lessons themselves come in more rapid succession. The more responsibility we assume, the greater the area of responsibility that comes into our awareness. Because we stand taller, we can see further and deeper.

The question often arises as to how we know the correct time and circumstance to make a change. There are a number of clearly defined checkpoints. We must be completely satisfied that the benefits of the change are of equal merit for all concerned. There must never be a shadow of doubt or a trace of guilt. There must never be a need to rationalize. If we are operating from the level of the I AM consciousness, we shall be clear of doubt, rationalizations and other humanhood misconceptions. If we are not operating from the I AM level, it is just another act in the darkness of occlusion for which we shall have to return to the conditions from which we tried to escape. The lessons or grades of spiritual growth in creative consciousness cannot be skipped. Marks for attendance are not enough. We must make A's on the course.

Another of the signs that we must look for in ourselves is the one that shows we are no longer reacting to 'old tapes'. As we learn to distinguish between reaction and response, we become more sure of our decisions and those decisions bear fruit one-hundredfold. We do this by recognizing the source of any input as divine consciousness. When someone invites us to partake in a joint undertaking, doing business, having dinner or a more meaningful relationship, if we make the recognition that the offer is coming to our humanhood from the I AM through the other person's humanhood, our response will be a creative one. As long as we are aware of the I AM in others we cannot fail to make the correct decision.

The 'pause' time in question is a mere fraction of a second, and how long is a fraction of a second in eternity? All that is required is a pause time that will allow us to make the recognition that the voice we hear is the voice of God. This, of course, does not mean that we have to accept any offer that is made to us. The real point of the matter is that it gives us the divine choice by hearing it as the voice of God. It raises our choice out of humanhood and into divinity. The odds are in favor of the person asking or giving the invitation operating not from the level of mere humanhood, but working from divine consciousness. This is the difference between the head response and the heart response. When we learn to live at the heart level of life we find ourselves more and more exposed to people who themselves work from this level of beingness.

When we have learned to accept our own actions, words and thoughts as the creations of our own consciousness we are well on our way to being successfully creative, and there is a way to hasten this process. We do so by giving reverence to that which we do, that which we say and that which we think. Also we give reverence to that which we see done, that which we hear and that which we learn about the thoughts of others. In this way we allow Divinity to manifest without judgment on our humanhood level.

Another area where we must give reverence is to our own "intuitional promptings". *Universal Divine Consciousness speaks through the self of 'individualized consciousness'*. This requires a total surrender of the "me" to the "I AM". We must abandon all false modesty of being unworthy of God's attention. We are the instruments of expression of the Divine Plan. Not to accept and serve is the real definition of Satanic Rebellion. To think that we have an existence apart from God would be the sin of pride. We must accept the responsibility of the creator if we are to fulfill our destiny. Again, it is best expressed in scripture: "Marvel ye not at the things that I do, for greater things than these shall ye do".

As we move more and more into this form of expression we shall find that we are already beginning to make the world a more beautiful place for ourselves to live in, wherever we may live. We find that we are adding style to our lives within all that we express. In a word, we put the magic back where it belongs.

The most important aspect in the creative developmental sphere is maintaining purpose in life. This means not doing things without knowing the feeling of why we are doing them. "I want to do it" is all right, but by having purpose in what we do we are putting our own beingness into the activity. The intentionality aspect is an integral part of the I AM Consciousness. When we do it with purpose we change a simple cooked meal into a banquet. In this way we create the enjoyment and the satisfaction which in its turn produces the full nourishment from the food intake. All of us know what it is like when we eat or drink something just to please another person – it does not give enjoyment. It is for this reason that people who eat for emotional comfort and an escape from their boredom with life put on all those extra pounds.

Being creative means to be creative even in the picayune details. There is no part of *life* that is not an expression of consciousness and is therefore sacred. All created things are sacred because they are created by divine consciousness. When we have learned to recognize things as a created item of consciousness, we are open to understanding how our own individual consciousness is the creator of our thoughts and the words which those thoughts produce.

The only reason people lack anything in life is that they have not yet recognized who it is that conducts the earthly Creation Program. There are some who do have an inkling, but they are only interested in starting in on the 'big' items, and cannot be bothered to even practice with the 'small'. Until we come to know that the first kingdom over which we have to assume dominion is the kingdom of "me", we will not be too successful in the 'big' creation business. We must assume dominion over the pettiness of the personality, with its hate, fear, jealousy, lies, cheating, greed, judgment, envy and all the other limitations by which it is beset. It is necessary that we look at the old tapes and 'decide' to discard them. We need to make a commitment to surrender our old personality pattern – the autonomous me – to the inner and higher authority of the individualized consciousness of the I AM. All we have to do to begin with is activate the desire to recognize and accept the fact that our individual consciousness is Universal Divine Consciousness in all our thoughts, words and deeds. From thereon, the outcome is never in doubt. We are the creators, and our only responsibility at this time is to initiate the desire and start the process. Our ultimate goal is to totally surrender our separatism and accept our beingness as Divinity in action. Creation has never paused. It is here and it is here to stay.

Consciousness is God and God is consciousness. It is that simple. When consciousness has become aware of a need, God has become aware of the need. Who will satisfy the need? God will satisfy the need, consciousness will satisfy the need. When attention on a need is focalized in consciousness the process of manifestation has begun. Continuing focalized attention maintains and finalizes the outer expression and satisfaction of the need. This is creation in action. It must first be ours in consciousness before it can be ours in the outer world of concrete manifestation. If it is not in the Mind of God it does not exist in the Cosmos.

Chapter 3

The Prodigal Son

Luke 15: vv.11-32

If the Bible is not a mere denominational historical document, what then is it? It is in fact a manual of personal spiritual psychological evolution. Therefore, the stories in the Bible are not in themselves oriented exactitudes; they are not reports of the day's events on an evening television news broadcast.

Unfortunately, the honor the Bible has acquired is not nearly as great as it might have been, the reason being that this monumental work of so many great minds has been reduced to an ethnic and denominational house organ. In the mind of many people it is little known or understood outside either of the groups mentioned here.

Once the Bible was moved within the parameters of the religious corporate domain or became a racial and historical boundary marker, it lost its universal inspirational benefit for planetary Man. Millions of well-meaning people have been deprived of a first-class work manual of self-development. The reasons for this state of affairs are not the concern of this book. The most likely and pervasive reason is an extensive occlusion of the mind of humanity as a whole.

So again, what is the Bible if it is *not* a historical document or a denominational exposition of religious doctrinal and ethnic structural beliefs? It *is* a great deal more. The stories in the Bible are not in themselves necessarily true stories in the sense that we normally hear in an evening newscast. The stories are about Divine Truth and its manifestation in the Cosmos. The stories are not limited to mere earthly happenings or even to solar system events. The purpose of the few stories that are true and factual is to illustrate a spiritual truth. They are used in much the same way as we would give an example from daily happenings to explain a fundamental meaning to someone who might not have the experience to understand the structure of the matter in question. The purpose of the Bible is to convey spiritual understanding beyond mere intellectual 'know about'.

Once we come to know that the Bible is a manual of Spiritual Psychological Development, there is no reason why we cannot choose to use it as such. It is true that we have to unlearn some of what we have previously understood in order to gain the newer and better benefits from our efforts. The scriptures have been written and assembled by enlightened Souls, but they have been presented so that we can use them only so long as we are prepared to take a little time to absorb the technique of their use.

There are a few simple things to learn about the method of presentation, the first of which is to know that the Bible is written in a code of symbols, and that these symbols transcend any mere intellectual interpretation in any one language at any time. The second factor we need to know is that there is an inner meaning to every outer meaning that is offered. These symbols, which can be spoken or written, are set out in parables, allegories, cryptics or numbers and, according to Pythagoras, "The world is built upon the power of numbers". For those who wish to pursue the study of the Bible at a more esoteric level, there is also the symbological discipline of the Holy Kabbalah. For our present purpose, we are confining our attention to the first three mentioned above.

One of the most learned of scriptural scholars, Geoffrey Hodson, provides the simplest and the most insightful of descriptions of this entire symbological process. He explains to us that many of the external historical events also occur within our own psyche, in our own consciousness. Each person referred to in a story represents a condition of our own consciousness. They are all personifications of the consciousness of the Divine. In addition, each story relayed is a graphic description of the experience of the Human Soul in its journey through evolution. This is so simple and beautiful that it is unsurpassed as a description of Divine Truth in action. Moreover, it is so germane and pragmatic in therapeutic application that it leaves no doubt as to its effective accuracy.

Our main point of attention here is the use of the parable, and our choice of an example is the story of the Prodigal Son. When we come to grips with this story in its esoteric (inner) meaning, we have a very good beginning for the understanding of the entire Spiritual Psychological process of involution and evolution. The involution of Spirit into material expression and its evolution therefrom is what this story is all about.

The first thing we note about this story is that it is a drama with three main characters, a father, an older son and a younger son. This immediately tells us that we are dealing with a situation that involves the concept of trinity. The trinity concept plays an enormous role in the whole drama of life for all of us. In life we have positive, negative and passive, and all three are substantive elements of the creation process. This then is the story/process of this involution of the Spirit into dense material expression and the re-emergence of the Spirit from that condition into the non-physical state of heavenly living.

The Father symbolizes the Infinite, the Eternal Parent from which the infinite is born. Let us look at this in terms of our own mortal daily life. If, for example, our normal condition (infinite) is cheerful, bright and easy-going and something upsets us, that upset would be finite (temporal), and would be limited to the period that we remained upset. Therefore, the eternal or infinite state of consciousness would be the on-going joyful, happy state and the finite or temporal state would be the upset condition that might have arisen because the water faucet leaked. Out of the infinite comes the finite. In daily living, when we get upset it means that we have forgotten that we are infinite consciousness, that we are the 'Father'. Once we begin to sense the feeling of the presence of this infinite consciousness, we are no longer alone 'out there'. When we read (if we read) the story of the Prodigal Son, we now know this is not just a story of two Jewish boys in Israel some thousands of years ago. With this realization we have stepped into the realm of Spiritual Psychology and Self-development. We have taken one of the first steps in the process towards at-one-ment.

Another and easier way to understand this concept is to think of the Father symbol as the source of all creation – the stuff of the universe. This also helps us to understand that everything that reaches us through our senses has an antecedent.

The elder of the two sons symbolizes the Angelic or Elohim level of consciousness. This is the level of expression which is never manifested in material form in the earth kingdom, but is nevertheless responsible for many of the things that are visible on earth. A particular example would be the Devas, who are directly connected to the plant life of the planet. In some esoteric literature these angelic beings are referred to as Earth Gods, because their function is to take care of the structure of the growing things of the earth such as trees, flowers, vegetables and plants of all sorts.

Because there is such an infinite variety of names for the same expression of consciousness, we often become confused as to what is being said. Throughout the various teachings there are a multiplicity of terms to describe the vibrations that surround an object or person on the earth plane. We have such names as magnetic field, aura, corona, force field and many, many more. All of these are titles and delineations for expressions of consciousness that are approximate to the solid earth plane. When we speak of the Elder Son (First Son) we are referring to that level called non-material Consciousness.

We are also referring to a level of Consciousness which does not become occluded from awareness of its origin. The plane or aspect of Consciousness in question remains detached from regular material expression, retaining near complete at-one-ment with the source of creation, that is the 'Father'.

The level of consciousness of the elder son is what many in society mean when they say Christ Consciousness. This is the state of consciousness in which the individual consciousness retains the feeling and the knowledge of at-one-ment. "I and the Father are one" or again "He that sees me sees Him who sent me". Both these expressions tell us of the presence of Divinity in the here and now. The elder son and/or Christ Consciousness plane also provides the level of awareness that allows us to recognize we have dominion over the earth, expressed in scripture in the words "My kingdom is not of this world". This entire phase of the story of the Prodigal is an account of the condition that prevails at all times in the planes of manifestation. There is always a non-material plane that inaugurates and governs the material plane of existence. The physical plane is always a reflection of the non-material plane. What we had in consciousness yesterday, we now have in material form today. In esoteric literature this is expressed in the words "as above so below". Scientists, painters, poets, writers and thinkers of all hues frequently call this consciousness creative intelligence, and it is just that.

Getting in touch with this level of consciousness is not nearly as difficult as many would have us believe. There is really no need to enroll in a secret society or to join a specific group of worshippers on a mountain top in Peru, or even to religiously attend the gatherings of a local denominational sect. As God is omnipresent and therefore everywhere, we only have to recognize this fact. One of the simplest and most effective ways of getting in touch is to spend five minutes each and every day repeating slowly and with composed attention "I AM That I AM". If this is done while looking in a mirror the attention factor will be enhanced. This is not being occult, but rather using spiritual psychology. What is in fact taking place is that we are re-focusing our attention upon the higher aspect of consciousness, which has always been the Christ Consciousness. As our attention is the agent of change in our psyche, that attention has to direct us to the right source. There is only one "I AM". We can never get a wrong number, and we will never find that the lights are on but there is nobody at home. "Ask and ye shall receive". This little exercise is not a miracle weapon for the lazy to become the world's next leading guru; it is a system of prayer which can lead us to the beginning of the straight and narrow path. It will not of necessity take us through the gates of heaven. Much more work, care and attention are needed for that. What this process will do is open our own inner sense of awareness of what is best for us on our path of personal spiritual unfoldment.

Many of us living in today's "New Age Thought" are caught up in the matrix of the metaphysical sciences, and this is as it should be at this stage of the evolutionary process. However, the time has come to look very carefully at what we are doing in this field of development. For those in the field of astrology there is a tendency to see the planetary arrangements as controlling their lives through both a long term and day-to-day scenario. Any who engage in this kind of practice, whether as a result of our faith in astrology or by studying the fall of an eagle feather, we are entering into the consciousness of the younger son, into the consciousness of separatism. In astrology this would begin with the concept of the twins, Castor and Pollux, who rule Gemini and who, in esoteric astrology, stand at the gate of birth of material expression. One of the twins – the elder son – remains in the non-material kingdom and the other twin – the younger son – descends into material expression. Following this separation in consciousness, the younger son continues to lower the vibratory rate of (his) consciousness throughout the multiplicity of 'below world' expressions, manifested in thought, emotion and effort, or through all the expressions of the personality.

The entry of the 'younger son' into the dense kingdom of matter and occlusion is the process of taking on the persona. It is the delusion of the personality's separatism that is referred to as the Far Country in the Prodigal story. Only when we make a deliberate attempt to return to our at-one-ment with our Divine self or source do we succeed in making our journey to the promised land. As long as we choose to remain in the land far from home we will be beset with the trials and tribulations of a life that is separated from its source. Living in the domain of greed, lust and envy keeps us as victims of our own created condition. Our pride in our 'independence' keeps us far from the nourishment that flows from the understanding of at-one-ment. As soon as we make the recognition that we are the 'younger son', that we have journeyed to the Far Country by choice and as part of a Divine plan, we are in a position to make our return. The whole purpose of the exercise outlined above is to facilitate that very process. Once we have focused our attention on the Father's House – I AM – we have begun to create the magnetic force that draws us home.

The younger son is, in fact, the indwelling Divine Light that embarks on a pilgrimage embracing matter and carrying with it the radiation of the Divine Creative Light. It is this Light, an aspect of Consciousness, that creates the entire physical plane in which we express our Divinity. We are this Light, and we must express the radiation of this Light. We carry the Divine Essence into everything we do, whether we are currently aware of it or not.

In the condition of unawareness which is called occlusion, we carry out our daily assignments as they were originally laid down by ourselves before our occlusion became absolute. We programmed ourselves to fulfill the mission of Divine Expression. Our condition of occlusion, or loss of conscious awareness of our Divinity, is spoken of in scripture when we read of the sheep that is lost from the fold. We are all lost sheep as long as we do not recognize who we are, because we all belong to one fold.

Since we belong to one fold, we all carry the Divine Essence into everything we do. While we continue to be unaware of our origins we are inhibited in all that we do, believing we have failed. This inhibition arises from the interrupted stream of consciousness. Only on a clear day can we see all the way to our 'Home" and forever. As the evening clouds of occlusion give way to the dawning light of Divinity we begin to lose the need to express the least and lowest aspects of the personality, and begin to exhibit the better qualities of the higher self. This is the stage in the Prodigal story where will is directed towards a given end. "I will arise and go now to my Father's House". This is the time when we recognize that the life we are living is not to our liking, and we are going to do something about it right here and now. Whether we join an ashram, go meditate on a mountain top or join a social service group makes no difference, for what we decide to do is what we need to do for our growth at this time. It is for this reason that we should never criticize anyone for their particular method of spiritual expression. There are no 'wrong' paths to spiritual enlightenment. Some may be slower than others, but that is par for the course.

The power we are using in our drive towards awakening is the One power. The power we use for our spiritual unfoldment is the same power we use to lift our toothbrush to brush our teeth. It is not the structure of the form of the power that alters the outcome. It is the quality of the consciousness utilizing the power that makes the difference. The only reason we have criminals and misfits in our society is that they do not know who they are, and therefore they cannot use the power they have in a creative and constructive manner for their own good or that of society. This situation exists in the highest offices of the world's governments all the way down to the most bereft citizen. Current evidence seems to indicate that there is little if any awareness of who they are among our present world leaders. Philosopher Gurdjieff refers to the state of humanity as being a 'state of sleep'.

Another description that can be applied to the younger son is 'Cosmic Christ'. As soon as you and I – the younger son – make the recognition of who we are we become the Cosmic Christ. The term Christ comes from the Greek word Christos, the Annointed One, and this in turn means the one who has come into the realization of their Godliness.

In our descent to the level of the gross material plane of matter we become mesmerized by our own successful results. In time this situation develops into a condition of the things of the world and 'me'. When this is our conscious outlook, the "I" sleeps. It is the reawakening of the I that signals the return to the Father's House. Again when we turn to another and profoundly meaningful statement in scripture, we find this view confirmed. Once again we read "Not me but the Father in me doeth the work". To say it is the me who does the work is like saying it is the car that takes us from one town to another, when in fact it is we who take the car to wherever we *choose* to go.

This process of the descent of Spirit into matter can best be seen through the use of a simple diagram (Diagram A), which shows the condition of Consciousness before any manifestation at all takes place. It is unmanifest. It is the condition of no-thing-ness or Cosmic Night. Then comes the Light of the first manifested frequency which, in its replication process, brings about the 'beings of light', the angelic kingdom, the soul-beings of all created form. The Elder Son is such a being and is of a lower frequency than the beingness of the Father. All expression in this realm resides in the Monadic level of consciousness. In the continuing journey downwards the frequency is continually reduced to the point where it is no longer immaterial, but becomes material. This is the Prodigal's entry into the realm of the physical expression. From here on we are in the realm of the physical and the domain of the lower nature and occluded consciousness.

We are now in the area of life where experience is primarily dominated by sensation, both physical and emotional. We, the Prodigal Son (for that is indeed what we are), suffer the "slings and arrows of outrageous fortune" in our daily sojourn in the solid world. Each effect that we feel – physical pain, harsh words, foul blows – are all the experiences which we programmed into our assignment. But now, in the experiencing, we can recall their purpose by accepting them for what they are, and by asking ourselves what is the next point of learning in our journey. As already indicated, once we reach the recognition that we are not satisfied with our daily life and begin to realize that what we are creating is bad temper, jealousy, hate, resentment and our last heart attack (not to mention our ongoing migraines!), we are in a prime position to start our journey to the Promised Land.

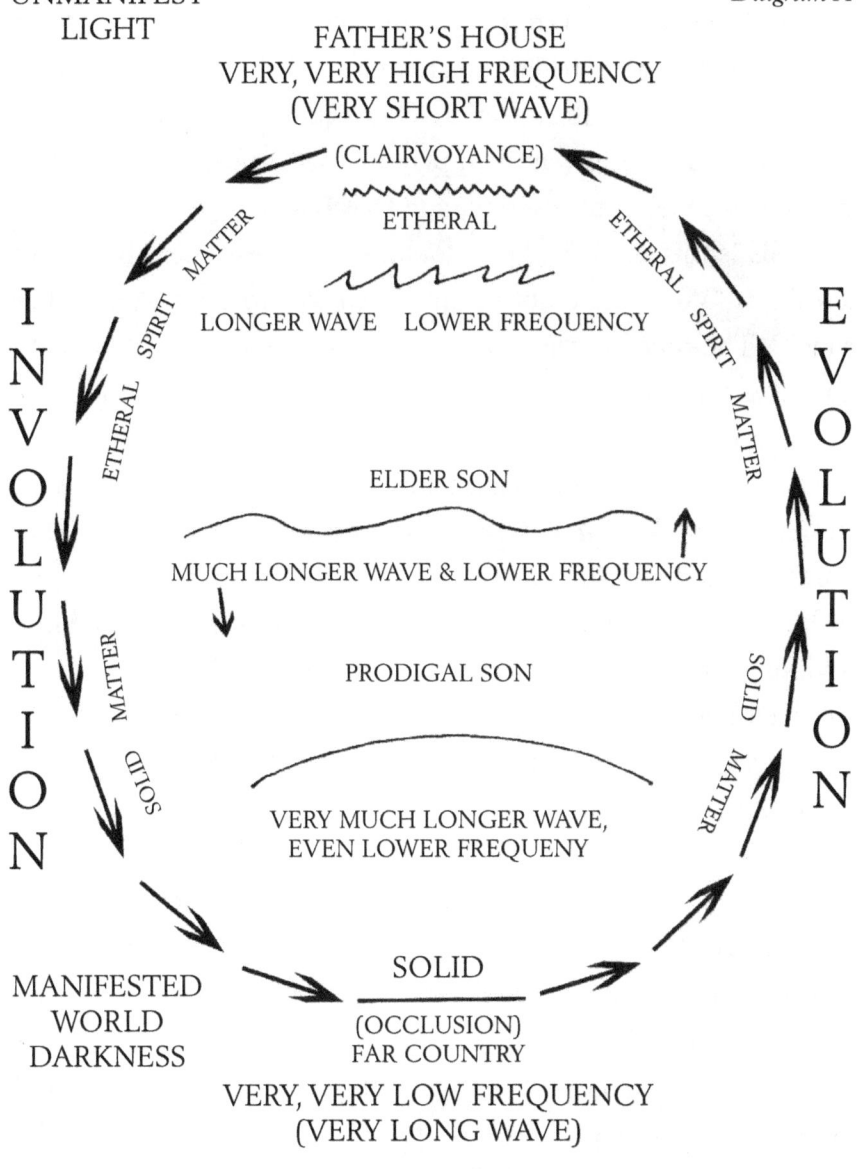

Diagram A

From here we can take every pain, every rebuff, every harsh word as signals of opportunity to advance our own redemption from the pit of occlusion – the Far Country. We start by accepting and blessing all of our experiences and recognizing them as an integral part of the Divine Expression. There can be no prevarication at this point. We cannot sit on a maybe about it, for rejection is a vote to stay in darkness. The question to be asked is "What do I do right now?". When the answer is provided – and it always is – respond to it with full faith. Often in the early stages of the process the answer given is simply one that provides an opportunity for us to learn to respond, and that is all.

This is the point in the unfoldment process where Scripture speaks of "Were there not ten made whole; where are the other nine?". The nine are those who do not respond, do not resonate to the incoming vibration of the Divine energy. These are the ones who are not healed, who do not have their prayers answered, who do not see what to do next and so remain in the quagmire of despondency. All our difficulties in life come from the fact that we do not accept our divinity and therefore we cannot be in the right place at the right time to receive the kingdom. "I know Mine and mine know Me". This is not an empty saying. It is pertinent to our well-being in all phases of our existence. If we wish to change our physical circumstances, our emotional climate or our mental environment, *we have to change our consciousness.*

In the crucifixion story Judas represents the characteristic of the contact with the gross world of physical matter. Judas sells the Jesus figure (the personality) for thirty pieces of silver. We sell our personality and our birthright several times a day for much less than thirty pieces of silver. Each time we lie, cheat, deceive or steal we sell for a mess of pottage, like Esau. The material world is our cross of crucifixion, and unless we overcome the material world by rising above the need to be lord of all we survey, we can never get on with the job of resurrecting our higher consciousness, going on to take dominion over the 'whole earth'. It is precisely this realization that the Prodigal makes in order to return to the Father's House (Diagram B on next page). The story of Jesus and the Prodigal Son are in essence the same story. They both tell of the descent and death of the Spirit and its entry into the dense matter of the tomb of occlusion and separatism. They both teach that the Spirit awakens to the light of a new dawn of resurrected consciousness, which goes on to assume dominion over the kingdom it had created in the first place. This is not a Middle East myth; it is a deep and personal drama on a grand Cosmic Scale.

As long as we are only concerned with the gross physical world, we are crucified and living in the rock tomb of material tyranny. It may be mink lined, but it is tyranny and we are its victim, we are never in charge.

We learn from the story of the Prodigal that we journey to a Far Country and spend our inheritance. This means that we have an inheritance to spend. It means that we utilize our spiritual beingness in the doing of all we do. It does not mean that what we do is not what we should be doing. We never have to apologize spiritually for what we do, but we do need to frequently check if it is time to do something else with our spiritual energy.

As we the Prodigal begin the journey home we recognize that there is a place to go to, that we are Divine Spirit. As we put our attention on this aspect of Divine Spirit, the personality level of our expression starts to transmute into a higher level of successful manifestation. We begin to replace the faulty parts in our engine of creation, and it now runs much more smoothly and gets us where we are going in far better style. Once we realize and accept who and what we are, we magnify the downpouring stream of Divine

Consciousness that has been there all the time. It is through this act that the story says the Prodigal is provided with new sandals. The sandals are the firm foundation of spiritual travel, which are given by the Father.

Diagram B

THE HUMAN SPIRIT AS THE PRODIGAL SON

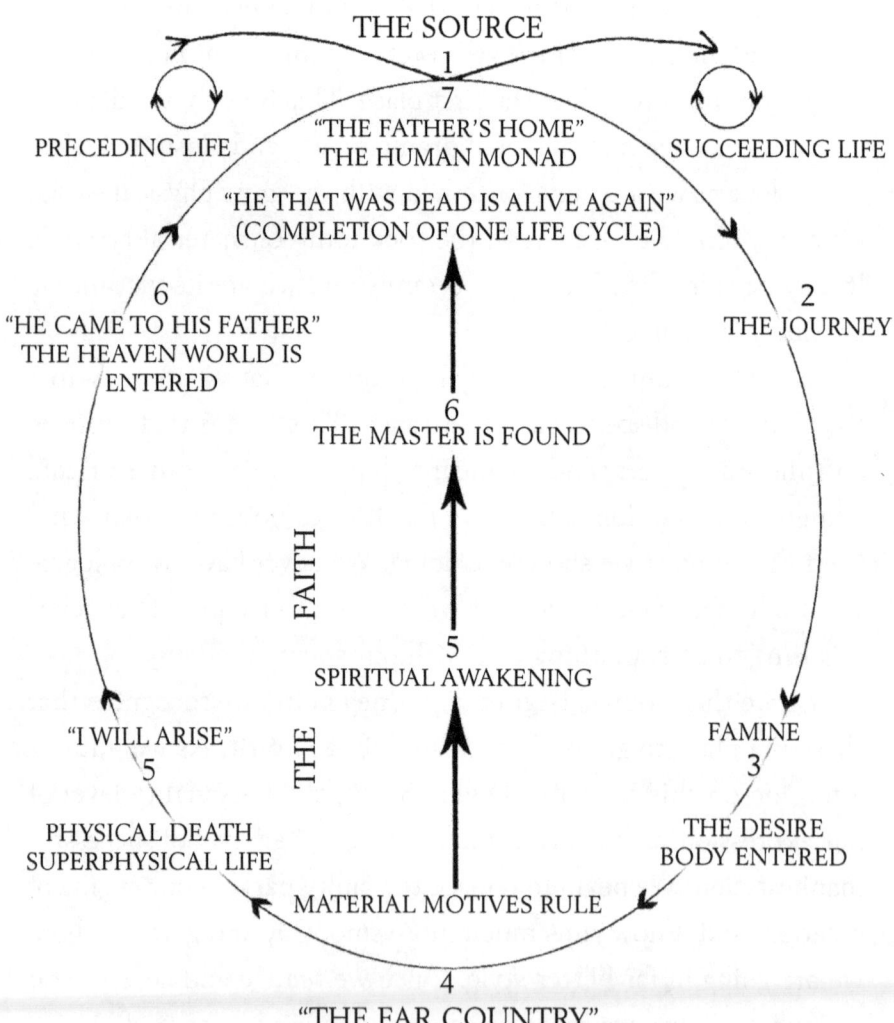

When we journey a way along this road of spiritual living we develop an additional dimension of understanding, which surrounds us like a robe. This is the Robe of Glory. It is the one which uplifted consciousness places around our mind. When at last we have risen above the need to possess the material kingdom for its own sake and ours, we pass on to the stage of receiving the Ring, which signifies our ascension into the realm of the universal, omnipotent, omnipresent and omniscient, the state of being from which we started our journey of manifestation. In this state we are constantly aware and continually focused on our Divinity.

There is a simple technique that assists us in our search for our Divine Expression. This small exercise can be practiced anywhere at any time as long as we are willing to put our own sincere dedicated intent behind what we are doing. There is no affirmation ever conceived that will give us results when we give it only lip service. The world is full of prayers, incantations, invocations and affirmations that are exclaimed on the barren wastes of non-existing intentness. In this exercise all we have to do while sitting still is:

A. Focus our attention upon our breathing, making no evaluation of its quality, but simply focusing;
B. Think of the left nostril while breathing in;
C. Think of the right nostril while breathing out.
D. While breathing in hold this concept in mind – "The Love and Power of God is All that there is".
E. While breathing out, hold this concept in mind – "I AM the Expression of that Love and Power here and now".

There should never be a set expectation, but change will occur. Once we have knocked and once we have asked, the door will be opened and the request will be heard. Being the Prodigal Son assures us of finding the welcome mat at the door of our Father's House.

Chapter 4

Getting Rid of Mistakes

There are few, if any, among us who have not made mistakes in our lives. Some of these mistakes have been of a quite serious nature with consequences that we would have been only too happy to have missed.

The first thing we have to realize is that in making mistakes we have only been functioning as mere humans, and as mere humans we can little afford to make too many mistakes. But as mere humans we can do little else than make 'human mistakes'.

The second thing we have to realize and accept is that there is nobody out there who is responsible for our errors. There is no one upon whom to lay the blame. It is not the fault of our families, it is not the fault of the government – it is *our* responsibility.

Even after we make the recognition that the mistakes we make are "too silly for words", we seem to go on making them. But in point of fact, it is often because of the words we use that we continue to make the very errors we are trying to eliminate from our lives – many phrases that we could well do without.

Among them is "Be patient with me, I am only human". Or again, "Be patient with me, God isn't finished with me yet". Both of these phrases are words of great limitation which severely restrict opportunities for getting rid of mistakes in our lives.

We must learn to let go of the need to allow our glib tongue dominate our conversations. With cliché remarks such as the ones quoted above we actively deny our divinity. Many of us do not seem to realize that our sub-conscious hears all that we say and receives it quite literally. Not only does it do this, but it then influences us in later activity in relation to the very thing that was involved at the time the remark was first made.

The sooner we become aware of our own divinity and its on-going power and presence in our lives, the sooner will we remove ourselves from the area of life in which mistakes are made. The more we become aware of the omnipresence, omnipotence and omniscience of our own divinity, the more quickly will we be able to improve the quality of our discernment. As we improve the quality of our discernment we become quite adept at seeing the pitfalls ahead, and so taking the necessary detour to reach our goal without hindrance.

No one wakes up in the morning and plans to have a day of errors. At least, if they do, they do not admit to doing so in public. That is not how we plan our day's activity, and yet by nightfall we have errors by the dozens. How do we make these mistakes? Better still, how do we cease to make them? The vital recognition we must make has to be the need to make a radical change in our vocabulary.

We need to banish such phrases as "I should have…", "I should not have…" or "they should not…". If we do not begin to eliminate these judgmental phrases from our daily life we are condemned to continue to bring the slavery of errors into those lives. We need to consciously withdraw ourselves from these patterns of speech, which we do by taking an objective view of what is going on out there in the world. We must learn that we no longer need to make subjective (personality) judgments. We must learn not to attach blame or preconceived moral evaluations to that which we are seeing before us in the present.

When we observe whatever is before us, we must simply make the recognition that what we are seeing is a manifestation of Divinity. Even if what we are seeing is beyond the limits of society's law and morals, we must go on to the realization that this could not be happening if the parties concerned were aware of their own individual Divinity. No one who has entered totally into the Consciousness of there being only One Source can ever again transgress against civil or moral law. When we come to know that there is only the I AM in expression at all times, we neither see 'wrong' nor do we perpetrate 'wrong' at any time.

In this context, 'wrong' simply means not being aware of being I AM, God Consciousness in all and any circumstances. By responding at the level of the I AM to all and every expression out there, we are exhibiting an awareness that there is only One Source of manifestation in the entire Cosmos. To condemn what has already taken place is to deny the Will of God in action and to set up an alternative power or duality. It is because we so often set up a duality that we become incapable of operating in this material kingdom.

When we have learned to accept that which is as the omnipresence, we begin to be aware of the presence of the divine as our own I AM Consciousness. By so doing, in that very moment, we remove ourselves from the *effects* of what is taking place in the outer world. As a result of this recognition we begin to be aware that our own individual consciousness is Universal Divine

Consciousness at all times. In so doing we come into the further realization of how impossible it is for any experience to come from any source other than the *One Divine Source*. The I AM Consciousness *is* that source.

Whenever we are faced with a situation in the outer world that is or has been a disturbing one for us, all we have to do to deal with it is remember a simple phrase such as "I know that there is but One Power and One Source of that Power".

Understanding and seeing beyond the appearance of what we are observing in our daily lives assists us to rise above the law. This means we rise above the *need* to break either the civil law or the law of nature because we see in both of these the Law of God. When we can do this, we cease to attract into our lives the kind of events which formerly tempted us into infractions of the civil law or nature's law. Natural law cannot affect us adversely when we no longer BELIEVE it to be an independent and unrelated power source. *It is that simple.*

Spiritual law is never complex, and the process we are referring to is a spiritual law. For generations culture has conditioned us to the belief that nature is an independent power source. The whole of our educational system is currently geared to promote this belief. We are instructed in physics, chemistry and biology to accept these sciences as absolutes and as founding 'cause' for life in the Cosmos. As long as we accept this belief we remain under the hypnotism of it and its effects. We cannot organize and successfully direct 'nature' if we believe it to be separate and outside of ourselves. The society that teaches there is an independent and separate natural law becomes subject to that which it teaches. Such a society enters into duality in every aspect of its expression – multiple gods, conflicting law, warring religions and personal violence. All of this disappears for us as soon as we realize that both natural law and civil law has its source in the One Source. For convenience in our society we call that source GOD. As there can never be a definition of God – because a part can never define a whole – the following description will have to suffice for our purpose here. *God is the sum of all that ever was, is or ever will be in the Cosmos.*

Whenever we look on the outside world and are tempted to say "Oh dear, what a shame", let us make the recognition that what we are seeing is an illusion. Let us also be aware that an illusion is something which is created by consciousness. Anything that is created by consciousness is an illusion. It is only when we forget that *we are* consciousness and have created what is out there that we enter into delusion and therefore become the effect of what we behold in our experience. There are no accidents – everything is caused. No matter how convincing the symptoms or the effects may be, they are never cause. There is only one cause, one source, and there is only one consciousness.

As we become aware of who we are and that we are consciousness individually, we cease to make mistakes – walking, talking, working, visiting or just relaxing.

Someone may think or say "How tiring to always be 'on'; I would be exhausted". Not true. When we know who we are, we remain plugged into the endless energy of the Source of all energy. It is no more energy consuming to act than to have an idea. Even thinking is very energy consuming if we believe we are merely human. In terms of this realm, thinking is the least valuable commodity we have in our inventory. "Have no thought for the morrow, what ye shall eat or what ye shall put on……" . Jesus was the best Jewish psychologist who ever lived. The sooner we all learn that, the sooner we will operate our lives with efficiency and with peaceful happiness. Anyone who thinks Jesus was not a psychologist does not know very much about psychology.

The process of removing or eliminating mistakes in our daily living is very simple. However, the execution of the process requires commitment, dedication and persistence. It is necessary to guide and direct the personality (persona) in transmuting its energy into the higher vibratory rate of the conscious psyche. By so doing it becomes easy to enter into the recognition that there is but One Source of all power. All energy stems from this One Source, and this One Source is the I AM Consciousness.

There is a long-honored statement in Scripture which is the most profound and powerful psychological tool ever devised for self-development. It is most appropriate in this circumstance – "Be Still And Know, I AM GOD". Whenever we are faced with any condition that is too much for the personality to handle all we have to do is pause, remember and repeat this potent affirmation. Once we have entered into God self-awareness, we immediately become capable of dealing with that by which we are faced. Having adopted this procedure for handling daily living, we soon become *constantly aware* of our own divinity, and we start to be more effective in our mundane daily efforts.

As we begin to live our lives from within this consciousness we rely less and less on our cultural training and thought analysis. We begin to tap into Cosmic Truth without recourse to our personal educational track, and thereby enter into our active intuitional creativity. How do we check our progress and our reality on this program? Quite early on we notice that we lose our sense of irritation with anyone or anything. Probably next in line, we lose our sense of disappointment with other people and their failings. We cease to be angry or disappointed. We are no longer surprised because we do not have expectations of anyone. We begin to live in the present. We live in the NOW.

If all evil, wrongdoing and mistakes are the result of a belief in duality or two powers, then as long as we choose to be part of that thinking we will automatically come under the law of that thinking. When we no longer accept that there are two powers and come back into the recognition of the One Power then we come directly under the Law of GOD, and there are no accidents and there are no errors. God does not goof.

In order that we may enjoy the full glory of this form of life we must learn not to fight evil (the appearance of two powers). This is what Jesus meant when He said "Resist not evil". We must not judge from the narrow perspective of the unenlightened personality. Judgment is always a characteristic of the personality and is marred and limited by its occlusion. It is the enlightened I AM that has created the Cosmos of symmetry and beauty which we behold every day of our lives.

Let us always remember that whenever we have doubts or fears we will be restored to at-one-ment.

Chapter 5

The Impersonal Life

*T*he only reason anyone ever makes a demand on life or themselves is because they are acting under the delusion there is a characteristic called duality in existence. We are operating with the concept of 'me and God', 'me and the Devil', an entity out there and a me in here. Our whole culture has promoted this concept for generations. We are taught at our mother's knee that there is a good and a bad, a good and an evil. We have been told that 'they' are wrong and 'we' are right.

The reason we make demands on society, family, friends, lovers is because we have accepted the belief that there is a separatism in Divine expression, which has come about for a very simple reason. We have been so expert and so prolific at creating, that we have become mesmerized by all that we have created. In so becoming we have also become occluded as to the origin of all we see out there, together with what we experience in life in general. From then on we personalize everything – Bill's house, Mary's car and so on.

The beginning of the personalized life was when we began to move away from the 'impersonal life'. It was when we began to accept the belief of a God out there and a me here. It was when we began to accept that there was a separation in any part of God's kingdom. It was when we began to accept that there could be something out there that was not created by God in the first place, or that anyone else had the power to create a single item other than with God's Will and Power. If such a thing as sin existed in the world, without doubt this belief would be the Original Sin.

If ever we seek a fundamental cause for the world's ills this is it and has been so since we lost our God-centered awareness. The loss in question was not a penalty, but rather a self-applied process. This is where all our problems in relationships start. We see the other person as an opponent and not as another aspect of self. We see the other person as stemming from some other source which is totally different from our own. We fail to see that the other person is part of the multiplicity of consciousness of our own Selfhood. We have accepted that there is a duality of consciousness in the universe, when in fact the only error we can ever perpetrate is to not realize there is only one consciousness, which is Father of all. What we have out there is a large variety of images, points of view, material expressions all initiated by us from the center of our I AM Consciousness.

We are talking about the personal and the impersonal life, both of which are an integral part of the creative process. We must not run away with the idea that the personal life is not a valuable part of the process of evolution. One of the chief aspects of the involutionary phase of evolution is precisely the 'personal' life stage of our development. Our mission is to spiritualize matter through the medium of spiritualizing the personality. There is a difficulty that most of us experience. We look at everything out there and we do not realize that everything that is did not get there without being created. The second thing we fail to realize is that *we have created them*. It is Consciousness that creates everything in the universe. When we say "I", it is Individualized Consciousness that is speaking. Let us not forget there is only one Consciousness in the entire Cosmos. There is only one word in every language throughout the world that describes individualized consciousness, and that word is "I". It is a word that describes a universal concept in consciousness.

Our difficulty in holding on to this concept at our present stage of development is due to the conditioning of the culture which has been our guideline for several thousands of years past. Evolution is a slow and gentle process. "The Mills of God grind slowly, but they grind exceeding small". We are surrounded by a society telling us that one day a Personalized God woke up from a cosmic sleep and decided to create a universe peopled by a bunch of folks, some of whom would make it to heaven while the remainder would have their heating arrangements taken care of for all eternity. If this scenario does not turn us on there is an alternative; there usually is in circumstances like this. One day there was a big bang in the 'nowhere' which set up a chain of molecular accidents, the latest of which can be seen on our favorite television channel any time we care to tune in. Both of these descriptions are most certainly over-simplifications, but they express the degree of occlusion as to our origin and evolutionary path we have reached in our recent past. What this culture has produced is not an impersonal life, but one that is indifferent and disconnected. When we are not consciously plugged in to the source of life we are unable to express life abundantly or even mildly successfully.

In order to break the chain of this irresponsible view on life and evolution we need to make a fundamental adjustment in our understanding of creation. It is not something that happened several billion years ago by accident or by miracle. It is something that is taking place at this very moment. It is taking place throughout the Cosmos within every moment of expression of consciousness. This is the first day of the rest of our creativity.

Every single object that we have in this solar system and beyond was first an idea in the 'mind plane' of consciousness. The very idea itself is constituted of the essence of consciousness. We cannot have an idea of something unless we have the consciousness with which to have it. Big Bang or no Big Bang, there never is a brain cell or its sub-atomic parts that has come out of a nowhere. As long as we cannot see or will not see our own responsibility for creation we will continue to blame others for the state of the world. "It is the President", "It is Congress", "It is my in-laws", and so the song goes on. From this condition of thinking comes all the physical, emotional and mental ills that we are heir to on this planet.

Life for all of us comes down to our relationships with people and with things. If we cannot attract and maintain a relationship with a person or an object, they or it drifts out of our orbit. The result of this in human terms is loneliness and poverty. And again in human terms, this is not the kind of life for anyone to live. Whatever relationships we have at the moment, *we have created them*. Unless we are prepared to face this fact we cannot successfully change the conditions which brought the relationship into being in the first place. Without spiritual responsibility we remain in life as material effects. There is no middle place between victim and creator. The only vehicle that can take us from the arena of victims is Individualized Consciousness and the awareness of it being focalized Universal Divine Consciousness.

There is a step beyond this which we must take in order to bring about the changes we need in our life. We must also accord the same quality of beingness to every person involved in our relationships. Unless we consciously commit ourselves to this realization, every relationship we set up in our life will run into rough seas, and founder on the rocks of 'separative' personality. If we fail to do this we find ourselves in situations where we are saying such things as "When we first met you were such a nice person, but now you are just rotten to the core". And there will also be many opportunities for it to be said to us. It is only when we try to establish a relationship in our state of occlusion that this can happen. When we come to realize and accept the Universal God Self in both ourselves and the other person we no longer have to experience the relationship breaks that formerly happened.

What then is the process of change by which we can bring this about? If we will commit ourselves to remember next time we are involved with another person in any form of relationship to see them and ourselves as expressions of the One Consciousness, manifesting through a multiplicity of expressions, we will open the door to a harmonious relationship. We can add to this by taking the very next opportunity to share the responsibility for whatever it is that goes off the track. We then can say with comfort "Gee! we blew that one. Maybe we better take another look at the blueprint.". With this form of action we have crossed the bridge over the river of personality separation and entered in the land of at-one-ment of responsibility, and this place is the foothills of the mount of the I AM Consciousness, in Scripture called Mount Sinai.

By using this method of dealing with the activities of a relationship we provide an opportunity to each other to accept our responsibility for what we have created in the situation and at the same time offer a path of new creative effort which both of us can walk in harmony. By recognizing our mutual divinity we remove the mote from our own eye ("I") and proceed to initiate dominion over our kingdom. This kingdom over which we exercise dominion is the kingdom of 'me'. Once we have begun to bring the 'me' under the guidance of the I AM we have begun to eliminate the occlusion that beset all our thoughts, words and deeds.

We are told in Scripture that Man has been given dominion over the earth, but we must be clear as to what it is the earth encompasses. The earth is not merely the planet upon which we conduct our physical expression. The planet is only the outer expression of the earth over which we have dominion. This earth has an inner expression, which is the personality. It is this personality over which we must first extend dominion before we can order the mineral, plant and animal aspects to be our servants. It is for lack of this understanding that so many of us fail in so many of the things we undertake in the course of our life on earth.

When we have recognized that there is only one consciousness and that consciousness has created everything, we no longer have a lack. We no longer have a need to fulfill. What we do have is an understanding of the opportunity to express the kingdom in all that we undertake. From the moment we become aware of this and of its source, the whole earth is activated on a magnetic vibratory level to bring into concrete manifestation that which we divinely wish to express. From this point forward all our ideas become facts because we are consciously aware that ideas have their birth in Universal Divine Consciousness. The consciousness we now have is at-one-ment consciousness, which is Impersonal and has no favorites.

Many people involved in New Age Thought have said that the time to express desires for manifested things and conditions is during our meditations. This is *not* advisable. All we should be seeking in meditation is at-one-ment consciousness. When we achieve that we will no longer need to express desires at the personality level of living. At any time, the whole purpose of meditation is to raise our own consciousness (individualized) to an awareness of the universality of all consciousness. All we have to do is to raise our own consciousness to the level where we become aware of the connection between individualized and universal consciousness. This is what Jesus meant when he said "The meek shall inherit the earth". The meek are those who no longer have a need to feel independent and separated from the Divine Stream of Consciousness – they have surrendered pride of personality.

In order that we may enter into the impersonal life as smoothly as possible we must be prepared to exercise great responsibility for what we inaugurate in our kingdom. When we create it we become responsible for cleaning, maintenance and repair, not to mention daily utilization. This is something which we must recognize and commit ourselves to even before being anointed. In fact, we can not become anointed unless we are prepared to undertake all responsibility in the earth plane. The state of grace does not permit free-loaders. The surrender of personality of which we speak is total and permanent.

In all categories of spiritual unfoldment – also known as "the journey of the soul" – until we finally and completely deal with them, the situations produced at the personality level will continue to return. If and when we are faced with a seemingly non-responsive ongoing situation, it can only be so because we are not treating it from the level of the I AM. As long as we try to deal with any matter at the normal earth plane level, it will stick around. Personality does not have the power to rectify its own shortcomings. This is the reason so much psychological therapy fails to give satisfaction to those who seek its help. There is an old Irish saying: "You cannot make a silk purse out of a sow's ear".

We must also realize that the more we spiritually advance the more responsibility we have to assume for the earth. Situations do not disappear from our lives; we simply get busier and better at handling them. Living the impersonal life does not mean having nothing to do while others labor for us. It means walking the straight and narrow path by removing the obstacles from it with spiritual acumen.

We have touched on the concept of commitment once or twice in this chapter, and a guideline about this concept may well be in order here. Many of us are all too willing to offer commitments to all and sundry. The real problem with commitments is that they are not made to a non-entity. They are made to the I AM Consciousness of whoever received the commitment at the time. That means they are made to ourselves. When we make and then break a commitment we interrupt the flow of Infinite Divine Consciousness, and thereby reduce the effectiveness of all Divine activity. In the process of giving a commitment we have participated in a Divine conception, and when we fail to fulfill our part in the birthing of that commitment we have actually aborted a mission of Divine activity. With each successive abortion we reduce the degree of our own creative fertility and thereby bring about a barrenness in our own individual womb of Creative Consciousness. It is much better to remain outside the marriage bed of creative commitment altogether. As long as we do not engage in commitment-breaking we do not reduce the health of our creative ability. It is far better to be in the state of spiritual rest than in the state of spiritual discord.

In order that we may move from the life of the restricted personality and enter the life of the I AM Consciousness or impersonal life, we must take active steps to achieve this transformation. We need to be on the alert for an opportunity to initiate the process, and the easiest way is to respond to the next intuitive urge that comes to us. For example, if we are driving along the freeway, not pressed for time, and find ourselves with an urge to get off at the next exit, the response is to do so. We will discover later why we were urged to get off at that particular exit. On this occasion it may be nothing more than an opportunity for learning to respond. However, next time it will be more meaningful, and as we develop this response mechanism we soon learn to discern when our I AM Self is at work. In this area of our development we need to learn to do without our slide rule or pocket computer. As we continue to use the process, we do become more proficient just as if we were learning to play guitar or piano. It is important to realize that we become proficient for our spiritual selves and not for display or boasting before others. "Go thy way and tell no man".

As we begin to recognize the threads in the fabric of life, we soon realize where the path to spiritual dominion lies for each and every day. The pillar of fire that leads us through our daily activities is the intuitive consciousness, which is in effect the Promethean Fire that descends from the heaven of Universal Consciousness.

Once we have learned who we are and have recognized the connections between cause and effect, we remove separatism from our life. This then enables us to find the peace of mind that provides us with the confidence to know what we are doing at all times.

The real starting point for entering the realm of the impersonal life is the recognition that we are going to have to accept responsibility for whatever condition we currently find ourselves in. We must learn that it does not matter what "they" did or said. In this instance, we are part of the cause. What we are really involved with is the transpersonal life. It is moving completely out of the 'me' into the 'I' within 'me'. 'Me' is merely the word 'I' uses to define and describe the persona. The persona is never more nor less than the outer expression of Inner Consciousness.

We do not have to take and devote a special time slot to getting rid of all our so-called bad habits. In any case, we do not actually have any to get rid of; what in fact happens is that by connecting to our I AM Self we change our vibratory rate of expression and therefore no longer have the old vibratory rate that expressed what we called our bad habits. When we change our Consciousness, the outer manifestation of that Consciousness has to change. There is nothing *wrong* about having a glass of wine or whiskey now and then. The greatest opportunity for developing our impersonal life is in the area of human versus spiritual love. They are not always one and the same, but they can be. It is when they are not the same that we are in the condition of occluded awareness of our at-one-ment. When we start to deal with this concept of love on the human level of male-female love relationships, one or other of the parties becomes the receiver and the other the giver. The roles may change from party to party – even sometimes between a particular couple – but for the most part it remains a static relationship. In most human relationships sharing is the exception. One party gives and the other receives, and so it remains all through the association. In such associations neither the man nor the woman sees the Divinity in each other, and so it remains a separatist condition of joint living. In effect, what is happening is that the man and the woman see only the outer effect of each other – body, actions, words and behavior in general. There is no awareness of an inner aspect to either one or the other. What is seen is the personality of each, and because both are occluded they are not aware that there is another dimension of beingness left untouched in the relationship.

This condition of non-awareness is the cause of all human relationship problems. We look at a person and say that they are this, that or the other, and then transfix them with a specific label from which we will not let them escape. We have only to sit in a restaurant or bar and listen to those around us as they talk about people they know. It seems that such remarks about those people are one dimensional – they are all bad or all wonderful – no mixes are allowed. We do not allow people we know to be multi-dimensional, nor do we allow them to grow.

When we hear, see and treat people in a fixed manner, we erect a 'stop sign' in their life and in our own. We totally ignore the dynamic of living creativity in their beingness or even that they might be connected to such a source of creativity. We can hardly call this love, whether it is between a couple who live together or between friends.

No matter how strong an original attraction may be between people, if it is a merely physical, emotional or mental one, it cannot sustain itself. It cannot do so because everything of the personality, as these three aspects are, quickly decays when deprived of the nourishment of the I AM Consciousness. There is no-thing of the personality or of the material world that can survive when disconnected from the I AM. Because none of us are perfect on the personality level, all of us find difficulty in living in close proximity with others. Living together is a learning process. There is such an infinite diversity and complexity of expression in what we have created over millions of years, that the personality completely occludes its creative responsibility when faced with a particular situation.

When we fail to see the Divinity in another person, all our faults become our graces and all their graces become their faults. At least, that is how we see them. There is an infinite variety of images that we are privy to in our daily experience, but it is in the comparing of them within their own orbit that we incur our difficulties. Our culture has trained us to do this in all aspects of life, but in truth we cannot compare since all images have a common origin in Universal Consciousness. When we learn this, and apply it in our relationships, we enter a whole new echelon of expression towards each other. We enter the domain of *peace*. Peace in this context can be defined in simple words, namely, peace is an absence of conflict, it is an absence of resistance to movement. Divinity and the humans through whom it expresses Itself is in a constant state of movement (expression).

Peace, harmony and love escape us until we re-unite our personality with our Consciousness and join both of them to Universal Consciousness. When we can do this we then have no difficulty in seeing Divinity expressed in all those by whom we are surrounded. Then it becomes very easy and simple to love anyone without having to love everyone in the same manner throughout our whole life. Once we recognize that the individual expression we are witnessing stems from a single source, we ourselves cease to be an adversary.

True love is when we can accept the *other* as being the total expression of God – not just a part of them, such as their generosity, but also their impatience and all of their characteristics. We have to be prepared not to "wish to change them for the better or for their own good". There is nobody else in them that is expressing except God, and as we begin to express this in our thoughts, words and deeds, we find ourselves with an increasing awareness of our own God Presence.

There is a very well-known and loved statement of this condition of awareness that has helped a great many people over many years, and we can all share it to our mutual benefit. *There is but one life, and that life is the perfect life, and that perfect life is my life right now.*

Let us be quite clear that when we are talking about the impersonal life, we are *not* talking about the indifferent life. We must be consciously aware of the needs of the 'other'. We do not have to be of service to those needs, but if we are aware of them and decide to serve them we are making a commitment to Universal Divine Consciousness. Even if we recognize that the service we are proposing to render is one that feeds a dependency, the commitment remains sacred. In this we must include normal physical attraction and emotional attachment or mental compatibility. When we enter into a relationship with this understanding, all of the aspects – physical, emotional and mental – are enhanced and uplifted. If in the act of love-making both parties are aware of the Divinity in each other and in themselves, the experience will transcend this world. Whenever the I AM is infused into a condition, that condition is transmuted into a spiritual experience. Indifference is separation. Conscious at-one-ment is the greatest of all love. There is nothing to equal the ecstasy of giving when we give from the I AM Consciousness of sharing.

In order to love someone on the impersonal level of love we must become aware of the interdependency of the love relationship. We must be prepared to receive and give in equal measure. We must never let the situation develop in such a way as to put the other person in the obligatory category. Relationships are a spiritual contract and must always be seen as such.

In all this activity of impersonal expression we must take great care to realize that it is not the expression that is God, but that which expresses the activity is God, which is also each of us. The pursuit of the impersonal life is the single most important undertaking of our entire incarnation. It is its purpose. The joy of the result is all the reward we need.

Chapter 6

Atlantis – The Creation Saga

Whenever Atlantis is mentioned in almost any group of spiritual seekers it never fails to evoke some inner response. Why is this so? It is because Atlantis is an integral part of all of our evolutionary and spiritual development. It is part of our spiritual heritage and is still a living factor in our psyche.

The basic facts about Atlantis are readily available. The first modern reference is contained in reports of early Egyptian history, and the primary evidence most frequently referred to is that found in the works of Plato, chiefly *Critias and Timaes*.

The story Plato relates is one he learned from a Greek traveler who had returned from a visit to Egypt. This story, told by the priests at Sais, recounted the events and the times of a land beyond the Pillars of Hercules (Gibraltar).

When the Egyptians referred to Atlantis they spoke of it as having already passed from view at least 10,000 years before the time of the Greek traveler's visit to Egypt.

Those who still believe that the world began just a mere 4,500 years ago are not able to handle a concept of existence that talks about living 12,000 years ago, let alone 2,700 million years ago. This is the time frame we have to deal with if we are to understand our own early spiritual and evolutionary development. Atlantis is not only a place of long ago. It was also a condition of consciousness of revered status in the process of involution for man's entry into earth living. It has been an essential step in our spiritual journey.

The second source of data available to us is that provided by Ignatius Donnelly, a one-time member of the United States Congress. Donnelly's work champions Plato, but goes far beyond in depth and research of Atlantis. The two books he wrote in the early 1880's, *Atlantis:The Antediluvian World* and *Ragnarok:The Age of Fire and Gravel*, are both long rational arguments for the physical existence of the Lost Continent. A third source is Lewis Spence's *The History of Atlantis*. But perhaps the most telling data on the Atlantean saga is found in the 'readings' of Edgar Cayce. In order to arrive at the information in Cayce it is necessary to wade through numerous readings because Cayce did not set out to validate the existence of Atlantis, and in fact such information was in conflict with his own religious beliefs. Nonetheless, the data emerged in individual readings undertaken on behalf of clients seeking help and guidance. In most instances he was tracking the client's evolutionary progress.

The most important source of data for enlightenment on Atlantis is our own process of meditative recall. Anyone with a little training can achieve this if they are sufficiently motivated to do so, but to regress ourselves merely to enjoy a good historical disaster 'movie' is a total waste of time, and is not the purpose of regression.

The first recognition we must make if we are to understand the world of Atlantis is that it is, as I said previously, an integral part of the creation saga. We must also realize that the material world in which we live has a single source of origin. Whether we choose to call that source God, Supreme Being, Jehovah, Allah or Cosmic Substance, we must still make the recognition that there is only once source of ALL CREATION. This creation has many expressions, of which Atlantis – continent and people – is only one. However, the part played by Atlantis is a major one in the total involutionary and evolutionary process of spiritual unfoldment of humankind. This process is that in which Divinity makes a descent from the state of non-physical manifestation to that of physical manifestation in pursuit of the Divine Idea. This descent stems from the state of Chaos (the unformed) outwards to the state of Cosmos. All manifestation in the Cosmos is material expression. It *is* the expression of the Divine.

The journey outward from Chaos is the involutionary process, while the journey inwards from Cosmos is the evolutionary process. As we have seen, this is the story of the Prodigal Son as related in Scripture. It is the story of Mankind journeying from Godhead to Humanhood and from Humanhood back to Godhead. Mankind is, in fact, Godhead in manifestation. This saga is expressed in Christianity as Crucifixion, Resurrection and Ascension. The outer material world is the physical body expression of God's consciousness.

Cosmos is not a miracle system. It is not an instantaneous expression mode. There is no such aspect in the creation process. Atlantis is a particular step in the overall descent of Divine Spirit into material expression. We must be quite clear what this 'descent' actually means. First and foremost it is not an angelic presence taking over an existing body, nor is it a sudden and miraculous 'appearance' in material form. It is a process whereby the Divine reduces its vibratory rate so as to manifest at an increasingly denser expression of material beingness. It is a process of Divinity organizing and structuring the elements of fine spiritual matter into the desired form of expression. No particle of matter on this planet is devoid of its "spiritual atom" structure. Humanhood is the most sublime expression of this spiritual creative process. It is not so easy to be aware of God in a piece of beautiful metal sculpture, but it is quite easy to be so aware with the 'feelings' we receive from each other as humans. If we in our daily life would accept ourselves as GOD in action, we would solve all our problems for evermore. God does not have problems.

All creation stems from a single source, the Unmanifested God, the first manifestation in the creation process being the outer expression of the Consciousness of God. This Consciousness then remains constant throughout all of the creation for the entire duration of the Cosmos. This is what is meant in Scripture when it states "In the beginning God created the Heaven and the Earth". Heaven is the Consciousness and Earth is the manifestation of that Consciousness. At this very moment, as we write and read, we are manifesting this very same Consciousness. We are One in the Spirit. We are not a separate entity which draws its power and sustenance from another source. There is no other source from which to draw, now or ever. All creation has emerged from this source and continues to do so every day as long as the Cosmos remains.

Anyone who is not prepared to make this recognition cannot as yet enjoy the benefits of living in the state of unlimited creative consciousness, for which the reason is quite simple. There is only one Mind, created by Consciousness, through which the entire creation is expressed. It is this Mind that permits us to be able to communicate with one another and to 'feel' the sense of each other at all levels of our being. The common denominator of understanding is the Consciousness of the Divine Source. This is the key to understanding the significance of the so-called Lost Continent of Atlantis. It is, together with other lost continents, a stage in the manifestation of the Divine Idea in the created Cosmos.

All of the Ancient Wisdom teachings expound this concept of the creation process. Long before there were modern written records in any of the world's scrolls, this wisdom was passed on through the oral method. The prophets who preceded the written word were the forerunners of the dissemination of the esoteric wisdom of the creation process. At that time awareness was not yet totally occluded. We had not yet reached the deepest levels of human material expression.

In order to understand the concept of Atlantis we have to adjust our mind-set to an idea of a time span and a duration of 2,700 million years. And let us bear in mind that Atlantis occupies even less than a quarter of that time span. Preceding Atlantis there were three major stages in the manifesting creation process, which are known as Polarian (Cosmic), Hyperborean (Monadic) and Lemurian (Higher Self), the parenthetical titles here being the names of the spiritual psychological levels of awareness. These divisions are also called root races, which in this context does not refer to European, Asian or other ethnic groups such as are spoken of in our contemporary books and journals.

Planet Earth is currently occupied by the Atlantean group or race. All of us are Atlanteans, whether or not we ever lived on the Continent of Atlantis itself. We are one of the sub-divisions of the Atlantean or fourth root race.

The creation process begins at the Polarian (Cosmic) level. This is the point when Divine Consciousness begins to express (focus) within the area where creation will be manifested. In esoteric language it is known as Fohat. In psychological terms this means Consciousness emerging from the state of rest. In Genesis it speaks of "....the Spirit of God moved upon the waters". This is not an expression in materiality, but rather an immaterial process. It is the creation of spiritual atoms from which material atoms stem. We can also call this the realm or condition wherein energy is inaugurated and is set to act as the positive and negative field at a later stage of manifestation.

The process of the descent of the vibratory expression of the Godhead at this stage covers millions of years. It is the period in which energy was diversified into positive (masculine) and negative (feminine). It is the forerunner of the physical male and female. Students of the Kabbalah will recognize this as Ain, Ain Soph. The significance for us today is the polarity of our life. Positive/negative, masculine/feminine is an integral part of the Godhead in an ongoing creative process.

As we move into the Hyperborean (Monadic) period we find the Divine Source subdividing the polarities into multiplicities of creative expressions. In the terms used in religious practice we would call these Archangels, Angels and so forth. These attributes are also the energy forms which provide the structure of the outer physical manifestations yet to come. Many of these attributes will not take physical form, but will remain non-physical, perhaps manifesting as the Devas who monitor and aid the Earth kingdom. Although many people have difficulty in accepting a Fairy or Deva entity, there are quite a number of highly evolved people who have managed to photograph these entities with a Polaroid camera, with which it is very difficult to fake a picture.

The third stage of descending developmental Consciousness is that of Lemurian (Higher Self), which expressed itself on the Continent of Lemuria, which was located in what we now know as the Pacific Ocean. It too is a lost continent, with very little of its land surface still showing above the waves. It was here that the chief work was carried out of organizing and structuring the human body we currently use. The form and the appearance were set at this time, but not the total density. Because the density was of minimal specific gravity it did not need tools or instruments. Therefore there are no artifacts remaining of this third root race. The major task of this group of incarnating beings was to perfect the technology of particle organization in the construction of atoms for use in a human body. They provided the blueprint and the detail drawings which we Atlanteans continue to use throughout our sojourn on this Planet Earth.

The group of the Monadic/Angelic Kingdom designated to actually build the bodies on Earth is – us. We are one of many groups each having their own particular assignments in the creation process. We never did ascend from the 'primordial slime'. We already knew from our Lemurian experience how to arrange and transmute energy into patterns of the particular body shapes required for specific purposes. This is the work of the Atlantean group – and we are they, doing the work we came to do here on Earth. We are spiritualizing matter, we are refining it into ever more complex multiplicities of expression. We began our incarnation on Atlantis in a state of low density, and set about assembling the energy particles to form the various organs of the body and the individual senses. We constructed the organs (faculties) of sight, hearing, smell, taste and touch. We perfected this structuring system many, many thousands of years ago (evolution), but we have as yet still to perfect the maintenance system. Because we have not yet done this we have an extensive dis-ease factor in our society.

Since we have already learned the technique of transmuting the vibratory rate of energy downwards, we now have little or no difficulty in assembling the particles of energy in the womb from the time of conception onwards, which is what the soul entity does in the womb. The cardinal issue for us during this Atlantean period of manifestation is to perfect the physical, emotional and mental levels of spiritual matter. We can make all the disaster movies we choose about the cataclysmic descent of the Lost Continent, but we still have to fulfill our commitment to the perfect expression of the Divine Idea in material form. We are, however, allowed grace periods.

How then do we go about our task of building a body. We begin as we always did – by focusing our *attention* upon a particular facet of energy during the act of physical union. This focalized point of energy later becomes the pineal gland. It is from this area of energy that the brain of the fetus is formed, and from this brain area the entire body is built. Even after physical birth, it is through the pineal that the Cosmic energies enter the human body. This portion of the body has the highest vibratory rate of the entire bodily form. If we speak to any pregnant woman she will readily admit that she had no conscious part in the initiating process, but we are reaching a point in our awareness where enlightened couples are consciously participating in a co-creation process in birthing as well as in other aspects of their soul expression. This is just the beginning of the re-awakening of creative soul awareness. It is the next step of the unfoldment process.

The question is frequently asked as to why a perfectly healthy fertile couple do not conceive at the highest point of their fertility cycle. Our answer is a simple one – namely, that the conditions prevailing do not provide a suitable entrance vehicle for any intending soul at that time. The choice of incarnation and the time and place is always selected by the incoming voyager. It is not the prerogative of an unaware consenting couple. Together with the question of fertile couples there is another question we must address.

There is a very informed body of opinion in the scientific community which claims that this process of which we write is out of step with known biological evolutionary facts. The chief claim is that consciousness is an effect of cellular activity. These claimants would say that DNA is the arbiter and creative force in the earthly domain. Yet, no matter how far down the ladder of disintegrating matter we proceed, we always finds matter in a state of becoming. It is admitted that matter is not solid, but it is not admitted that the particles of energy of which it is constructed are arranged and structured by an Intelligent Consciousness. This scientific assumption is *not* a proven fact. The next step for science to discover is the realization that what they work with and what they observe are symptoms and effects. They are not causes. All of us, scientists and laymen, have to realize that Consciousness is the Source of all manifestation, both visible and invisible. It is not that Darwin is wrong; it is simply that he mistakes modus operandi for cause. He does not grant directive Intelligent Consciousness a role in the process of natural selection.

A large part of the history of Atlantis is now lost in occlusion. This occlusion is also an integral part of the creation process, because without it the work of total immersion in the physical domain of living could not take place. As we re-awake from our 'entombment' of Consciousness we will begin to be more aware of our true place in the evolution saga. We have traveled through seven developmental sub-groups of Atlantean Consciousness to reach the advanced and sophisticated state and condition we now find ourselves undergoing. Each of these sub-groups developed a specific aspect of humanhood in order that we might become totally physical in our expression. The first developed sensation was pain and pleasure. Next came memory and ambition. We had to develop ambition in order to want to be physical expressions in the first place, and we had to have memory so that we could find our way back to our original state of awareness. The third grouping introduced idolatory out of the need to worship their (one) own God-like beingness at a previous state of their (our) existence. The group following this developed 'independent thought', the essential tool of intellectual survival once we had given up total awareness. Now we could no longer be intuitive, but we would retain the seed of our renewal, and therefore this group has the nomenclature of 'the chosen'. This deeply buried seed, which is carried in the psyche of humanity, is there so that the entire level of humanhood will be uplifted to glory. This particular concept has been kept alive by Hebrews and Christians; although most Hebrews and Christians are not aware of the fact, the concept remains at the very kernel of their religion. The concept in question is that the I AM Consciousness is the preeminent factor of all Creation. Moses taught this as also did Jesus, but few of their followers have maintained a loyalty to it in this present age. Only in Cosmic Christianity does the I AM Consciousness occupy its rightful place.

The sixth group are not highly commendable from our present view. They introduced sacrifice and barbarism. Knowing there was a God-like state, we attempted to communicate with it through offering bribes of animals and humans. The bribery system seems to be still alive and well in our society. The last of the groups is the one that carries "refinement of thought" to the nth degree. They are the ones who raise miniaturization to the apex of refinement in our society. If we think a little about these latter groups it will not be too difficult to pinpoint them in our midst; they are ourselves.

Alongside all of these are those among us who have already begun to move towards a more open and less occluded sense of spiritual awareness. These are the pathfinders of the army of Resurrected Consciousness. These are those among us who are already expressing deep concern and compassion for people of every color, hue and caste. Most of these have no denominational ties with any organized religious structure, and they have no need of such to sustain them. This is because within each and every one of us there resides the I AM Presence, even when we are not aware of it being there. There is never a time and never a place where Divinity is not expressing. If only the leaders of the world were already aware of this we would have no need of a defense system because there would not be anything to defend against.

So what then is our responsibility? Our responsibility is that when we begin to recognize *who* we are we must begin to behave as *what* we are. As soon as we recognize our Divinity we must implement our Divinity, otherwise we become a "barren fig tree". It is insufficient to sit on a mountain top and meditate or to repeat constantly "I am God". "Faith without good works is dead" says St. Paul. Perhaps the words of Shakespeare are more appropriate for this day and age: "Caesar's wife must not only be above suspicion, she must be seen to be above suspicion". Our responsibility is to actively pursue, with whatever talent or skill we possess, the job of expressing our Godliness. It is not necessary to find all new things to express through. It is only desirable that we use what we already have with the full knowledge of their Source. We cannot be sainted by renouncing the material world. We have to take that world and spiritualize it through our own spiritualized consciousness. That is what transmutation is actually about. When we do this we are doing the job we are here to accomplish. Our body and mind are designed to express the DIVINE IDEA. It has no other purpose. It never had anything else —— so why don't we just accept and BE.

Chapter 7

Ambassadors of the Spiritual World

The cause of most human destructiveness and sorrow can be traced, very simply and very easily, to an absence of knowledge and understanding between what uplifts and what holds down. Many people live lives of quiet desperation. We can have enough money, clothes, furnishings and holidays, and yet we may not be happy. The chief reason for this is the lack of awareness of the unity of all expression. The mere recognition of the unity of Life is enough to immediately open the channels of new-born energy. The re-opening of the channel will eventually present the understanding and knowledge.

It is the recognition of unity which must come first. All life that seems real to the senses represents neither reality nor eternity. They are simply representations of reality. No matter what we look at, whether it is each other, a building, a table, a motor car, it is not reality, nor is it eternity. What we see out there is a reflection or impression of reality. Everything we sense out there is temporal and temporary. There is a phrase: "This too shall pass". And if we ever make the mistake of thinking that this earth is the real thing and somebody takes it away from us, we are in serious trouble.

Have you ever had anything stolen? Have you ever had your home robbed? We lose sight of the essence of things at times like this. We can get so tied up with our possessions, children, husband, wife, car or even a tape recorder, we lose sight of the eternal. We create an albatross for ourselves and then put the blame on our relatives. We forget that everything in life is temporary. We must bear in mind that the underlying cause of all phenomena in our life is the expression of Eternal Life.

On the world scene there is only one political problem that divides all countries and peoples generally – they do not recognize that there is only one Source of all manifestation. We have to start with ourselves. All aspects of us stem from that one Source. Our government and humanity in general are not going to make a move until we start with ourselves individually. This is what is meant by the phrase let there be peace on Earth and let it begin with me. I cannot expect you to be peaceful towards me while I am not peaceful towards others. I must first be peaceful, or how otherwise can I expect to attract peace to me. I can only attract to me what I already am at this time. This is why so many of us make the mistake of saying such things like "As soon as I get out of this neighborhood….." No, all we do is take our disordered and crushing life with us, no matter where we go.

By changing the conditions we do not change the people. We cannot change the society in which we live unless we change ourselves as individuals. The majority of people still proceed to act for personal and national gain. Listen to the speeches of any world leader. He or she wants their country to be superior – not equal.

I have never yet heard a world leader stand up and say: "If you people will only become more peaceful in your own hearts….". Instead the speech is: "Give me more weapons so I can threaten or eliminate the people who don't agree with me". Just imagine if for one moment all of us in this country were to sit down at one time and focus our consciousness on the concept of non-violence and peace! The Maharishi Yoga has said if we could get 10% of the world population to meditate we could change the world. That is what Scripture says when it refers to ten just men saving a city. Why? Because the other 90% are not paying attention. By being awake we can be the cause of at-one-ness. There is enough evidence in the world situation and its capacity for nuclear destruction. If the leaders and a few more people responsible for world security knew of a way to change what is going on, they would do so because they know very well they are not running the show anymore. There is little doubt of that. And the more we listen to these people talk, the more convinced we become that they are not running things, but are all reacting to a given situation. They have no center of focus because they are thinking in terms of division. They are not thinking in terms of unity of consciousness. If instead of 10% of the world population we could get the world leaders to sit down in one place (a good such place would be Hiroshima) and focus their attention on the at-one-ment consciousness, agreements would be happening so fast the copying machines would break down from heat exhaustion.

There are a lot of people in the world really afraid of imminent nuclear war. There is not going to be a nuclear war; there cannot be a nuclear war. Why? Because the earth rotates. If the Russians were to strike the United States, in 24 hours the nuclear cloud would be over Russia. We do not have to respond to retaliate, and they know that. The reason this threat is going on at all is economic.

Technologically, business does not know how to transform or reorganize the basis of industry from a defense industry to a peace industry. The current economic system has been running for over fifty years, and it is very difficult to change. This is a case where the system is running the people.

This sense of division is the cause of wars. Physical societal peace is not attainable by physical means alone. Therefore we cannot rush out and sign a peace treaty – which is only a piece of paper – stating "I will destroy my weapons if you destroy your weapons". Nor can we make a lasting agreement with a person with whom we have had a confrontation. How many times have we heard people make promises never to be nasty again? It may last for a day, a week or two, even a month before the next confrontation. We have made the agreement on a personality level rather than a spiritual level, so they have no basis upon which to endure. Freedom from personal, national and international confrontations is not possible until we make the recognition that at all times, without exception, *each one of us* is an ambassador of the spiritual world. The material world, including our lives, is not going to change until we make the recognition that the person who confronts us is also the expression of spiritual essence. It can be difficult to recognize and accept this when someone is holding us by the throat. It is not easy to accept that this is spiritual essence before us. The first time we apply this idea it is never easy. Therefore we do not start practicing in a high intensity area. We start to practice with the individual we do not get along with at the office, maybe because they never say good morning to us. That is a good place to start. It is not good to start with an intense situation between two people living in a narrow space of interaction – a husband and wife, parent and child, etc. – who have already been confronting each other for several years. Our beginning or low level of 'spiritual recognition' can only handle low level difficulties. If there is an intense conflict situation between two human beings where they get nasty every time they see each other – "Oh, not you again. I didn't think you would come home, and was hoping you wouldn't. I wanted some peace and quiet around here for a change" – this is not a good place to start practicing your spiritual awareness concepts. We start practicing on our weak spiritual legs so to speak, like a baby, who can hardly stand up, first learning to walk. We start in an area of relationship where there is not that intensity, such as a situation of someone's unfriendliness rather than antagonism. We make the recognition that whatever this person is expressing at this particular moment is temporary and temporal, and that they are also the manifestation of spiritual divine essence.

When we have that situation licked we then take on a bigger one, and eventually we go to the big league! We do not start with high intensity low vibration (bad vibes), but with the low intensity situations. Once success is attained in the lower levels it releases additional spiritual energy, which can make it easier taking on the higher or more difficult levels of confrontation. How does a weight lifter start? With his top potential weight? No, he picks up a five or ten pound weight, and he adds to that the next day.

We are here in whatever state of rotten personality or stinking thinking we have developed in the past, so instead of saying that in future we shall be all sweetness and light, smiling at everyone, let us begin by using a simple affirmation. A good example would be: "I surrender body, mind and soul, here now and hereafter. Let there not be me and mine, but Thee and Thine alone. Be Thou me". We are saying this from the level of the personality ('me') and at that moment are surrendering to our own higher I AM God-self. What we are saying in effect is that in future, when we get annoyed with someone, we will let the personality surrender to a higher level of functioning. At that moment we are actively transmuting energy from one level to another. We are extending our awareness of our own individualized higher Consciousness, and are turning the show over to our own ever present indwelling I AM Consciousness. Soon we will discover, for example, that we have not screamed at anyone for two whole weeks.

The whole problem was division – keeping things separate, saying this is good, that is bad. It is division and a sense of separatism which keeps us from our spiritual expression. The confrontations, or our part in them, came about because we forgot that the people we were putting down or arguing with are the I AM God Consciousness in expression. Every time we confront someone, we must think silently within "You too are the Father's expression". It is we who must recognize that there are no divisions. We must recognize the spiritual essence of everyone's personality, no matter how atrocious that personality may seem to us. Whenever we get into the 'separation valence', it becomes the father of all fear. "They threaten me, and make me feel so insecure". When we speak with people we must look into their eyes instead of, as most times, averting our attention. We must make soul level contact. In time their body fades from focus because we begin to communicate on a soul level with those to whom we speak. We cease to be aware that this is a person of whichever sex, age or bulk, for that is no longer what they are to us. Age, sex and bulk are simply what a fellow soul is manifesting. They are Divine.

We must be consciously aware, not merely intellectually, because intellectual awareness is not conscious awareness. Our intellectual understanding is only "knowing about". Conscious awareness is experiential – it is what we feel. It is an inner knowing which, in most cases, we cannot find words to describe.

We manifest according to our state of Consciousness. This Consciousness, which is God, is the Creative Principle of All. It will manifest in whatever form is necessary for us at the moment. This is the pearl of great price. If it is necessary for us to have the experience of someone scream at us, that is the experience we will have in that moment. And it is *not* a bad experience. When we are faced with expressions of Consciousness that make us uncomfortable, it is because our attention is being directed to an area of our life that requires some remedial action. It is because of something we have not *resolved* within ourselves.

We have to start with ourselves. It is for this reason we say in the affirmation "Be Thou me", because then the 'me' becomes perfected and now does not have any problems since the "I" is now in total charge. Harmonious and cooperative relationships can only come to fruition after many disappointments and false starts, because for most of the time, when we start on this particular path, we attempt to move mountains first. There is nothing wrong with enthusiasm. We must remember that starting on any form of spiritual growth is still a personal interest. "I no longer want to behave like that". In most instances when we start this process we do not even consider the other person's needs. By 'me' finding the answer, we might very well be removing from his environment an experience needed in order to grow.

We do not have to buy a particular trip at this particular moment from anyone. It is very important to realize this, because it is here that we enter into idolatry. Idolatry is not bowing down and adoring stone or wooden statues. Idolatry is buying somebody else's intellectual presentation or postulation. In the final analysis our own inner feeling must be our guide. Otherwise, as soon as we have found him or her or 'me' as our guru, we have set up a false god. We have gotten into a form of idolatry. If we say he only can lead me out of my morass, we are denying our activity, our intellectual power, our experience and saying we can only reach God through our "false god". That is no different from a Roman Catholic who walks into a church and worships a statue. They have lost the symbology of the statue. Are we condemning this? No, but when we do this we lose touch with Divinity. We lose touch with our own indwelling Divine Self. It is what Jesus meant when he said: "The Kingdom of God is within you". The whole direction has to be inwards. Once we go inwards, what we express on the outside will be changed. It must start with us and it starts inside.

It is frequently asked: "Don't we need teachers to give the message to 'prime the pump'?" This is true in most cases, but having listened to the teacher and the message it must still be an *inner* response and decision. We have to be extremely careful *not* to set up a dependence on the *outside*. Depending on a person is exactly the same as the worshipper who depends upon a statue. St. Paul advises to "Prove all things" (Thessalonians 5:21).

A fundamental aspect of all this rests on the direction or condition of self-spiritualization. Peace of mind and peace of heart depend on the recognition of the powers of the spiritual realm and aspect of being within oneself. It is this which makes it possible for us to discern what is our nourishment when we hear it. That is what makes it possible to go to the spiritual smorgasbord and pick from it what is truly beneficial for us. Whenever somebody comes to us and asks a question, we must not respond to it on the personality level. Pause and then answer. We do not have to know. The answer will be given to us, otherwise the question would not be asked of us. That is the other side of the coin in the phrase: "When the student is ready, the teacher will appear". Maybe the next day we will find out that we were only 50% right, but the part that was 50% right was the 50% that was needed, and the remaining 50% did not matter. We must never adopt, particularly in spiritual teaching, the concept that we do not know enough to help. That is a separation and a division. That is working from the level of the personality. We must practice at being God, as we must practice the piano. We do not wait for it to happen. We respond when we are asked. We do not refuse to heal a person when they ask us to heal them because until then we have never done any healing. We have just become a healer since we were asked, and at that moment we let go and let God. How? Very simply, by reaching out and touching the person who has made the request. While doing so we hold in our consciousness for about twenty seconds the concept "I and the Father are one" and then add "Be Thou me". Divinity knows the location of the problem, and we have no need to know at the intellectual or personality level.

If we look at the last 500 years in society, all the major changes take place within the last 25 years of any given century. The drawbridge between the spiritual and the material worlds seems to be lowered every hundred years during the period of the last 25 years of the century, in which the outflow of the energy from the Chalice of Christ Consciousness pours down with tremendous power and significance. We have recently moved from one century to another, and have witnessed the end of an age. We are already into Armageddon, which has nothing to do with wars in Iraq or Afghanistan or troubles between Jews and Arabs in the Middle East. It is the war between spiritual living and material living. We are experiencing tremendous pressures at this particular point in our consciousness. We are now in a transition time where we are learning to distinguish between spiritual needs and material wants. This is a process whereby we learn to get rid of the false wants that hold us in bondage to the material plane. We are having career problems, we are having relationship problems.

We are having more relationship problems today than ever before. Those of us who have the good fortune to be exposed to the knowledge of the higher consciousness teachings have a great duty to ourselves; we know what we have to do in order to raise our own Consciousness. By raising our Consciousness we raise the overall level of the Consciousness of the world. We pull the world up with us.

At no time must we judge a person unready for spiritual help when they ask for it. We must never make the decision that such a person is not ready for our level of spirituality. Because we are at this "One" level of spirituality we will be quite capable of reaching them through compassion. We respond to a person at their level when they ask.

There are many people who would say this compassion is what is meant by the concept of Christ Consciousness. This is not completely accurate. Compassion is, without a doubt, a major part of Christ Consciousness, but only a part. Christ Consciousness is the *recognition* of at-one-ment with the Divine Consciousness at all times. When we have surrendered our illusion of separateness and accepted 'our' at-one-ment, we enter into Christ Consciousness. Mere utterance of the descriptive words of the concept is insufficient. It must have the depth of feeling of the *Inner Being*, the Divine God Being within. This recognition is the Christ Consciousness – there is none other. It is constant. It never leaves us. Once we accept and apply that recognition, Christ Consciousness opens up. First we narrow in to the recognition. It is called: Straight is the Path and narrow is the Gate. In Kabbalah it is some times called the Central Pillar. What has caused confusion for us is that over 2,000 years we have been told Jesus is THE Christ and only Jesus has Christ Consciousness. Jesus made a number of very specific statements which guide us quite distinctly in this area of consciousness expression. For example, "I and the Father are One", shows quite clearly that Jesus had entered into awareness of his at-one-ment. And again, "He who see 'Me' sees him that sent me", whereby Jesus illustrates that the personality (me) which he then is, is God in action on the earth plane. Now there is no longer separation between Divine Beingness and earth plane expression.

Because of the limitation of earth dwelling consciousness we sometimes look at the development of Jesus and his work as being in the order of the miraculous. Nothing could be further from the facts. No-one, neither Jesus, Buddha, Krishna nor any other Avatar, let alone people in general, go from slob to saint overnight. It is a slow process through many incarnations. It takes a considerable period of earth time to crystallize in concretized form an *original concept of spiritual essence*.

How many times have we promised to improve ourselves for someone else's sake? How many times have we made promises to stop doing this or that in a relationship? It is no use for us to go home and promise our spouse or children that we are going to stop doing whatever it is. We can go home and say to them: "I am going to do something about this, but I will need your help and encouragement. Maybe tomorrow I will only do it ten times instead of the usual 25, and the next day I will only do it 9 times". What we have to do is change the vibration of energy around the effects we have already created, and one of the effects we have already created – the greatest effect of all – is habituation. Most of us have a routine when we get up in the morning. Some of us go directly to the bathroom and some of us go straight to the coffeepot. Some of us go out and breathe in a lung-full of air. We have routines, and we have routines of behavior towards the people with whom we live, which we automatically assume are acceptable and only theirs are wrong. We cannot understand why they dislike what *we* do, but for us what they do is terrible and nothing could live with that. It is a slow gradual growth to change the vibration of our habituation.

Then we move into the vacuum from the old habituation. It is referred to in esoteric scripture as the ring-pass-not; the area of manifestation. You see, manifestation has to take place in an area of activity. Once again, it is what Shakespeare is talking about when he says that Caesar's wife must not only BE above suspicion, she must be SEEN to be above suspicion. It must be manifested. It is no good our sitting in our room and writing books and meditating, feeling holy, pious and wonderful, and sending good thoughts to all and sundry, and then go walking into the living room yelling about our dinner not being ready or our spouse not being back from an errand by the time we want to use the car. These are not "bad" things to say, but these are the things we do, and these are the things we have to change. However, we do not change them by waving a wand and saying abracadabra! We change them by changing the vibration of the habituation and creating a vacuum into which the new concept can move and manifest. Spirituality needs a stage on which to perform. If the old play is still running in the theater, the new production cannot perform, so it hangs in the shadows of the wings.

How then do we change the vibration of habituation? When we have a habit that we observe to "not be in our best interest", the first thing we need to do is look at the effect of this habit upon ourselves and other people who are subjected to it. At this moment also we must allow ourselves to become aware of and accept the responsibility for initiating the habit and its effects on all concerned, including ourselves. We look at it in terms of the thought and the effects on self. We look at the emotions and the effects on self and others. Lastly we look at the action and the effects on all those involved. We accept this is what we have been doing and the situation we are experiencing is the outcome. Having done this we can now begin to look at the habit by saying: "I, you and the Father are one". We make the recognition that what we have been doing was a spiritual action, constituting spiritual essence, even if until now we have not been aware of the fact. No action is ever devoid of spiritual essence, for it is the only Source from which the entire universe manifests. Since we have already accepted our responsibility for our actions (habits) and have linked them to the Father, we are now in the most favored position and situation to undertake the next step, the one of transmutation. From our position of spiritual dominion we can now say: "I do not intend to continue this habit….", naming the item that it is. At this point we must not declare a time factor to what we are doing. We must not ever attempt to place the Father within the dimension of time. There is no need to do so. There is no 'time' in the Kingdom of Spirit, only sequentialism.

This entire evolutionary process is best expressed by the late Geoffrey Hodson, who wrote: "……humankind would seem to be treading a pathway towards destruction, sensually, militarily and ecologically. If this be true – and support visibly exists for the view – the salvation of the race from this suicidal procedure must depend to a considerable extent, if not entirely, upon spiritually illumined human beings arising and appearing. The life of such completely dedicated occultists may justly be described as an ambassadorship. The earth is passing through the deepest and therefore the darkest – from the spiritual point of view – phase of the great involutionary and evolutionary journey of the One Life. In consequence, matter – particularly in its inertial attribute – is in a position of great power; it over-emphasizes materiality in the motives, methods of fulfillment, the modes of life, and the day to day waking consciousness of the bodily selves with which the spiritual Monad-Egos of man are associated. However, at this time the earth is emerging from the position of deepest descent of spirit into matter – or involution."

To be ambassadors of the spiritual world we all need to apply our individualized spiritual essence in the routine activities of our daily life. It is in this way lies resurrection and ascension.

Chapter 8
Spirit Teachers and Guides

The term spiritual teacher or guide became known and popular about 1848 and has remained with us soundly ever since. Alternative descriptions had, however, been used previously and also interchanged with the word prophets.

The basic principle of spiritualism is the belief in the continuance of life after earthly bodily death, and that the entities in this so-called after-life may be contacted through a living medium residing here on earth. A medium is, by definition, a person who enters into a state of self-hypnotic trance and brings through information from those who are functioning and communicating from the 'other side' – the spirit world.

One thing we must understand from the outset: when a person transits from this side of the veil to the other, they do not automatically become spiritually enlightened. The consciousness we carry with us at the moment of transition is the same consciousness we carry on the other side as well. Assume that at the moment of reading this, as we each sit in our respective locations, our building explodes, leaving very little of our bodies remaining. Few among us would automatically become spiritually enlightened from that experience. Departure from the habitation of the physical body is far from meaning we have become totally aware. We will be just as ignorant, just as emotionally distraught, just as mentally upset as we were immediately before the transition. Transference does not immediately bring enlightenment. Therefore, when we sit with a medium, the person communicating with that medium is not necessarily better informed than the person listening to the medium. Truly spiritual mediums, through meditation and study, can, of course, raise their own consciousness to an extremely high level, but a medium can only operate at the level of their own consciousness at the time of the session, and cannot communicate at that moment with someone of a far higher level. The only reason this point is made is because we are addressing the issue of whether what we receive is beneficial to our individual needs in terms of our personal unfoldment. All of us are on a general track with a general direction of self-discovery, self-unfoldment, self-improvement, spiritual upliftment or whatever term we may chose to use, but not one of us, in whatever physical location, is on the same track as another. We may be very close, but we are not all traveling on the exact same track at the exact same time at the exact same rate.

The whole field of spiritualism was very much influenced in 1848 by the Fox sisters, Leah, Kate and Margaret, because of reported rappings in their home in Hydesville, New York. In Europe, however, interest was much aroused in the late 16th century through the work of Dr. Franz Antoine Mesmer in the field of animal magnetism

We now move into the area of what I refer to as "authenticity". The level of a medium's work relates directly to the person who is posing the questions. For example, if my position on the scale of awareness is that of only being concerned as to where grandfather hid his will and I go to a medium with this question, I will get the level of response that my Consciousness is capable of receiving and accepting. There is nothing wrong with that. There is nothing wrong with so-called mundane information from a mundane soul in a state of Altered Consciousness. The only mistake, in this instance, would be to think it is not mundane and is something more. In this world of mediums, spirit guides and teachers there are two groupings of teachers available for each and every level of Consciousness.

The means of help offered is always appropriate to the need of where we are on an ongoing daily basis. Earlier reference has been made to a statement in the Ten Commandments, as pronounced by Moses – "I Am The Lord The God". A person who carries this in their Consciousness will have an entirely different style of communication, teaching and advice from the 'other side' than a person who does not. It has nothing to do with lip service. It is not sufficient to *say* "I Am the Lord the God and I shall not have strange gods before me" and then turn around and call someone an idiot. In order to receive inspirational help from the other side or through a spiritual teacher, either on this side or the other side, we must still have the comparative level of consciousness to receive. So many people seem to think they can go on living their life with their current 'stinking thinking', and some miraculous being is going to appear in their driveway or through their medium or psychic, wave a magic wand and everything is going to be wonderful. It is not going to happen that way. We are told quite clearly in Scripture: "By the sweat of thy brow thou shalt eat". Eat what? Bread? Butter? Hamburgers from Wendy's? No, no, no. Eat the food of the Spiritual Kingdom. That means we must select, and we must select where we are at this moment to dine at such a table. We must be prepared, first and foremost, to accept ourselves where we are. If we are a thief we must start by saying we are a thief but no longer desire to be so. We must not condemn ourself for being a thief. Here is the crossover point. We accept, for example, that what we are expressing is labeled 'cheat'. We do not say it is bad to be a cheat, it is wrong to be a cheat, it is evil to be a cheat. As soon as we introduce a morality concept we are saying there are *two sources* of expression and power in this universe. We are saying there is good and bad, right and wrong. To say we are cheats is to say that the expression of God we are is acting as a cheat. That is seeing actuality, but to say that God is wrong in expressing through us as a cheat is divisive thinking. We usually decide that this has nothing to do with God because He is only good. As soon as we do this we are at once introducing an evil or a devil, and we are thereby saying there is more than one God in the universe. There can be no equivocation here. The only thing we can receive, the only information we can receive, either from this side or the other, is from people who are of like Consciousness.

If, however, we achieve a new and higher level of Consciousness that differs from our chronic level, then we will attract to ourselves entities of that level. All of us regularly function with two alternating levels of Consciousness, chronic and acute. The chronic is not usually as elevated as the acute. When the acute is raised higher than normal, maybe after a period of meditation, it helps raise the chronic level as well. We have the best possible chance of being inspired by messengers from the other side, who have no need to identify themselves, at the end of a meditative period. Some people get their best ideas walking the beach. We must not make the mistake of thinking we only get these ideas when in the 'church-consciousness'. What we do is raise our consciousness through the process of meditation, and having raised it we maintain it in the action that follows, by a conscious and deliberate act of will. We extend that expanded awareness into not only the first act, but also the second, the third, the fourth, the fifth and so on. Having expanded our action level in the new consciousness our inspirations will come. It is no good getting ourselves all high and holy, and then walking out into the level of not being high and holy. *The action we now initiate and implement must be in line with the new level of consciousness, otherwise the action drives the consciousness back down again because we are behaving on the level of habituation.*

How many times have we heard people say "I'm going to quit this and I'm going to quit that"? All of us, without exception, have done so. To guarantee an additional input of spiritual uplift at a new level of consciousness we must express it in our most immediate activity. When we do our meditations, whether for a few minutes or longer, we must come to realize that it is the quality of the meditation that counts, not the extent. If we want to know how long we should meditate, the answer is very simple – we meditate until we are completely at ease with being God. We end our meditation when we totally accept that we are nothing other than the expression of the Divine. Once we reach that point, we immediately get up and get on with our daily life. We get up from our chair, and in the act of getting up we recognize that it is our Divinity that has made the decision to rise from the chair.

The level of consciousness achieved in a meditative state can only be maintained by an active decision of our soul being to implement it in direct action. "By their works you shall know them". We finish our meditation and we consciously operate our body, raising it to the perpendicular position and starting to walk towards the kitchen or den, or we take the trash out or get the vacuum cleaner out. These are really exciting spiritual activities, aren't they? But if we do not come into the realization of our Divinity in action in the instant of time, we never will come into it. That is dogmatic, and being dogmatic is needed here. As Jesus said: "All those who say 'Lord, Lord' will not be saved.". We can pray and we can hope, but that alone is not going to save us. There is nobody out there who is going to lean down and pick us up, saying "You have been a good boy, you can be in charge". When we conduct our daily routine tasks in the Consciousness that we are an expression of the Divine, we have implemented the Divine Impulse of Creation. Now we will get the inspirations; now the Angel Gabriel or whomever will call us on the hot line. They will not even have to identify themselves; the inspiration itself is enough.

All of us are born into a highly complex and culturized society, yet the Kingdom of God is at hand. Having made our decision to actively implement our new level of Consciousness we very quickly get the opportunity to check our faith in the Consciousness (God). The next step is usually the appearance of an urge to do something that does not seem to have a rational base. We may be impelled to get in our car and drive to a place we would not ordinarily visit. Very likely nothing of an exciting nature happens on the journey. We may just turn around and make for home, but what we have learned to respond to is inspiration. This is the *spiritual* message. It is complete. Let us get away from the idea that the only time it is only a spiritual message is if we are sent out to convert the 10,000. Let us start by converting ourselves, and let us continue the process. Then we will begin to find that we are inspired to do this, that and the other, which will produce immediate effects that we can see.

This is truly the 'pearl of great price' of which Scripture speaks. If and when we move out of our Divine expression, we lose our contact with our Source or God. We can now pray as much as we like, but nothing is going to happen. Not only is God out to lunch, but He is on vacation in the Far East. Our prayers are never answered because we keep God separate from ourselves. We do not allow God to become a conscious part of us. We put God in some far away place, Pluto perhaps, and we live on Earth pleading "Please God, help me with the mortgage". If we separate God from ourselves there is *no communication*. What happens in a household when the couple in question only see each other at a personality level? In next to no time their communication diminishes and eventually disappears altogether. Neither of them can do anything right. As soon as we can only see people at a personality level we can only expect from them a personality response, and that level of response is no longer sufficient. We cannot get Divine response from that which we do not see as Divine. We cannot expect love from our spouse if we consider them to be 'no good'; we will only receive what we have projected.

Once we begin to accept who we are, it all begins to work very smoothly. There are no problems – only solutions. When situations are presented to our attention we are also presented with the technology for dealing with them. If the technology does not emerge immediately it is because the time for dealing with the situation has not yet arrived.

We cannot receive messages from spirit guides or anyone else because of our own limitations, not theirs. We cannot expect to be crowned Queen of the May while still living in a pigsty consciousness. We have to raise our Consciousness to the level where we hear the message. We cannot do it for one another; we can only do it for ourselves. Yes, we can help each other by letting others be themselves without interference from us. We *only give help when it is asked of us*. This is why it is said "By the sweat of thy brow thou shalt eat". We simply must devote ourselves to the raising of our own individual Consciousness to the level whereby we can receive the inspirational information that goes beyond what we read in books and hear by word of mouth. That is one side of the coin; as always, there is another. When we learn and accept this, we also learn to hear the spiritual messages that are meant for us in the voices of those that speak in our presence, even if we are eavesdropping. An example of this is expressed in the following incident.

A man was sitting in a restaurant eating breakfast and reading a magazine. At a nearby table a group of ladies were also having breakfast and talking quietly with each other. Very soon the man's attention began to wander from the printed page and, even though he did feel he was not being too polite, to focus on his fellow-diners' conversation. One sentence in the overheard conversation came through clear as a bell, and carried the answer to a question the man had asked several weeks before. The speaker never knew she was a 'spiritual guide', but she was. We must learn to listen and to not expect inspiration on a so-called psychic level only. We must learn not to discriminate in that way. The peasant can tell the king an important message. We can discriminate as to what is needful for us to utilize. We cannot discriminate upon the Source of the message, because that Source is always the same. It is the channel that alters. In the case described above it was a middle-aged lady eating breakfast with her friends in a restaurant in York, Pennsylvania. We will get our messages, but not necessarily from a disincarnate entity. Be aware if, as you walk into a bookshop and walk along an aisle of books, a book falls out at your feet. Pick it up and flip through the pages. You do not necessarily have to buy it … … your message may well be right there.

There is a third way we can get our message, and it is a little more subtle. Sometimes, when we are talking or lecturing or sermonizing or teaching or helping other people, we suddenly get on a roll. We are explaining to him or her what it is they need to do, and suddenly we find out that what we are saying is not really for them, but for ourself. This is also a spirit message for us, which can very well be coming from a spirit guide on the other side, but we do not have to identify the channel in order to validate the message. If, stemming from the message, the result of what we do works, it is genuine. The proof of the pudding is in the eating. Or, if it is not practical, it is not spiritual, and if it is not spiritual, it is not practical. If it can happen, it is spiritual, and if it cannot happen, it is not spiritual and therefore it does not happen. There is only one Source.

There is only one Source – it is that simple. We start with God, Jehovah, Allah, Logos or whatever name we give to Divinity. As we come down the scale of vibratory differentiation we reach the other Divine expressions – teacher, mother, father, minister or psychiatrist. They can all be channels. Even as we listen or speak with someone we are channels to each other, once we accept there is only *One Source*. Therefore, we listen to ourselves as we speak. We are also our own spiritual guides. Guides are other and varying levels of Consciousness. If it is not working in our life it is probably because it is stemming only from the level immediately above us. This is probably due to our own 'stinking thinking' or our own emotional confusion, which has been adulterated with separatism. As soon as we make the decision that I and God are two separate expressions we are in trouble, for now we are suffering from the sin of pride. "I and God cannot be the same". This is real and total pride. People ask how can you be so prideful as to think you and God are One? The answer is how can we be so arrogant as to think we are not. This is what Scripture means when it says "Unless the Lord build the house, they labor in vain that build it". That is the secret right there. If we only build it on the humanhood level, the roof is going to cave in the day after we build it. If we build in the full knowledge of our Divinity it will work. And here we are talking about the relationships in our lives. Each and every one of our problems has to do with relationships, either with other people or with things and conditions. "If only there were no people, if only there were no things it would be a wonderful world!" It is so easy to be a saint when you live in a mountain cave. Anybody can be a saint when they become a recluse. A real saint is somebody who lives in the inner city, with all the problems that the inner city may have, because it is in dealing with the daily situations on a pragmatic, down-to-earth basis while in the Consciousness of our 'Divinity' that we improve the standard of the expression of Divinity. Put another way, God needs you and me to fulfill the creation plan. The only way the Divine Plan can be implemented is through us.

We are the point in the Kingdom where God becomes visible at the material level of expression. The following exercise helps to focus on the Godliness of our expression.

Close your eyes and place your feet flat on the floor, and then focus your attention on your breathing, making no attempt to alter it in any way, but just focusing your attention on it. Now attempt to think of a time in the past before you existed, not as a body but as a conscious being. Maintain this focus for about 30 seconds, and then attempt to think of a time in the future when you will no longer exist as a conscious being. You will very soon find that it cannot be done, because we cannot uncreate our immortality. We cannot create the condition of our own non-existence. Not only do we exist, we exist eternally. It is this quality of soul that is the accepting self in the recognition of our Divinity. It has nothing to do with our morality, with our culture, or racial heritage or our economic status or our standing in society. It certainly has nothing to do with our nationality. We are talking about that which transcends all these temporal things. We are talking about that which transcends humanhood, which is the most limited expression we will ever experience. And when we finish the series of incarnations we are on this Earth to complete, we will never have to experience it again. There are no specific numbers of incarnations we have to go through. There are those who "take heaven by storm", those among us who have totally and completely surrendered their personality to their I AM Consciousness. When we get a perfect balance between the negative and the positive expression in our daily living we become capable of following the straight and narrow path. We must not let ourselves be too compassionate or too severe. When we learn to do this the messages start to come through, to give the right answer to a question, even if we never heard the question – or indeed the answer – before in our life.

We are talking of the acceptance of Divinity. There is no Source in this entire universe other than God. We are talking about God always being present at all times and under all circumstances. We must make the recognition that whatever is taking place in our environment at any moment is still an expression and manifestation of God, even if the person is jumping up and down and beating their chest. As we proceed into this ambience of living and move more and more into this acceptance of there being only one God, the problems begin to fly out of the window. It is not so much that everything out there changes, but rather that we change and become different in our relationship to the environment. This is what Jesus was talking about when he said: "I am in this world, but not of it", and what he is saying is simple. He is saying: "My World is really the World of Consciousness, which creates the forms". "You would not have power if it were not given you from above". These words, spoken to Pilate, epitomize the teachings of Jesus.

Through the actions of both church and science we have lost the core of these teachings. We have lost it because church and science would each like to have the only key. We have no need of them. We have no need other than a connection to our Source. We get all the nourishment, spiritual messages or whatever we need and require from the host of messengers both here and on the other side. Whether the Angel Gabriel is used or not does not matter. Mrs. Smith who works at Kentucky Fried Chicken will do just as well. She does not need to have golden wings.

When we raise our consciousness, we must immediately implement it, otherwise it just slips away again. It is like putting on a locking nut. It is no good being way up in sanctified holiness and mystical splendor when nobody can reach us, and where we cannot reach anybody else. People say: "Ah yes, but if you start mixing with those sort of people you lose your spirituality". No we do not. We expand our spirituality because we are living from up there, but acting on the dense or mundane level. We are in this world but not of it. We must have practice. This is what St. Paul meant when he said: "Faith without good works is dead". St. Paul did not mean we should run around doing charitable and nice things for other people, but rather about you and I coming out of our meditative state, our spiritual or our praying state, and getting on with our daily chores. Paul went back into his workshop and made sails for ships, and then he came back out again and delivered a sermon to the Corinthians, after which he returned to the shop and made a belt. We must practice constantly on a practical basis. We must practice it in our private life, not only with our neighbors, not only with our family, but also in our most intimate private life, as we make a cup of tea, as we clean a toilet. Nothing is more spiritual than cleaning the toilet. This is the secret of spiritual life: there is no action that is not Divine in essence. There is only one fundamental lesson to learn – that there is always *only* One *Source* present at all times and that it is this Source that manifests *all power.* When we learn and accept this Conscious Awareness we never have to be afraid of anyone or anything, jealous of anyone or envy anyone. We never have to hate or even dislike anyone and no-one ever causes us distress or pain. We can remain open and alert to the Voice of God all around us. At no time when we are *Consciously Divine* can we act other than *Divinely.* "This day thou shalt be with Me in Paradise".

Chapter 9

The Rise of Aquarian Consciousness

For the convenience of spiritual mechanics, the Cosmos is divided into categories. The category with which we are currently dealing is known in esoteric circles as a 'precessional cycle' consisting of 25,900 years. This figure breaks down into twelve divisions of 2,160, each of which has a specific symbolic astrological name.

We are concerned here with two of these divisions – the Piscean and the Aquarian, the former phasing out and the latter phasing in. Whether or not we are all knowledgeable in astrology, we are all touched by the Cosmic influences filtered through the characteristics of each of the individual categories in the 25,900 year cycle. These named categories are, in fact, epochs or Ages of cosmological history. The Aquarian signifies the Buddhic vehicle of the Spirit. It is the container of truth. In the Tarot it is the figure of the water carrier pouring forth the waters of truth from the vessel borne on his shoulder.

For those active seekers in the field of self-development, this Age now provides the opportunity to meld all that has been learned in the material and emotional areas of life. These two energy fields may now be more readily transmuted into spiritual awareness and expression than heretofore. Unfortunately many people seem to think that in the unfoldment process a whole new and unused body of spiritual energy is especially provided to those who now consider themselves to be on the 'path'. This is not so – all spiritual development starts within the already existing body of energy expressed in the Cosmos. The Cosmos does not discard or waste, it is not a throw-away society. We always have to start from where we are and with what we have already received. We already have all the Divine substance we require to remake our lives.

There are differences of opinion among scholars about the actual beginning date of the Aquarian Age, but there is no dispute about its significance and esoteric essence. Many people will say the Beatles ushered in the Aquarian Age with their music. This could well be, for it is in the arena of outward material expression that all spiritual development first manifests. The movement of Spirit in matter becomes apparent to us once we allow ourselves to see beyond the mere physical phenomena we are witnessing. The area where this physical expression is by far the most obvious is in the field of electronics. This is a spiritual revolution born primarily from the mind of a man named Einstein, as it all stems from his unified field theory. Anyone who has read his works will know that it flowed from his dedication to his science combined with his openness to this intuitive capacity. This meld brought about his enormous contribution to the entire field of spiritual manifestation in matter.

What is really involved in this revolution is a quickening of the consciousness of all of humanity. This in effect means a rise in the focus of consciousness from the lower physical through the emotional to the mental plane of expression. It does not mean that each and every individual is experiencing this activity to the same degree. It *does* mean that many have already begun to 'feel' the infusion of the spiritual realm into their thinking. This feeling is entered into in the sense of concern and compassion we have for the well-being of people and the environment as a whole. These are the positive signs of the movement of consciousness into the field of at-one-ment, which is the forerunner of the Cosmic Consciousness active in all mankind.

We have all felt a distinct quickening in the society in which we live our daily lives. Many among us seem never to have the time to "stand and stare". We are hurried from place to place in work situations, in living locations and in all manner of our activities. This feeling of no time or not enough time comes from the quickening of our own individual Consciousness. In our occluded state we have forgotten that time is a purely arbitrary tool we have inserted into duration. It is not so very long ago that our days and their divisions were noted by the ringing of bells in the local monastery tower.

This quickening of Consciousness first manifests on the physical plane. We are now processing information at galactic speeds, compared to the days of our grandparents. There are many among us who, on first contacting the notion of spiritual unfoldment, think that their initial task is to eliminate the physical/material from their lives. They begin to give up all sorts of physical things in their living because they have been told that the physical is gross, evil or unspiritual. Nothing could be further from the truth. If the physical/material is evil, we then have to ask ourselves why God created it in the first place. To be spiritual does not mean being anti-material. We are not asked to surrender our goods, but rather to surrender lies, deceit, jealousy, envy, hatred and other such expressions that separate us from our Impersonal Divine Consciousness. We are asked to realize that all physical/material expression stems from the One Source. To think that there is any other source of manifestation in the Universe is to deny the Omnipresence of God.

We have already referred to the idea of consciousness formerly manifesting only at a non-material level of expression and subsequently manifesting as physical/material expression. We have now reached the stage in our evolutionary journey at which consciousness is beginning its ascent towards the non-material level of expression. This Aquarian Age is the point in the journey where we begin to be aware of our own inner self, and try to relate it to all that is taking place around us in our society. At first we question why God allows so much suffering in the world. A little later on, we ask ourselves what we can do about it, what we can do to help. This sort of question is the early indication of our growing sense of spiritual awareness. We may not as yet accept that we were the cause of these conditions in the first place, but at least we accept that there is something we can do to alter them. All forms of the sense of responsibility stem from our own inner God-self. These feelings of concern are the early movements in the process of our resurrection from the tomb of our occlusion.

This awakening from occlusion and its concomitant awareness, manifests as our understanding that we are not controlled by the material world, but that maybe – just maybe – we are the ones that control the material world. This is exactly what our scientific fraternity is doing at this time. The only difficulty many scientists have is thinking their ability and decision making capability is a happy molecular accident. Those of us who are aware that we are not a happy accident are also beginning to be aware that we can manifest spiritually at an actively conscious level. Already we have among us many people who are consciously creating circumstances with a high degree of success. That success, however, is in ratio to the degree of awareness of the inner I AM Consciousness of the individual in question.

We have a great number of organizations in the world teaching people to assume control of their mental processes and to direct them towards specific goals. Although there is a modicum of success, the long term outcome cannot be total success. We cannot acquire total control of our mental processes until we have gained a release from the tyranny of our emotions. We *must* learn that we are the spiritual master of our emotions. They are never caused by conditions that exist outside of ourselves. If we allow ourselves to think they are we are reacting, not responding. We are giving power to control our energy field to outside events. In esoteric terms, we are setting up 'strange gods before us'. Until we, as individuals and organizations, learn that the Source of all Man's attributes is Divine Consciousness, we can never have total success in material expression. We must also learn that the consciousness we are expressing is Divine Consciousness and no other. There is no other. These realizations are all an integral part of Aquarian Consciousness. Unless we allow ourselves to enter into this Aquarian attribute of consciousness, we cannot correctly express our creative ability. We must be aware of and actively feel our Divinity.

Aquarian Consciousness is also concerned with another aspect of our spiritual growth. It causes a great many people to look for a philosophy of living that deals with the *NOW*, rather than looking for rewards in a hereafter. It begins to provide the capacity to act and function in the here and now in all our relationships. We cease to see the world out there as something we have to combat or compete against on a daily or lifelong basis. Aquarian Consciousness allows us to see the Hand of God in all that surrounds us and the Presence of God in all by whom we are confronted. All people who enter into the domain of this Consciousness immediately seek a modus operandi which permits them to live a life of higher quality. They also desire that this higher life is available to their fellows. This Consciousness does not permit us to go off into a cave in the mountains and involve ourselves in continuous and detached meditation. Meditation remains a part of the daily activity of the Aquarian psyche, but involvement with life in the market place takes precedence. Aquarian Consciousness is very much aware that a diamond becomes a beautiful asset only when it has been pressed against an abrasive wheel. We learn that the obstacles we encounter in our daily life are no more and no less than the stepping stones on our Mount of Ascension.

We are witnessing a definite movement towards togetherness. This is the activity of Spiritual Consciousness that is already moving people towards a climate of thinking that urges them to undertake ever more responsibility for ever greater amounts of material possessions. Most of those engaged in the acquisition process are not even aware of the power behind their actions. They simply think that it would be neat to own this or that for its own sake. Such people are in the nursery school of spiritual material responsibility. Many of the older generation are none too pleased with the younger ones in our society with their demands for the good things of life right now. Most older people have had to wait half a lifetime to attain much that the younger ones acquire in their twenties, but the speed up is in all departments of life. The later generations are learning to gain control of matter at an earlier age than their forebears. Until we master the mechanical methods of organizing and controlling matter, we cannot move on to the processes whereby we control consciously through thought. This is one of the most important lessons of the Aquarian Age, and we must learn it quickly.

We have now reached the stage where more and more people are aware that we cannot go forward from here in the old separative consciousness pattern. It is no longer possible to be a hermit in the desert and live on locusts. Our society is becoming a totally interactive and interrelated union. International corporative enterprises have been the first to make this recognition, and let us not think that this has happened while God was out to lunch. Business may be doing it just for profits, but little does it know that it is conforming to a Divine Plan. It is essential that we release our old concepts and the limitations we have placed on God's methods of creation. At-one-ment is our destiny, and if it takes a one world super-corporate entity to achieve this, that is how it will be. However, that is not the script, for the consciousness of the world corporate mind is also in the process of Aquarian transformation.

The onset of Aquarian Consciousness brings another enlightening facet of life's diamond to our attention. For those who are living in the ten million dollar home with the four Mercedes out front, life is no longer good enough. With all that material wealth, there is still something missing. We begin to feel that of itself quantity of life does not give quality to our lives, and so we seek that quality in the realms of self-discovery. But here again, if it is not sought in the areas of Impersonal Divine Consciousness, we soon find ourselves to be shortchanged. The manner of turning quantity into quality is really quite simple. All it requires is that we set out to help others without expectation of reward or commendation, and this is already happening on a wide scale. Many successful business people are asking what they can do to help. We do not need special skills or training to be of help; all we need is the willingness to listen to those who seek our help. We will find that we can at least help and advise the individual on how to get the help they need, and even maybe do more. Man *is* the instrument of God's help to His people, and when we become aware of this and accept our role in the creation process, we fulfill our destiny. The next time we are thinking of buying a gift for someone, let us pause and think about what that person might like done for them that we could very well do. This way we would be sharing the very essence of ourselves, serving them on a spiritual soul level of consciousness.

Whatever amount of knowledge we have gained in our studies and search for unfoldment is of very little value unless we put that knowledge to work for others. St. Paul states it very concisely: "By their works ye shall know them". The best and surest way we can know and feel our inner Divinity is when selfless love fills our hearts and there is a strong compelling urge to help someone, relieve their suffering or bring them happiness. No matter how we have lived in the past, it can all be changed in "the twinkling of an eye". All we need is a little guidance and that guidance does not have to come from a guru or an earthbound avatar. We can receive the guidance from people with whom we interact every day of our lives. As stated before, they are the ones who provide the obstacles out of which we weave the opportunities for our spiritual expression. The Kingdom of God is at hand constantly. We do not have to seek it in some far away place or in some future time. We have but to learn to accept it in present time. All the knowledge of all the universities in the world is not wisdom, but one idea of spiritual service put into practice is expressed spiritual wisdom. The Spirit of God cannot express in a vacuum; it needs expressing through the focalized consciousness of each and every one of us in the here and now.

When we serve others, Aquarian Consciousness allows us to *know and feel* that what we do is the expression of God in this earthly plane. "Not I, but the Father in me, doeth the work". It is being able to translate acquired knowledge into practical expression in the service of God, and as we advance further into this Consciousness, we will find ourselves responding to situations on an intuitive pragmatical level without the aid of thinking. We begin to know exactly what to do next. As we learn to trust this inner knowingness we will begin to eliminate mistakes from our actions and our sayings. Mistakes in life come from firing on only three cylinders, when we leave our Divine Nature out of the act, and reduce ourselves to a mental guessing game. The inclusion of our Divinity in our thoughts and deeds transmutes quantity into quality. This is the Aquarian Consciousness in action.

As has been said on many occasions, there is one step we must take in order to enter into any level of higher consciousness, whatever name it may have. We *must* cease to condemn ourselves for anything we have done on any particular day. We *must* accept that what is done is the Will of God, therefore, if we condemn we are condemning and rebelling against the Will of God.

We started out by saying that the Aquarian Age is a period of time within cosmological duration, a cycle of manifestation. We now find that it is really an individualized experience along our own spiritual evolutionary track. As this plane of Consciousness is now available to us, so is every other plane in a similar manner. They are, however, only available to those willing to accept the responsibility of their Divinity. No amount of begging, bargaining or manipulating of mental processes will get us a free pass into the Kingdom.

Aquarian Consciousness is that which initiates the process of elimination of the divisions of the sub-conscious, conscious and super-conscious. There is not and never has been a separation in consciousness. The belief there is such a separation is the prime cause of the ills in this world. There is but One Source, and from this Source flows the One Consciousness that is the substance of the entire material and spiritual world. It is of this Consciousness that Jesus speaks when He tells the man who has been healed: "Go thy way. Thy faith hath made thee whole". The faith here referred to is the knowledge of the One Consciousness. When we cease to separate our thoughts, words and deeds from our Divinity, we have to become whole. We start by imagining that we are Divine and by behaving accordingly.

The main emphasis of the Aquarian Age is that it is the beginning of the path towards At-one-ment. The Piscean Age was one of analysis, fragmentation and separation. It has been an age of division in politics, religion and sociology, not to mention our communities and individual families. In order to consciously achieve At-one-ment, we all have to seek our unfoldment on an active level. Passivity will not serve the purpose. We have to set forth a philosophy for ourselves which assists us in maintaining an awareness of the consequences of our thoughts, words and actions in the very moment of their expression. Our hereafter is firmly and irrevocably conditioned by how we act here and now. We create in our thought today the experiences that will occur tomorrow. There is no escape. We do not escape destiny by the death of the physical body – the soul is immortal and carries with it in its varying incarnations the seeds from its past creative actions. We are always the sum total of *all* we have ever been.

This development towards an at-one-ment is evident in all parts of our society. The most important and fruitful area of activity is in the scientific fraternity and the religious community. They have been pursuing separate paths since the latter part of the 16th century. Religion is looking at science in the areas of medicine and psychology. It has entered the field of psychology and is attempting to spiritualize it by taking it out of the domain of molecular accident physics. Many psychologists are now refocusing their attention away from the belief that people are an accident of genes. Science is glancing coyly towards religion in its approach toward the more fundamental aspects of para-physics. Both science and religion are reaching towards a universalism of understanding and expression. This is Aquarianism in practice. In the 23rd Psalm we read: "He restoreth my soul". In this Age we are marrying that which has been lacking in each other. We are connecting the physical to the spiritual – the 'me' to the 'I'. This state is advanced by our individual daily actions, which do not have to be of world-shaking significance. To begin with, all we need do is take those daily actions we already perform and add to each of them the conscious awareness of who it is that is performing them in the here and now. As soon as we admit to our Divinity, our Divinity begins to express itself through the 'me'. It has always done so in the past; we just did not recognize it before.

There is only One Source of all creation, and once we place our attention upon it, it begins to flow into the personality. This results in our thinking being cleaned up and our behavior modified. This is the true key to behavioral psychology. This is how we come into our sense of at-one-ment with our own I AM Consciousness, the Consciousness that Jesus, Krishna, Moses, Muhammad and all the great spiritual teachers speak of in their teachings. The At-One-Ment of their teaching is our most illuminating beacon in this Aquarian Age.

Chapter 10

Karmic Law and Spiritual Ignorance

The learning of spiritual principles is not nearly as important as the practice of them in our daily lives. We would be best advised to take one or two fundamental principles, learn them thoroughly, practice them sincerely, and allow the fruits of this expression to guide us in our spiritual search from there on. As we learn the principles of truth through study and practice we begin to develop our consciousness to the state where we "resist not evil" (Matthew 5:39). We need to look at this phrase in terms of our spiritual ignorance and our Karma. When we encounter the word 'evil' in Scripture we must first make the recognition that it has nothing to do with that of which we disapprove.

'Evil' is not what our enemies are, nor is it what we have done that we need to rectify. 'Evil' is not any of the so-called sins of society or of people.

'Evil' is actually no more and no less than the *Presence of God in the moment*. It is not resisting AS IS. When we say resist not evil we are saying resist not that which *is* expressing. We are further saying that which is expressing is the Presence of God. We are saying there is only One Source and all that is expressed is the manifestation of that Source. There can be no hedging of bets on this issue. We cannot have an Omnipresent God and an expression that stems from another source.

We cannot look at someone or something and claim that it is evil, because if we do so we are resisting evil, which is the Presence of God. For us to *judge* any expression of God is flagrant spiritual arrogance. As soon as we begin to criticize or judge any manifestation we are resisting. The very moment we resist, we begin to move away from the sense of our own spiritual awareness.

Once we enter into this mode of thinking we move away from the totality of the expression of God in the universe. In fact, we move into a more limited view of God's universal expression, and as we are made in the image and likeness of God, we now move into a more limited capacity to express our Divinity. What this means for us in real terms is that we deprive the personality of its main source of nourishment, and we already know that a "house divided against itself cannot stand".

So that we may clearly understand what we are dealing with in regard to this concept, let us visualize a blank circle with a single dot in the middle. The circle represents the universe where God's creation will be manifested and the dot represents the Source (God). All manifestation is expressed within this 360 degree circle – there is no other universe. Any individual expression within this circle has to be a manifestation of the Source. When we as individuals stand at any point in this circle, we are expressing the Source, and so are all individuals. This is true not only of humanity, but of every single object and circumstance in the universe.

Wherever we stand within this circle or on its periphery, we are seeing the Presence of the Source. The Presence is all that is. Every time we denigrate, ridicule, debase, judge or resist the Presence, we close down a part of our awareness and we shut out a whole dimension of God's Kingdom. As we do so, we become more and more the unwilling and victimized effect of the society in which we live.

When we look outwards into the world and see something that causes us concern, we are looking at a reminder of our own area of beingness that needs our care and attention. If we are looking at our leaders, seeing them as insensitive, unjust, deceitful, dishonest or just plain gross, we are being reminded that these characteristics are still in active restimulation in ourselves. If we see our friends and relatives being unkind, untrusting or unhelpful, we must look to ourselves and find out where we are failing in these areas of our own life. As we begin to work out our own limitations we expand the awareness of our own Consciousness, and thereby absorb and transmute the energy of that upon which our attention has focused. We may not change the habits of our relatives overnight, but we will change and have contributed to the domain of Consciousness that will help them to change.

It is at this stage of our development that we need to give our attention to the most important aspect of our growth. We must pay some attention to our own Divine Expression. We need to desist from self-condemnation of any sort, such as "I am not pretty enough", "I am not tall enough", "I am not worthy" and so on. All judgments of self such as these must be eliminated, for they are also denigrations and denials of the Presence of God. Whatever we are at any moment is "sufficient unto the day". We can, nonetheless, decide to be different in the future, in appearance and in behavior. Whatever level of performance we express is always what is needed at that time. We can never do too much or too little. We must accept what *is* about ourselves in the present, otherwise we are saying: "I am not accepting the expression of God as me in this moment". When we judge ourselves in this way we close ourselves out from the inner peace and awareness of grace, and leave ourselves to be victims of Karma.

Inner peace has always been a goal for most people. No-one ever willingly seeks turmoil, but many of us quite often find ourselves in turmoil. What then is peace? Peace is not an absence of motion or change. Peace is an absence of resistance to motion or change. Change is, in fact, the one constant in this universe. This does not mean that everything is getting older. It means that the relationships of the particles of cosmic matter are involved in a cosmic dance in which they are constantly changing partners. For us, in our human guise, peace is when we learn to accept that what we are exposed to at any time is God in Action, and respond instead of reacting with concern, fear or resistance. When we learn to remain at peace through our acceptance, we initiate ourselves into the realm of grace. Grace is the descent of the uninterrupted flow of Divine Presence into our daily life. As we achieve this way of living, there is nothing left to fear and we are now open to receive all the gifts of the Kingdom.

If we consider grace to be an attribute of Divinity which is poured down from above (higher vibratory frequency), and begin to be selective as to which parts or attributes we will respond to, we soon find we have blocked the flow. There is little point in asking God to provide us with the bounty of life when we have already closed the door of our receiving depot. In our personality (lower self) level of functioning we are not capable of providing for ourselves in this material world. Once we have blocked the flow we are reduced to the world of chance and guesswork, which brings us directly under the Law of Karma. We continue to live under this law as long as we remain ignorant of spiritual law. Spiritual law states quite clearly that there is only One Source which provides all that is manifested in this universe. If we cannot accept this we separate ourselves from the free expression of our Divinity.

Living in the state of grace permits us to function "without taking thought for the morrow". It permits us to move and take action, knowing that all we need is available for our use at all times. "Therefore, take no thought for your life, what you shall eat or what you shall drink... ..." (Matthew 6.25-34). We accept with equanimity what is happening in life as being that which needs to happen. In this condition we are no longer exposed to the less desirable aspects of daily living. We can only experience in life that which is still a part of our Consciousness. If we choose to watch on television and read in our newspapers of the activities of those functioning at the less desirable levels of life, that is our prerogative, but we must remember that is what we are putting in our Consciousness, which becomes a magnet which attracts it own expression – a lesson we must learn.

When we cease to resist that which is at any given moment, we begin to set in motion the diminution of the separate 'me' which, in time, completely disappears, leaving only the I AM in total ascendancy. It is the 'me' that has "the wants" because it resides only in the material world, without the knowledge of how that world is supplied. The I AM spoken of here is Divine Consciousness, and as such does not have needs. I AM Divine Consciousness expresses in material form all that is required at any time to fulfill its own Idea. As we move ever more into awareness of our Divine I AM Self, we find that our wants decrease because we realize we do not need to 'have things' for some unforeseen and unfortunate future event. Therefore our savings companies are not assets which have interest bearing value in the spiritual development area. The pot of gold at the end of the rainbow is the knowledge we do not need to have security in the spiritual realm – we are immortal.

Having reached the stage where we no longer resist evil and have ceased to condemn ourselves, we can move on to the practice of our Godliness. We do so in a very easy and gentle manner by simply adding a short exercise to whatever spiritual ritual we currently practice. Having completed our earlier exercise, we pause in the state of grace, keeping silent and still for a few moments, and then repeat affirmatively: "God now functions as me", and we can repeat this phrase several times throughout our working day. Having affirmed it, we can then go forward to whatever we need to do at that moment, while maintaining our awareness of Who and What we are.

Having *created* this new condition of Consciousness, we must now pronounce our creation good. An essential part of the creation process is the blessing of that which is created, as the Biblical creation story firmly tells us. This is a necessary step for moving into the state of grace where we can continue to express our Divinity, not just for the exercise, but so that we can become an active and conscious co-creator in the overall Divine Plan. In a comparatively short time we can find ourselves not having to forgive ourselves for anything we have done because we know that what is done is the Divine in expression. Having reached this stage in our growth we are released from all Karmic effect. We know that our Consciousness is the I AM Presence. Now we can truly serve the Kingdom.

Chapter 11

Spiritual Growth and Sexual Unfoldment

As most of us are aware, there is a tremendous growth explosion in the field of sex education liberation and in the area of expanding spiritual awareness. They are, however, seldom spoken of in the same voice. Nevertheless, they are intimately related.

It is a subject most spiritual teachers and community leaders would rather leave to the confines of theology, because there it is safe as long as we keep it in the abstract. Those who hope to find the 'abstract' here may be a little disappointed because, while we may or may not be involved in sexual unfoldment and spirituality in this incarnation, we are going to face it in a future one.

Our quest for peace and serenity, which is an ongoing daily process for each and every one of us, is a quest for self-enlightenment, which cannot be limited to any narrow area that may be currently fashionable or desirable. Also, it cannot be restricted by any area that is not fashionable nor currently popular. It must be pursued across the entire area or spectrum of our lives.

In order to do this it is essential – in fact, it is mandatory – that we go through the process of letting go of outworn illusions, shibboleths, regulations and rules that we have placed upon ourselves, together with many of the outworn ideas we have about sex.

The first delusion, and the one that stands largest in our society, is that the state of ultimate satisfaction can be gained through the 'right' sexual relationship. Sexual perfection as portrayed in our action novels, on our television and movie screens and in many other ways, is sought for itself, as an end in itself. And when it is sought for itself alone, all it brings is disillusionment, impotence and frigidity. The reason why there are so many in society who are impotent and frigid, is because of the emphasis and isolation of the 'use of sex' as a single separated tool from the general pageant of life and its unfoldment.

Sex is no more and no less than the effect or outcome of the thought that creates its expression. It is just as simple as that. Like all of Divine Truth, it has no complexity in it. It is simple and direct in its cause and effect process. Divine Truth is never baffling. Divine Truth is never contradictory. Divine Truth is never other than nourishing. And perfection, as far as sex is concerned, is only reached when the act itself, the very act of sex, is set within the context and its place in the totality of creation. We cannot take part of creation and highlight it, emphasize it, bend and twist it out of proportion, and make it work successfully. We cannot take prosperity out of creation, isolate it, distort it and make it work successfully. This is important to understand. Any physical manifestation in this society, without exception, is an outcome of the creative thought that precedes it. Unfortunately, in the societal idea of perfection, we have the perfected male hero and the perfected female heroine, both of which change fashion from time to time. At one time the lady had to be Rubenesque (a polite way of saying plump); then she had to look underfed and undernourished, which is now called slim.

Sexual perfection, in terms of the individual involved, assumes a separateness for the process that divides it from its Divine expression. The fantasy of sexual perfection – and it is a fantasy in this instance – assumes a separateness which is opposite from at-one-ment. In fact, there is no physical condition that is perfect when it is separated from its Source and restricted to the physical alone. That means to say we cannot have a perfect physical body operating harmoniously unless within the Consciousness using that body is the concept of the at-one-ment with its Source, and this is the Divine.

No matter how far we carry our medical practice of today, no matter how good our holistic health program may be, unless there is included in their work Consciousness the concept of the presence of the Divine, it cannot be perfect. "Not me, but the Father in me doeth the work". The most it can ever become is good human action. We cannot develop a perfect physical body on this plane until we make the total recognition of the Source of that physical body. All physical bodies stem from Consciousness which is filtered through our minds.

We are not talking about the brain. The brain is a physiological entity which is the result of the work of Consciousness working through the human mind. This is important to understand because if we do not, we get lost in society's activity and if we are lost we cannot use sex for spiritual growth.

The second delusion we must erase from our thinking is that sex is evil and that physical desire is wrong and sinful. There is a concept in our society that by talking about, thinking about or being involved with sex is evil, and evil means we shut ourselves out of the spiritual realm, from the Kingdom of God. We must come to understand very clearly and make a positive decision that this is not so; that all past sexual activity, whether society considered it moral, amoral or immoral, has not been evil per se. It is a strange type of purity and a strange form of perfection that states or advocates the denial of the normal God-created process. Make no mistake, only God generates sex. How can a God-created body, with its infinite variety of appetites, be called evil? How can we say that any one of these appetites is not stemming from God? As there is only One Source, there can only be one Stream of Consciousness creation. There is only one Law of God, and most of us share an appreciation of sex. How can it be non-harmonious? How can it be non-peaceful? How can it be non-creative? We cannot take one aspect of Life and say it is wrong, that God made a mistake. It is part of our growth process, either in our current incarnation or another, for celibacy or sexual activity to be present. There is nothing wrong with *celibacy*. There is nothing wrong with *sexual activity*.

We must relinquish the delusion of possession, the concept of possessing our partner, our loved one, whether husband, wife or indeed whatever term we choose to use. We must make a conscious decision to surrender possessiveness. No soul owns another soul, therefore no soul can own the body, the temple of another soul. Consequently there is literally no one who can own another person. In fact, possession is the root of all sexual jealousy, which instigates havoc and disorder in the heart area and generates numerous disorders in the pelvic region.

No one has the right to feel they possess their mate. Love and loyalty can only be given, never appropriated or captured. They are not a piece of territory to war over. We must note and be aware of what happens to children of possessive parents. Love, caring and compassion can only be shared, either between couples or groups – never captured or imprisoned. It cannot be bought, for it is not a commodity offered on the commodity market.

Most of all, love and loyalty can never be used as a tool of enslavement. A tremendous number of people in our society use those we love or those who love us as tools, and we enslave them with that love. We *use* them as slaves.

We are not talking about theory. Possessiveness, which is the delusion we must let go of, is the enemy of love. If we try to possess the loved one, we will kill the love of that loved one for us. We will also kill our own ability to love. We cannot be possessive and loving at the same time.

There is a law in physics and the same law in metaphysics, that two solids cannot occupy the same point in space at the same time. In metaphysics there is also another law, that two contradictory expressions cannot occupy the same position in a relationship if the relationship is to survive. Therefore, we cannot love and possess at the same time – we will either love or possess. This is important to understand. We cannot love and possess; we will have one or the other. When we try to combine them, we destroy. When we begin to possess, we destroy love. When we begin to love, we begin to eliminate possession.

In a marriage the celebrant or the official only performs the ceremony. The marriage can only be effected by the parties concerned, which brings us to the next factor in this whole question.

One thing we must let go of is the concept that the wedding day is the greatest day in our life, something that has been pumped into women more than men. Think of the concept here, think of the consciousness. If the wedding day is the greatest day of our lives, a day when two people commit themselves to share a life, it means it is all downhill from then on. If we enter into it with that concept, the relationship is doomed. This is important to understand. We must consciously and deliberately release this concept from our mind. It is essential if we do not want to come back next time and do the same trip all over again.

Let us instead hold the concept that the wedding day is the *first* day of *all* the greatest days of our life yet to come.

Marriage, as spoken of here, does not necessarily mean a religious or civil contract arrangement. It simply means two people who have agreed to live together in love.

There are four levels of consciousness in which the sex act is pursued, whether within a religious or civil contract setting. The first of these is the security level of a relationship. It is that level at which a woman or a man provides sex for their partner as a security blanket. Security blanket number one is when the woman provides sex for the man because he is a meal ticket to live in the high rent district, what is known in metaphysical circles as legal whoring. Fortunately that is the level of consciousness that is not too prevalent in our society anymore. It is beginning to fade out, but is still there, and if there is even an inkling in our consciousness of finding someone who is going to keep us in comfort in our old age, we are already beginning to produce a situation which is doomed to failure.

We should not leave the man out of this, so let us talk about him. There are tremendous numbers of men who marry women for their money so that they do not have to work too hard. That is at the higher level. There is an even lower more unfortunate level – they marry women so they will have a cook and caretaker for their children. What an insult to the beauty of womanhood! What an insult! Why not hire someone? That is security consciousness.

The second level is the use of sex purely for sensation. This is the playboy and the playgirl in our society, concerned with one thing and one thing only – the immediate and the non-responsible. Enjoy now and hope not to pay later. We will return to them very extensively in a little while, because unfortunately this is where the majority of people in society are right now. Whether or not we belong to this group personally does not make any difference. We are surrounded by this consciousness.

There is a third not very large group, but it is still with us. It is known as the power group level. This is the type of individual who uses sex as the scalp hunting technique. With this particular type of person the more unobtainable the male or female is, the more desirable he or she becomes. The more unobtainable – now hear what is involved – the more unobtainable the person is the more desirable that person becomes as a triumph trophy. It becomes a challenge of one's masculinity on the one hand or one's femininity on the other. I am sorry to say that women play the same game as the men, but they play it by a different set of rules.

The fourth category is known as the love level. This is the level where the deliberate use of the experience flows more lovingly and more acceptingly throughout the whole of our life. They are in the minority just now, but those who are already moving into this level are producing magnificent results in their lives.

We do not need to spend too much time on group number one, the security group. It is self-evident what is involved here, because when a person marries only for security it never lasts too long. A lady living in New Jersey many years ago explained that all through her childhood her mother had drummed into her, practically on a daily basis, what a pretty girl she was and therefore had no need ever to fear poverty at any time in her life. With no difficulties at all she could find and marry a rich beau. She did. She found and married a rich beau, and beggared them both. Her later behavior, because of her fear of her security blanket and meal ticket being taken away, drove her husband to distraction, to such a degree that he became incapable of handling a multi-million dollar business he inherited from his father. She destroyed him and the business. Admittedly this is an exaggerated case, but it is the consciousness process we are involved with when we use sex to purchase a meal ticket. We are thus abusing a most important part of the Divine expression. Do not let us forget that what we are talking about is a Divine expression, not an expression of man that is separate from the Divine. It is Divine expression.

Let us now look at group number two in some detail, because this is the area we must really study because the greatest percentage of people in our society belong, and where the church in our society is at this time. It is the level that is most common, that is concerned with mere sensory enjoyment for its own sake. This is where we are using each other as objects of self-gratification, eliminating, occluding and excluding totally that the person we are using is an expression of the Divine, while forgetting that we ourselves, in the process, are also an expression of the Divine. This is no more and no less than a base objective that *deprives* us of the higher level of feeling that is obtainable in a one-to-one relationship. It deprives us of the opportunity to experience at a deep level, and this particular process leaves us extremely vulnerable, extremely weak. It leaves us in a state of vulnerability where we begin to compare yesterday with today and worry if tomorrow will be better.

When we use sex for sensory gratification all we have to compare is last night with tonight and hope tomorrow will be better or not as bad. We know this is true, as there are many of us who have been through this particular form of experience.

We are talking about the start of the comparison process. Because we are working with the sensory only, we enter into a very strange situation in which we lose completely the awareness of the here and now and, as a result, the fulfillment. Listen to the word – the full-fill-ment – which takes us a step further. But there is something even worse involved in this which, when we realize it, is more degrading as an individual.

We are using a manipulative focus which keeps us from being completely satisfied. We are always *looking* for the ideal when we confine our sexual relationship to the purely sensory. We are always *looking* for the Goddess or Apollo. We are looking for the descended god.

When we are working on the sensation level we miss the beauty of the company, the joy of the intellectual exchange, the spiritual upliftment and inspiration from the sharing over dinner, in the intervals at the theater, during the party, or whatever it is we are involved in.

It sometimes takes us years to learn that lovemaking begins at the moment we meet our date. Listen to the word – lovemaking – or would we prefer to say love manufacturing? That is what it is. It is building an atmosphere and a climate of love, building a vibration of lovingness. When we work only on the sensory level we nullify this. We cannot build a state and a condition and an atmosphere of lovingness when we work on the sensory level, but this is what most of society is doing at this particular time.

The whole television bombardment of our senses is purely sensory, almost totally devoid of any inspiration or uplift. We watch television and all we learn about is what we should eat, what we should put on our underarms, what we should put on our hair, what we should put here, what we should put there, and then what we should wear. Having put it on, we learn how we can get to where we are going, which particular vehicle we should use and, having got there, what we should do and what we should see. This is all purely sensory bombardment, and the purpose behind it is to make us buy all the objects for the satisfaction of sensory enjoyment. Rarely do we find in advertising in any medium anything whatever to do with an aspect that might be uplifting. We are talking here only about the advertising field, not about programming on television or radio. There are worthwhile programs on television and radio, and there are good articles in magazines. We are concentrating on the advertising aspect, so let us look at it and see what is happening.

This is a constant battle on the plains of Armageddon, which is the sensory on one side and the spiritual or inspirational on the other. It is the battle between the lower self and the higher inspirational self. It has nothing to do with the Jews, the Egyptians, the Iranis, the Iraqis or the Saudi Arabians.

We have talked about wining and dining and losing the benefits, but there is another factor – missing the here and now of the person with whom we are spending time. Many people do not even know each other after six months or six years of marriage. They do not know what their partner thinks or feels. When asked why they got married many couples reply with statements such as they both love tennis or they both love the Moody Blues. At least with the second we are getting a little into feeling, and that much is good.

Even for married people, let alone the casual date, this state of affairs produces a condition wherein the gentle loving kiss or the loving caress are unimportant and we do not get the full benefit of them because the attention is already projected forward to what comes later. We slip out of present time into a projection of something that may never happen, and if it does not we feel cheated.

With this emphasis on the sensory, we are so focused on the ever-heightened sensory response and gratification that we cannot get the full enjoyment of the inner qualities of the experience. A relationship with another human being is a complete totality of the physical, emotional, mental and spiritual. If we are confining ourselves to just eating the red, raw meat, we are cheating ourselves at the banquet. If our attention is so fixed we can only focus on one aspect of the relationship, we are impoverished. There is so much more to be enjoyed.

This has nothing whatsoever to do with being young or old. Age has nothing to do with this. A lot of young people make this mistake. Do not make the error of thinking that elderly people are incapable of making the same mistake. Many of the elderly have become impotent or frigid because of their behavior on the sensory level when they were younger. They are now walking around in a fit of jealousy or envy of the young people because they have not yet also become impotent or frigid.

If we operate on this level we too will become impotent and frigid. When we operate this way – taking only a part of the whole – we are always a bridesmaid or best man, never a bride or groom. We never get the full measure of what we are worth, and each and every one of us is worth the full measure.

Scalp hunting, the third level, need not concern us here. It is no longer a major factor in our society; permissiveness has seen to that. Everyone can be loaded with conquests if that is their wish.

When we operate on the fourth level, the love level, we can unfold. This is where we lift the whole of our beingness into an entirely new realm of consciousness. When we operate on the fourth level we begin to expand our total awareness of the now – not just in the area of personal physical relationships on a one-to-one basis. It is important to recognize this. This is why lovemaking is the most potent tool in the hands of the Divine 'angelic man' that is available to us now for the upliftment of our consciousness. *This brings us into contact with the highest level of the eternal that we can experience while incarnated, through the process of sharing.*

Now, instead of the original mere sensory, which is self-gratification, we enter into an entirely new field – the field of giving, which means pouring forth. The entire purpose of the love act becomes different. We are there to serve the loved one. We are there to give to the loved one. And once we begin to realize who we are, when we make the recognition that we are God in action, bringing joy, pleasure, ecstasy and exaltation, we change the entire experience. We have just spiritualized the act. "Behold, 'I' make all things new".

Our entire purpose on this earth is to spiritualize the earth and the lower nature. We do not spiritualize the lower nature by getting rid of it and abandoning it. We spiritualize it by raising it an entire octave in its expression. That is why sex is not evil. That is why sex is not wrong. That is why sex is not dirty. That is why sex is not a sin.

Sex is designed to be an initiation into a higher level of Divine expression. Being currently celibate does not mean that we can never again utilize this particular process. This is most important to understand. Some celibacy would appear to be enforced, some celibacy is enjoined and some celibacy is sought for different reasons at different times.

Whatever takes place in the act of lovemaking and giving becomes blessed and hallowed within itself. The taking of the hand of a loved one becomes a sublime spiritual sexual act. One of the mistakes made in sex is to think that the ten seconds of orgasm is it. It is not. Lovemaking can go on for hours and hours without ever having an orgasm. In fact, even without touching or being touched we can be making love. And if we have not been through the experience of lovemaking on that level, we have not yet lived.

The ecstasy of that state can be so stunning that further physical expression would be a corruption.

When we are giving on the fourth level is the point at which we start being really and truly sensitive to the needs of our partner. We know it becomes an equipoised shared enjoyment in which we *feel*, and we are not referring to the tactile. We *feel* what it is the partner needs at that moment, what the partner requires at that moment. It means that it is sufficient unto the day, which word means a period in eternity. It is the moving into the here and now, and once we begin to learn to give, to serve, to worship (because this is worship), we receive a hundred fold. This is the temple of the spirit in action. We begin to *feel* – notice that word again – more and more. This feeling becomes the actual presence of the Divine operating within us. We lose all sense of the mere physical.

We begin to touch the "hem of the garment"; we begin to touch the level from which the physical stems, the causation level, as we move into this consciousness. We begin to be aware of the true inner beauty of the individual with whom we are relating. We begin to become 'one'. We begin to enter the lower echelons of at-one-ment, all because we have put ourselves in the position of being the giver. We begin to feel a *deeper* and *definite* level of being-ness. Deeper, not lower. Our consciousness is freed totally from the conceptualization of the subjective and objective. Consciousness is freed of this. All because we chose to *give*.

When this takes place, a heightened sense of awareness of the moment touches us, not only while lovemaking, but within conditions outside of and beyond the time and place of lovemaking. Our awareness of the moment is never lost from this point on. We learn to see the Divine in all aspects of human expression.

The highest level of exaltation the human being can experience while incarnated is the instant and moment of coitis. The human being can never rise to a higher level of Divine creative consciousness than the moment that creation takes place, which is why conception takes place. A soul that chooses to enter into a womb at that moment would be nothing other than a beautiful soul. Do we want beautiful children in our lives? Do we want to attract beautiful children? Do we wish to be parents of a Jesus? Let us not walk away from that. We need to understand what is involved.

Mary the mother of Jesus and Joseph his father were Essenes, and the Essenes were keenly aware of three things involved with birth – firstly, what we have just referred to above; secondly, the fertility cycle of the woman, and thirdly, the fertility ability of the father. Therefore, if we want our son or daughter to be "born of a virgin", it is not a virgin womb that is meant, but a virgin consciousness that is required. A virgin consciousness is when we reach that level of at-one-ment, in coitis, to bring forth the purified, to make a gateway, to provide an entry, to make a home, to make a place in society for an anointed one. That is what it is all about.

This is when we begin to allow ourselves to be used as an instrument of the Divine; when we allow ourselves to take all of our physical abilities, whatever they may be, and offer them as a chalice into which Divine Truth and expression can pour. This is consciously taking sexuality, which has been provided for this very purpose, and using it as a tool of spiritual unfoldment and awareness. It is within the province of all of us to do this at will.

There is only one thing we have to do – *we have to make the decision to do it*. It does not matter whether we are young, middle-aged or old. We are all coming back. We are coming back to express on an ever higher harmonic everything we have learned to achieve in this incarnation. It is an entirely selfish concept to assume that having gained particular abilities in this life we do not come back to share them with others. If we decide that having achieved a particular level of spiritual attainment, this is neat and we are not coming back, it is guaranteed we will have lost the higher level of consciousness. The very act of deciding we do not wish to share means we lose it. "The Father and I are One". "Behold I am with you all days, even unto the consummation of the world". This is what it means – coming back. We are all coming back until this particular earth which we are treading at this juncture, is spiritualized at all levels, in all ways, by all mankind.

Chapter 12

Endless Love, Here and Now

Most people, when they talk about love, have one of three misconceptions. The first thing that usually pops out is some sort of sentimentality, some sort of wishy-washy, non-definable, very non-concrete concept of love. It is usually about being loved, rarely about loving. The second misconception is that somehow it is all to do with the physical and only with the physical. In other words, it is totally and completely tied up with sex, and nothing else is involved. Usually that relates to jealousy, control and absence of liberty and space for the other person. Third, and by no means least, there is some sort of idea that we are somehow in touch with an abstraction that does not need any pragmatical expression. Somewhere out there is a being called God, and if we go to church on Sunday and we do not lie or cheat, if we do not try to tip the scales and give poor measure or whatever it is, we will be loved by God, and we have it made. These three broad descriptions are the common-place in our society.

Some may say: "Hey, I don't believe that", but then we need to ask a question – "How many normal people do you work with?" For the most part those of us who are involved in the spiritual unfoldment field are a minority. We do not represent the largest majority of the practicing people in the world. Seven or ten may be the percentage figure, but it is small. In our daily lives, if we remain within the narrow confines of the spiritual unfoldment group, we are dealing with an active minority. To the broad body of people out there we are "a bunch of flakes".

The first thing we must understand is that love is not an abstraction. It is not something that comes in from a distant point in space from which we can fill our buckets. It is a down-to-earth, pragmatical interaction with universal consciousness. There is *a* definition for it – not *the* definition – *a* definition. It is "the sense of at-one-ment at all times for all things". There are many other definitions which may be more apposite, more appropriate.

Most of us at this particular stage in our development are not capable of having this sense, nor of having this sense at all times, and certainly not for all things. It is a little difficult sometimes for us to love her or him or it when her, him or it would seem to be behaving totally and utterly contrary to all the principles and the whole body of beliefs we have. It is very easy to love those who are carrying the same belief structures as ourselves, those whose general daily performance is exactly the same as our own (which means we are the ethical ones because we never see ourselves as the unethical ones). It is very easy to relate with that, but how easy is it to relate with somebody who is in prison for murder or rape, or for beating an old lady over the head and stealing her purse? Can we get in our car tomorrow, drive to a prison and really feel at-one-ment by going into the maximum security block and sitting down with some man who is doing fifteen to twenty years in there because he murdered a child? When we read in our newspapers that someone in Santa Barbara, New York or Chicago has murdered a very pretty little girl who happens to be a Catholic, and we see a picture of her on her seventh birthday making her First Communion, all dressed in white and looking beautiful, can we really now love the murderer? Or do we allow our emotions of repugnance to take over and refuse to recognize the Divinity of the perpetrator of the act?

Let us take it right from the bottom level at this point before moving into the higher echelons of analysis. It is all very well to talk about this thing intellectually and say we should be able to love the murderer of the pretty little girl. If we do not (and we are not to be criticized because we do not), how then are we going to move our Consciousness up from the displeasure and abhorrence of a condition without placing that abhorrence of the condition on the perpetrator?

The more we abhor the person rather than the condition, the longer will we perpetuate that very condition. Even as this is being written the thought is going out on a Cosmic wave, and whatever is being projected from the writer's Consciousness through these words is now reaching every conscious being in the universe who is tuned into this particular vibration. Every time we think or speak from whatever vibration – resentment, hatred or love – we reach every individual who is on a similar vibratory frequency.

Having established the principle under consideration, let us return to our murderer. If we are sitting there seething with abhorrence and hatred for this 'foul person', what are we sending him? We are sending out more of the same foul, hateful vibration. We are sending a non-optimum vibration to that individual. We are not in the process of reconstitution, rejuvenation or resurrection. We are in the process of condemnation and burial. We are projecting hate, malice and abhorrence. So, the next time we pick up our newspaper, the next time we watch our television and see the heinous villain being apprehended and dragged before his peers to be judged, we had better be aware of the vibrations we are narrow-casting.

Let us start at the very beginning. If we want to be a channel of love for all those neat folks with whom we normally associate, if we want to be a clear channel of love to all those whom we already love, if we want to be a clear channel of love to all those beautiful people who are all meditating all over the world – none of them need it! They are not the ones who need it. Why did Jesus tell the rabbis in His time: "The whores are getting into heaven before you"? Why do you think He said this? He said it because so many of us involved in spiritual unfoldment work are trying to establish a closed shop. We want only to work with the noble, the just, the enlightened, the good, the fruitful, the bountiful, the beautiful.

With whom did Jesus work? He worked with the blind, the lame, the lepers, and He worked with them physically, emotionally and mentally – all three. So our lesson is very simple. When we see our villain on our television screen or named in our newspaper the first thing we have to remember to do is to not be abhorred by this person, which requires a conscious concrete decision in advance. "I will not be abhorred by the personality because within that personality is the Divinity of Soul". We then give thanks that we as ourselves are no longer in that consciousness. We have taken the first step of love (because love always pours downwards and outwards) to one who needs our love. We make the recognition that we are no longer in the consciousness where we have to perform unlawfully, and with that recognition goes an obligation – the obligation to serve. That does not mean that we have to run down to the jailhouse, but what we do have to do is very simple. For only a few seconds (we do not have to sit there hour after hour) we hold the person's image in our mind and remember him in our prayers.

How do we remember the person in our prayers? What is our prayer? What is prayer? Prayer is when we identify with God, and as we hold the image of that individual in our consciousness we repeat to ourselves: "You, I and the Father are One. I bless you and pronounce you whole". Let us understand what "whole" means in this sense. At this particular moment we are making the recognition that the aspect that committed the crime is the *personality*, which is only the lesser part of the total Divine manifestation. In addition to this there are three other parts of that manifestation – the Higher Self, the Angelic Self and the Cosmic Self. If we see and accept this concept, we can go on to say "I bless you and pronounce you whole". At that moment we are seeing the additional parts of the Divinity and are not focusing only on the lowest part.

We have now taken a practical step, not just in the propagation of the concept of love or intellectual wrangling about love. We have taken a dynamic step in the extension of the love vibration from the abstract to the concrete. This is very simple to understand, but a little harder to do. At this stage, for most of us who are normal, the natural action is to be abhorred, horrified and traumatized by such an event as committed by the "villainous" individual. If we talk to the average parent about the murder of a child, the response is that it could have been their child, because the first thing they do is personalize it. They attach it to the lowest quadrant of our being. They relate to it on an intimate, personal, pragmatical and physical relationship level. This makes us feel as bad as the parents or relatives, and if we think we are being of any help at that moment to the parents of the victim, we are not. By being sad and sorrowful with them we are not being of any help, but compassionate is another matter. That is the next step – to move from the victim to the sufferer. We are concerned with what we are doing and how we use love. We now move from the perpetrator and the victim to those who are suffering – the parents or relatives involved. What can we do for these people in these circumstances? Do we say "How terrible. We know exactly how you feel and we feel just as you do". Do we write them a letter of sympathy and demand that the perpetrator be strung up with piano wire? Why do we want to perpetuate a person's misery, which is exactly what we are doing with that consciousness. We are perpetuating and reinforcing their misery and their sadness.

If we are a spiritual being and are functioning on a spiritual plane, that is not what we do. Instead we will act in a spiritual manner in all circumstances, making absolutely sure we do not descend into the level of personality where we are being controlled by the emotion rather than by the Higher Self, Angelic Self or Cosmic Self level of beingness. We cannot help by jumping into the water and drowning with the already drowning man. We begin very simply by raising our own consciousness to the highest level we can through whatever may be our process. If it is meditation, fine. If we happen to be a Catholic or an Episcopalian, we can use the Rosary. Whatever our tool, whatever our instrument is fine as long as we raise our own consciousness to the highest possible level we can achieve, and then we *visualize the sufferers in the same consciousness as ourselves.*

If we cannot do it by affirmation or by ritual, then we do it at least by visualization on an abstract level, because *where attention goes, energy follows*. This is the Cosmic Law. We do not even need to have an actual picture or image; when we say abstract level we mean an abstract feeling or idea, not an actual picture. We visualize ourselves in a state of contentment, in a state of joy, and possibly in a state of serenity. We then immediately refocus our attention upon the sufferers, and see them enlightened. Think of the words enlightened, enjoyed, ennobled, enriched – enriched by the Consciousness of Divine and sublime Love. As we focus our attention upon them, it may be in that moment the sufferers have said "O God, please help us".

How many times in the course of our life, even in agnosticism, have we cried out: "O God, help me"? Whom do we think replies? How do we think God channels energy to us? Direct by satellite conduit or through a coaxial cable? No way! That is not how the help arrives.

After a dog had caused a leg and foot injury to him, a spiritual teacher made a very definite decision. He decided he would immediately engage himself in a self-restoration of the bodily injury. In this instance, the first thing he did was to get up and walk around the house for five minutes. He knew the injury was there and was not denying it. While walking, he decided to instigate self-healing. A little while after that he also asked God for help. A few days later he met a friend who greeted him with the statement: "David, I hope you felt the help you were getting during last week". He had indeed felt it, and it had not come by coaxial cable. It came from some of the good people in the community acting in their "Godliness".

This is how the Love of God reaches us. It does not matter how many churches we have been in. It does not matter how many synagogues we have been in. It does not matter how many mosques we have been in. We never yet have received a vibration of love from a brass sculpture, from a stone sculpture or from a vaulted ceiling, Gothic or otherwise. We have most certainly got it from those physical human beings by whom we are surrounded. This is how the Love of God reaches us. We are all constantly expressing it all the time. Every time we project a loving consciousness toward another being, it is guaranteed that persona had recently asked for help. Divinity functions through people.

Let us, therefore, take the third stage of this process. We now know how to deal with the perpetrator. We have a method for dealing with sufferers. Now we come to people or events we do not read about in newspapers or see on our television screens. Why do we think that often while showering, driving along the motorway or eating a meal, we suddenly think of someone? It is not because we once shared a meal with them. It is at least ninety-nine percent certain that person has just put out an appeal for help. The reason it reached us at the particular moment in time is that we were in the specific octave of vibration of the seeker, and therefore have the opportunity of becoming the giver. Our response is to pause in whatever we are doing, and hold that person in benign Consciousness, repeating to ourselves the mantra we have used before, namely "You, I and the Father are One. I bless you and pronounce you whole".

God never comes to visit us in a golden chariot with the Archangel Michael as chauffeur; we will never see that vehicle pull up in front of our house. What we may well see pull up is a 1990 Ford, with a teenager climbing out of it and saying "Hello, I love being with you folks and have come over to talk with you". Do not forget who it is that has spoken to us – none other than the Indwelling God. If we turn away the owner of that old Ford because we need to keep the entry-way clear for the golden chariot, we are in serious trouble and had better not start looking for love in our life. We will soon know that it is no longer there to find, and if we do not have love in our life, we need to look at what it is we are turning away.

All of us need to look at the times throughout our lives in which we have turned away love, not least the love of an animal. Love is a very important quality, even in animals. They do love us. It is interesting to note and understand that every vibration level on the scale of the hierarchy always directs its love to the level above it. The animal kingdom directs its love to the kingdom of man, in all sorts of ways. Our cats, dogs, birds and even members of the vegetable kingdom render unto us. We in turn are genuinely seeking to love our fellowman and to love God. For the most part it is performed as an abstraction until we get into the areas of practice we have been referring to. To us, love very often means being loved.

That is the general, but how about the particular? That we will discuss in the next essay.

Chapter 13

Endless Love and the Seven Sacred Planets

Most of us have heard the phrases "the Seven Spirits before the Throne", "the Seven Rays" and "the Seven Sacred Planets", but have not realized there is a direct relationship between these three entities and the seven days of the week. Each day of the week has a specific and particular vibration that we can tune into and utilize.

We need to develop an understanding of the seven days of the week and how we can utilize the vibration of a particular day to augment and uplift ourselves (because as a man thinks, so he becomes) and all those to whom we direct our attention.

Let it be understood that "attention" is *Divinity in action*. We never have to seek far for the Divine as it is no more and no less than our attention. When Patrick focuses his attention on Julie, however fleetingly, Divinity is focusing attention on Julie. And as Julie receives and returns that attention, Divinity is focusing attention on Patrick. We do not have to seek far for God. Another way of spelling God is ATTENTION. What do we think our attention is? What do we think it is that moves above the speed of sound, way above the speed of light, way beyond the confines of the galaxy, way beyond the confines of time and space itself? Our attention *is our immortality*, and there is never a time when we are not applying our attention. Our attention is constantly manifesting, even if it is focusing on the banal, on the trite or on the profane. It is even more delicate than an angel's wing.

Therefore, when we put our attention on a particular vibratory level – the Seven Spirits before the Throne or the Seven Sacred Planets – we as Divinity are augmenting and implementing that particular vibration in the Universe at that moment. We are in an active position of 'co-creator', not a benign, not an inactive, but a positive co-creator. There is only us to do it – there is no-one else.

We will begin with the vibration of Thursday, the day whose sacred planet is Jupiter. It is not necessary to go into all the astrological aspects of this here, but it is necessary to understand the consciousness of Jupiter. If we are into astrology we know that Jupiter rules Pisces. What is Pisces? Pisces is the ocean Mother of Creation, the Virgin exalted, the Virgin Consciousness exalted, exalted meaning primed for creative action. So what are we talking about? We are talking about the consciousness and the vibratory rhythm of a planet that is particularly apposite on the day Thursday, known in Nordic mythology as Thor's Day.

We normally like to think that Thor is the god of war, but he is not. Thor is the bountiful god of emanation or creation, therefore the concept that we hold in our consciousness on Thursdays is a simple one – "So God created man in his own image". Who is God? I AM God. Therefore, I have created myself in the image that I have created, and whatever I am manifesting at this very moment is what I created in consciousness in the past.

What I am expressing in the physical and emotional plane of my existence now, I have already created in the Cosmic plane of my Consciousness. Let us not make the mistake of thinking we are never in Cosmic Consciousness. We are constantly floating in and out of Cosmic Consciousness all day long. It is what Jesus talked about when he said: "For a little while I AM with you, and again in a while I AM not with you, and yet again in a while I AM with you". How many times in the course of the day do we slip out of our I AM Consciousness? How many times in the day do we concretely and deliberately move back into our I AM Consciousness? At the moment we move into our I AM Consciousness we are in Cosmic Consciousness. If in that moment of Cosmic Consciousness we decide to go to the market, the I AM has made a decision and has begun to manifest in the Angelic Kingdom. "Not me, but the Father in me doeth the work". The I AM has begun to transform and to transmute the energy downward into the physical action of going to the market. As we move into the action we carry with us our direct connection with the Cosmic Consciousness. We sometimes forget who decided to go to the market in the first place, and wish that we had not come that day because it is so crowded.

This is the day to be particularly aware of the condition we are in, physically, emotionally and mentally, and *accept* it as the creation of self. Nobody, nobody out there, has done it to us. If we are feeling "lousy", it is because some time back we decided to do that which has now made us feel that way.

Next, the sacred planet for Friday is Venus, the goddess of love, and the concept we focus our attention on is "He that dwelleth in love dwelleth in God". We need to understand this concept and how we translate it into practical use. By projecting the love vibration, the at-one-ment vibration to a murderer, to suffering parents or to whomever, we are actively dwelling in our Godliness. Understand that "dwelling" means the totality of our manifestation, our expression, at the moment. It has nothing to do with a physical level of beingness and living in some kind of a place called 'heaven'. At that particular moment, consciousness is total in its concept of giving, in its sharing, in its compassion, in its understanding, in its mercy toward that upon which we put our attention. In that moment we are living in God. We that are dwelling in love are expressing our Godliness.

The days of the week are not accidental nor are the months of the year, or that there are 365 days in a year. We do not live in a happenstance universe, where God goes to bed at night *hoping* the sun will come up in the morning, but in a structured and ordered Universe. For Saturday the sacred planet is Saturn; 'Sat' is another name for the god and 'urn' is the resting place of the god. The name Seth means the same thing in Egyptian. The concept for Saturday is "Let the Christ be formed in me". We must get this very clear, because in a Western Christian civilization there is great confusion here. A whole lot of people immediately see a character bowed, struggling, carrying a cross on his shoulder and making for the nearest hill, with another couple of people following behind him carrying a hammer and some nails. This is not what we are talking about.

It is necessary to define very simply the actual meaning of Christ Consciousness, which is that consciousness we have when we see *no separation between ourselves and anything we observe*. No holds barred here, no limitations. No saying: "Well, how about Chicanos? How about Chinese? How about young people? How about old people? How about boys? How about girls? How about surfers? How....? *No* exceptions. If we want to know right now the degree of our Christ Consciousness, let us take a look at all those people and things we object to and we will find how far we are from Christ Consciousness. *Any* form of discrimination – discrimination as we normally use it in our society, as distinct from discernment – is a lack of Christ Consciousness. We must not make the mistake that discernment is discrimination. Discernment is one thing, discrimination is another. Christ Consciousness is that state of consciousness where we see no separation between us and them. It is that part in an affirmation meditative poem we hear sometimes:

> *In the deeps of our being, I AM,*
> *Within the innermost reaches of our thoughts and thoughtlessness,*
>   *I AM.*
> *May we come to understand that there is no place where I AM not,*
> *For I AM you and you are me,*
> *And we are all together in the knowing.*

That is what Christ Consciousness is.

A specifically beautiful and wonderful day of the week to practice this is Saturday, but not only on Saturday but everyday. Practice, practice, practice, practice is the key. No-one who has practiced spiritual unfoldment has been unsuccessful. There are no 'also-rans'. They may not have won the Preakness or the Kentucky Derby, but they *have* won the self-development stakes. There are no failures when we practice spiritual unfoldment, but do not make the mistake of trying to put a time barrier on the development. That is where most of us go wrong, by insisting it has to happen by five o'clock on Saturday afternoon or thinking God is out to lunch if it does not happen by the time set within spiritual parameters.

For our next area of attention, Sunday, not surprisingly the sacred planet is the Sun, and the concept is "Love is the fulfillment of the law". What does this mean? Love *is* the fulfillment of the law. The law is the acceptance of the at-one-ment, together with the fact that where attention goes, energy follows. *That is the law.* Therefore, when we focus our loving attention, it is the fulfillment of the law. The law is in complete and total manifestation through this alignment. Let us be quite clear on this, with no hold-outs. It does not matter how weak we think we may be in our ability to love, whatever we are expressing our love toward. If we only have a pint, that is all the loved person or thing needs from us, they do not need a gallon. The amount of love we give to that which we love is the amount they *need* from us.

This is what Shakespeare is talking about in *The Merchant of Venice*, when Shylock is told he may not have one drop of blood from Antonio. Not one drop of blood. One pound of flesh. No more, no less. *We cannot give more than is required, and we cannot give less than is needed.* Therefore, whatever action we carry out for one another, or even for ourselves or for our own body, is just what is needed. We have got to move out of the concept of being incompetent. We have got to move out of the concept of being unworthy. We are always a worthy vessel. We always produce the perfect effect at any given moment of manifested time. *There is only one Perfect Source of all effects.*

"Love is the fulfillment of the law", and when we make the recognition of this, we can never give less than is needed. God does not goof! God always picks the right measure. God always picks the right vessel and he always picks the right ingredient. From some a smile, from others a dollar, and we must never make the mistake of thinking there is any difference between the hug, the handshake and the dollar. There is no difference; it is all Divine

Energy in manifestation. This is what "Love is the fulfillment of the law" is all about. The fulfillment means there is never short measure. We must let go of the idea that we have ever been short-changed at any time. It is not always easy to do this, but it is very simple to understand it. We change it first of all by deciding we have never been short-changed. We have to let go of all the decisions we have made that we have been short-changed, such as we should have been taller, shorter, broader, fatter, thinner, richer, better-looking, blonde, brunette, redhead or whatever. At this particular moment we are the perfect expression of Divinity, and we can never be other than the perfect expression of Divinity in every moment of our living.

This brings us to Monday, for which the sacred planet is the Moon (Monday/Moonday). "But if we walk in the Light, as He is the Light, we have fellowship one with another" is the concept for this day. The Light we are talking about is the light we have just referred to. If we walk in the Light of our open realization of the at-one-ment, we will never be able to see anybody else other than at one with ourselves. If we maintain this Light of realization, there are no Monday-morning blues. Why do we have Monday-morning blues? Only because we lose our awareness of at-one-ment. If we live and practice "Love is the fulfillment" of the law we will never have Monday-morning blues again.

The next day for attention is Tuesday. The sacred planet is Mars, sometimes referred to as the red planet. This is the day in which the concept is "Behold, I make all things new". This is probably the most important day of the week, because on this day we take the world as it is, creation as it now stands, and we accept it in its totality. We cannot change the world by fantasy thinking. The creation process is done with that which is already created. The raw material of our future is what we have in our consciousness today. We do not and can not live in fantasy-land and say: "I wish this gas was 20 cents a gallon". It is not so anymore. Nor can we say: "I wish the Russians did not do that, and I wish the Germans did not do the other". We must stop wishing and hoping at the level of the personality. There is no hope in the Kingdom of God, there is only creative decision allied with action. Hope is the last redoubt of the damned. Whenever we hope against hope that something is not going to happen, it always does. Whenever we hope it will not be, it happens; whenever we hope it will be, it does not. Hope is the reneging and rejection of responsibility for the creation of which we are the co-creators. Hope is the rejection of responsibility.

Therefore, on Tuesday "I" make all things new. This means that we take the existing condition and transform and transmute it into the desired state of beingness that we wish to manifest. "Behold, 'I' make all things new", not he does or they do. As soon as we make this recognition and make this concept active, even if it is doing the washing up after dinner, we have changed our life. This is what is known in literature as 'a moment of truth'. It is what William Blake called the Divine Aspect. Goethe called it the 'moment of illumination'. This means that at the very moment we look at all the turmoil around us, all the disorder, we no longer see disorder in our presence. We see a thriving, structured, uniform, optimum and active universe. The greatest thing we have to offer is our ability to restore confidence in our own creation.

We now come to the last day – Wednesday – whose sacred planet is Mercury. Having gone through from Thursday to Wednesday, we come to the most beautiful, the most serene and the most uplifting of all the concepts we can carry throughout the week. It comes from the 46th Psalm – "Be still and know I AM God". Here is one that is so simple and yet so sublime, so beautiful, so resonant, so harmonious. Because of its simplicity we tend to gloss over it without realizing just exactly what it is saying. How then do we take this beautiful, resonant affirmation or concept and translate it into a fruitful and functioning reality? Again, it is very simple.

As soon as we open our eyes, at the very moment we awake on a Wednesday morning, while addressing our own physical body, we repeat "Be still and know I AM God". We are not now asking the body to become paralyzed. Stillness is not an absence of motion, nor is peace an absence of motion. Stillness and peace, which are synonymous in this instance, are both an absence of resistance to motion. It is harmony. It is peace. It is the glowingness of the sense of God within. If we then go through our day and the various tasks we undertake repeating this affirmation, we will calm our own erratic behavior. We learn to control our own erratic emotions, our scatterbrained thinking.

If we find ourselves not to be in total control of our body actions or mental processes, all we have to do is consciously fractionally pause and command our body and our thoughts to 'be still'. "Be still and know I AM God", and we become more nimble on our feet and clearer in our thinking. If we find ourselves getting emotionally disturbed about anything, we pause fractionally in the same way and command our emotions to 'be still'. This is the temple of the Holy Spirit. It is not us. *We command it.* Therefore, we can command this emotional body of flesh. If we find our thoughts flitting all over the place when we need to concentrate, there is nothing better to focus attention upon than a particular thought. Let us focus our attention, let us focus our thought. "Be still and know I AM God".

We do not have to work with all seven concepts every day. It is much easier if we select one particular day in the week to do those which are most applicable. Rome was not built in a day. A journey of 10,000 miles begins with the first step. This is practicing love in action. It is love of self, which is necessary. It is love of our own personal Divine expression, which is not only desirable but is also uplifting. It is the practicing of love toward those by whom we are surrounded, whether we are intimately related to them on a day-to-day, one-on-one basis, or whether they are further removed from us. For we are One in the Spirit, we are One in the Lord, and we *know* that our unity has been restored at that moment when we do knowingly express our Divinity

---

The days of the week, their planets and concepts:

Thursday	Jupiter	So God created man in his own image
Friday	Venus	He that dwelleth in love, dwelleth in God
Saturday	Saturn	Let the Christ be formed in me
Sunday	Sun	Love is the fulfillment of the law
Monday	Moon	But if we walk in the Light, as He is the Light, we have fellowship one with another
Tuesday	Mars	Behold, I make all things new
Wednesday	Mercury	Be still and know I AM God

Chapter 14

Is Satan for Real?

In this Western world of ours the name Satan is almost as well known as the name of God. Very often, in certain circles, Satan receives more frequent billing.

Whether or not we are religious, the mere use of these names in our daily utterances brings us into the active domain of Spiritual Psychology. Any form of utterance involves the thought forms generated through our mind. Both God and Satan are terms that are constantly used in conjunction with Holy Scripture, which for us in the Western world means the Judaic/Christian Old and New Testaments. Unfortunately no benefit is derived from these scriptures by the vast majority who read them because the Bible is not a book of worship. Rather it is a spiritual psychology manual, and only becomes a useful tool when the code in which it is written is understood. To read scriptures at the literal level alone is pointless, as it provides little if any spiritual nourishment.

Before deciding whether or not Satan is real, it is as well to have some understanding of the basis of scriptural writing and the code used in presenting its psychological insights.

Scripture is not written for those who have not yet entered upon the path of spiritual enlightenment and are still looking outward for their personal salvation. It is an aid and a work manual for those who have decided to take responsibility for their own spiritual growth.

There are several major keys to the Biblical code, and there are at least four levels of comprehension to address in understanding the message of scripture. It is not a job for the lazy. It is not until we 'sicken and die' from outward unproductive Bible readings that we can turn inwards to our Soul Being and obtain the soul nourishment that leads us into the Light of our Divine expression.

As we read literature written about the Bible we frequently come across references to the character of Satan and the diabolic deeds he inspires in the unwary. In a culturally Christian society many of us carry within our consciousness a sort of quasi-belief that somewhere out there behind us is an entity or persona pushing us towards what we really do not want to do. This is only partially true. We are impelled but never forced, and we are only directed along a divine path.

Let us take a look at what this entity called Satan is and see if it has the power to direct us anywhere, be it our own choosing or not.

The word Satan is actually derived from the word Sat-Urn, and is also the word used to designate one of the sacred planets in the solar system. This does not mean that Satan as an entity came from the planet Saturn. Satan is the title given to the separative tendency in Creative Consciousness which manifests the entire concrete material world. This is the angelic Consciousness that creates the physical universe in the full consciousness of its at-one-ment with the Universal Divine. This Consciousness is intrinsically spiritual matter, and in no way can it be perceived to be physical matter. It is the tendency in the mind towards the Creative which is a focus center in the One Consciousness. Once we begin to understand this fact we can begin to glimpse the connection of the relationship between God and Man. This is best expressed in Exodus, Chapter 3, Verse 14: And God said unto Moses, I AM THAT I AM: Thus shalt thou say unto the children of Israel, I AM hath sent me unto you. This is the most profound and yet the most simple statement of the relationship between God and Mankind.

So that creation may advance, a separative aspect is initiated in Universal Divine Consciousness (God). If this were not so, Divinity would have remained in a state of Chaos, the condition of formless non-structured Be-ingness. Without the urge to create there is no creation, no-thing manifested. Therefore, the urge to create in Divine Consciousness is called Satan (Lucifer, Prince of Light). Any modern scientist will tell us that all concrete things are the effect of light waves, so we are talking about a process that both the religious and the scientific communities can agree upon.

This urge in all of us to create is how God uses the instruments of his creation to continue and maintain that creation which is still taking place on an ongoing daily basis. Contrary to common and ignorant belief, God did not create the world in the past, in the short time of six days of twenty-four hours each, with a union-organized rest day to follow. The attempt of many people to make God an extension of their limited personality causes a great deal of the confusion in the world regarding the symbols and coding of Holy Scripture. The use of Scripture in recent centuries was solely for the purpose of keeping attention on the concept of a Supreme Being during the long night of our spiritual occlusion.

Let us examine this separative-consciousness from the point of view of the material world we see around us in our daily life. If we were to maintain what the French call the 'idee fixe' (the fixed idea), we would never create anything because our attention would be transfixed on the last thing we thought of. We would be remaining in a static or non-vibratory condition. No creation can take place without the interplay of the polarities of energy. If urge and attention is missing from our consciousness, no-thing can be manifested and we would be in a state of suspended spiritual animation.

If we understand that the urges within consciousness, or the separative aspects, are the action of Divine Will wishing to express creation, we begin to understand our relationship with God. In this state of awareness we are being tempted by Satanic consciousness, God's urge to express himself. This has to be so because God is omnipotent, omniscient and omnipresent. There is only one source of all creation, therefore it is that source which creates the urge to create, which we call Satan. It is only in our ignorance and personality demand for duality that an evil alternative source power can be entertained.

If we stayed home, so to speak, and never left the heavenly state, we would not have a planet earth, we would not have a solar system nor a cosmos, nor indeed would we have coffee on the table each morning. In order for us to have that morning coffee we have to separate ourselves from our bed or from our sleep state.

We are talking about the creative process that has brought about separative consciousness. If we are complacent and satisfied we will never ever make spiritual progress. If we are complacent and satisfied we will never ever make scientific progress. If we are complacent and satisfied we will never make educational and cultural progress. In fact, we will make no progress at all. Therefore, when we hear people speak of Satan urging us to do wrong, it is not Satan who is doing the urging but rather Satanism or the Satanic energies of separativism urging us to manifest differently from that we have already manifested.

What we are really saying is that Satan or Satanism (or whatever word our society uses to describe it) is no more and no less than the essence created by God from which all of the *remainder* of creation is manifested. In Sanskrit it is called Daiviprakriti. Carl Sagan calls it the stuff of the universe. His program *Cosmos* is probably one of the best, if not *the* best, spiritually scientific programs ever put on television.

Not only is this essence the stuff of the universe, but it is the stuff of the universe projected outwards and maintained by the One Life. There is only One Life. There is only One Life, and that Life is the Perfect Life, and that Perfect Life is my life right now. Which means we take the Divine Essence, the stuff of the universe, and we implement it into the beingness of our consciousness in the here and now. Which means that when we read this book or when we walk downstairs and pour ourselves a cup of tea or make ourselves a cup of coffee or we turn to speak to someone, we do it in the total and complete knowledge of our Divinity.

It is not that something in the past, an exalted Being called God, residing somewhere in the Middle East or some other exotic location, did something and it all happened back then; nor that an entity called Satan or Devil upset the plan and is still doing so today. Creation is perfect, present and here to stay. God is perfect and *no entity can upset the plan of an Omnipotent God.*

If we talk about Separative Consciousness, which is Satanic Consciousness, that Consciousness is a degree lower, vibratorily speaking. We are, therefore, into a process of descending the scale of vibratory frequencies. This is what Scripture speaks of when it refers to the Fall, the fall of man or man being driven from the garden, the Edenic state of consciousness. The Fall in this instance refers to the conscious descent by self-directed expression in the direction of material manifestation. It is the descent from non-dimensional into three-dimensional Beingness.

In terms of physics, there is no dimension as such in Spiritual Beingness, but there is dimension in material spiritual Beingness. We are Soul Beings, angels who have descended into material form in the bodies we have created – the bodies we have created and the bodies we use, not the bodies that we are. We are not just bodies. The bodies we use have been created to become vehicles of ongoing creation. These bodies become our vehicles of manifestation, and we use them to continue the creation process.

When two people stand before a microphone to share their music with us, that is a creative process. Before they decided to share with us we could not hear the music nor could we hear the words of their song, but through the use of their spiritual entity, their spiritual creative beingness, they are able to vocalize, structure and organize the airwaves, which had passed into their lungs and come out again in the form of harmony, so that we listen to a particular category of musical expression. A violin does not play itself. The bow does not caress the strings unless it is in the hand of the creator. The song is not heard unless the voice of the creator is at work.

So when we talk about the Fall we are talking about a descent into material expression. Some of us may have wondered why, after more than 2000 years of monasteries, convents and holy people, the world is not in better shape. The answer is that very, very few of us have taken our spirituality into our praying or coffee-making, let alone into our love-making. If we make love with a member of the opposite sex and conception takes place, if we are not doing so in our awareness of our Divine Consciousness, what sort of soul are we inviting to enter the fetus? A highly spiritualized and aware soul? Never. Our spiritual decision-making process is what produces the spiritualized effect. This brings us directly to the concept of the Tree of Knowledge of Good and Evil.

What then is the Tree of Knowledge, this tree that stands in the Garden of Eden? It is not a citrus nor a fig tree; it is a fruit-bearing tree, but you will notice that we only talk about the fruits of the Tree of Knowledge without identifying them. What then are they?

The Tree of Knowledge is the active Life Force of the creative process, and the characteristics and the attributes that arrive as the result of the use and application of that process are the fruits of the tree. The Tree does not give ordinary fruit. If we have a Spiritual Consciousness which we maintain and keep hidden from all mankind, it is a barren tree that does not produce fruit. But when we consciously go about the prosaic act of making a cup of tea or coffee for another person, we have brought the spirituality of the Tree of Knowledge into concrete spiritual manifestation. It is not good to say "I love you" unless we are prepared to show it in action. We also need to be aware that *we* are God, currently in action. The smile upon our face, the look of joy in our eyes as we say "I love you" is the expression of the soul. How many people have we heard say "I love you" without even looking us in the eye. We are lucky even to hear it.

The utilization of Divine Creative ability is the very simple act of the conscious focusing of *Divine Self*. And there is only one *Self*, there is no other. The only thing that is separative about us in consciousness is our chosen ability to manifest and to spiritualize matter. This is what the Tree of Knowledge actually represents. Sometimes it is expressed as the kundalini fire. Kundalini is a Sanskrit word which translates as the union of the positive (Ida) and negative (Pingala) forces. When these two forces are perfectly combined we produce a third aspect of energy, balanced expression, which in Sanskrit is called Sushumna. It is in the moment of the perfect balance between the positive and negative poles that a creative urge takes place. It is the moment of total acceptance of our will being Divine Will, an utter and complete surrender on our part.

What is this balance? How do we achieve it? How do we produce the creative fire?

We produce the creative fire in our awareness when we speak and listen, actively aware that we are the I AM Consciousness speaking and listening. We must recognize that we are the singer and the song. It is in moments like this that we bring forth the fruit of the Tree. At that moment we have brought into active concrete manifestation the teachings we find in Scripture. "I AM the Way, the Truth and the Life". The song, the piece of music or the word would have no life were the I AM Consciousness not present. In music this is the difference between the various artists; some are spiritually aware and some are not. Hence we say that a particular piece has no soul. It is the feeling in the mind, Consciousness, of the performer that makes the difference. Whether the performance is the playing of the Mendelssohn Violin Concerto, making the cup of tea or coffee, it is all the same. If we are a simple toiler or a royal personage, it is all the same. Remember, when we are in the act of doing we are the I AM Consciousness, knowingly or not. What we have done becomes a part of us, and anything we do while in this state of Consciousness raises the spiritual level of all of the community in which we live.

What then is evil? Evil is manifestation in the outer realm, thought, word or deed that is separated from God Consciousness. Evil is the expression of spirit in the material plane without the one expressing it being consciously aware of its spirituality. When we use the laws of nature or the scientific laws, as in gravity, without being aware that these laws are subject to the Divine

I AM Consciousness, we are expressing evil. This is so even if we are doing it as good humans. This is why Jesus said: "Call no man good". What then is good?

Good is the opposite of evil. It is the state of Consciousness we enter after we have learned to transmute the expressions of the lower nature or lower self into the expressions of the higher nature or higher self. Then, and only then, does all action become good.

It is really that simple. There is no complexity to spiritual law. Hence, Jesus says: "He that seeth me, seeth Him that sent Me". Jesus did not say "me and only me"; He meant the me of all mankind, of each and everyone of us when consciously aware of our own individualized God Consciousness. When we recognize and accept that our own me-ness is the expression of the I AM Divine Consciousness in what we do, we have entered into heaven. We have ascended from the state of occlusion into the awareness of who we are, and in so doing we have begun our own resurrection and the process of our individual spiritual ascension. We do not have to become Lutherans, Roman Catholics, Jews or Mohammedans, or even Scientists, in order to make this ascension. We do not have to have a label. We simply have to be aware of who we are.

Once we have started to be aware of our real identity, we have begun to limit or end the Satanic or Separative Consciousness. We have begun to rejoin the Father, Who is in Heaven, as spoken of in Scripture. Now we can live our life without thought of 'what we shall eat or what we shall put on', for now we know we are living in the Kingdom of God. There is no longer such an entity as mere man, the separative entity. Man is no more and no less than the lowest point at which God becomes Consciously visible in the material universe. This tells us that we are God in Manifestation, in all that we think, say and do.

There is another factor that is very important to understand because it is directly related to the above. We are told that after Adam and Eve shared an apple they fell from grace and were banished from the Garden. The use of the word fell suggests involuntary departure, force from outside of self, but it is really the descent of Spirit into matter.

The descent into matter does not mean that matter is something that is already there for Spirit to descend *into* at will. Instead, it means that Spirit is decreasing the frequency of its vibration and lengthening its wave until it expresses at a lower frequency and a longer wave, and becomes solid. This means that Spirit (Consciousness) is the heart and source of all matter. Matter is the expression and material body of Consciousness. Our body is an expression of Consciousness, as are granite, lead, apples and all electro-magnetics.

Human physical form is the highest expression of what we refer to as the material plane of Life. We can get no higher than this without transmuting ourselves into the invisible spectrum.

Good humanhood is most acceptable in polite society, but it is still lacking its awareness of the Presence of God in thought, word and deed. Science might take a look at this dimension, the state of Godliness – the fourth dimension. The fourth dimension is actually the realm of the Conscious Awareness of Godliness. There is no fourth dimension in matter.

What we must understand is that the fall is not a fall of Spirit or matter, but a controlled descent from the Angelic level through the changing vibrations of the Light Kingdom (Elohim) and 'taking on skin' or the wearing of skins as quoted in Scripture, which means becoming flesh Beings. This is a deliberate conscious descent in accordance with Divine Will. Not only this, but everything we do is in accordance with Divine Will. To think otherwise is spiritual arrogance and satanic pride. If we wish to improve what we are doing right now, we do not begin by divesting ourselves of our Divine heritage, our image and likeness of God. This image and likeness is our individualized Divine Consciousness.

The serpent in the Garden is the symbol of the urge to manifest. In the unified Consciousness of God before the process of creation begins, positive and negative are blended as One. The energies of positive and negative are blended as One in the unity of God – in the state of chaos, the state of the non-manifested God (Ain in Hebrew). Before manifestation begins we have, in this state of Ain, a combined polarity. We do not have the electrical polarity between positive and negative. We do not have the situation of what we call male and female, masculine and feminine. God is the perfect blending of masculine and feminine, of positive and negative. There is nothing in creation that has a perfect blending. If we had a perfect blending we would no longer be in the physical state. We cannot have a perfect blending in the physical state. It does not mean that when we die, leave this incarnation and pass over to the astral world that we will have a perfect blending.

"In the beginning God created the heaven and the earth". In the beginning God created positive and negative; in the beginning He created masculine and feminine. He created an energy force. And it is the feminine aspect of that energy force that becomes the leader in the downward path into material manifestation.

It is the pure Spirit Essence of the monad (the feminine aspect) that proceeds with the creative process, becomes the vehicle of the creative process. It even becomes the physical vehicle of manifestation. It is not the man who carries a child in the womb – it is the female. It is the female who provides the vehicle for the incoming soul. It is the female aspect of Godhead.

There is an aspect of the serpent to which we must give recognition. All over this world, no matter where we go – China is probably the best example; others are the United Kingdom and Adams County in Ohio – we will find large masses of land that are structured in a serpentine fashion. All rivers flow in a serpentine fashion; we never see a river that flows in a straight line. The reason is very simple: this whole earth and every other planet in the cosmos have two prime energies working, a positive and a negative. It is the same energy that is circulating around the spine (which, incidentally, is indicated by the Caduceus) in a spiraletic movement, crossing each other. And this serpent power is the power of magnetic-electrical energy. The dragon power that is talked about in China is the same thing. Most of the land mass in China has been hand-structured, as has a great proportion of the land mass of the United Kingdom. These places are made and placed along what are known as ley lines, or lines of spiritual energy.

When traveling anywhere in the British Isles one will find a tremendous number of towns with their names ending in 'ley' or 'ly'. If a traveler took an ordinary survey map and, starting with the northernmost town, drew a straight line to the southwest, that line would pass through all of those towns that are many centuries old (it may well not apply to the later arrivals on the scene of history), and all of those older towns are meridian points for ley lines. The same situation prevails in our bodies in relation to the meridian points used in acupuncture. They are the points where the lines of force intersect, the primary energy of creation. We are talking about getting in touch with the individualized energy in our own body and, in the case of the countryside, getting in touch with individual energy within the planet. In times past, large masses of people foregathered at a goodly number of these magnetic energy intersection points, Stonehenge being one of the most famous. The whole purpose of these gatherings was to consciously participate in harmonious and balanced energy interchanges.

Another of the things we must get away from when reading Scripture is the concept that, as a result of the fall, we are on this terrible place called Earth and we must get away just as soon as possible to heaven or better. The most devastating idea we have to rid ourselves of is the one which claims that there is an entity out there called Satan, the Devil, who is bent on our personal destruction. As long as we are carrying that concept in our mind, we cannot utilize the energy and power we have been talking about for our own upward movement, because it acts as a screen on our path. There is *nothing* that can stop us. The serpent power or Satan power is the power of manifestation itself. There is nothing to fear!

The Bible was written in code right from the beginning. It was always intended to be used as a work manual, an aid, for the seeker after spiritual development on a personal level. Primarily it was written in three languages – Hebrew, Greek and Latin. In the course of time it has been translated into several hundred other languages. During the period when the New Testament was being written there were no less than four different tongues being spoken in Israel. There was Hebrew, the language of the Jewish religious fraternity. There was Greek (which has survived from the days when Alexander ruled the world all the way to India), the commercial language of the Middle East, which many of the learned also spoke. With the coming of the Romans the official language of the period was Latin, and for the non-academically educated there was also the Aramaic tongue, the ordinary vehicle of communication of the carpenter and the peasant in the field. So it is not too difficult to understand the problems involved in interpreting the gospels of the four evangelists. In the case of the Old Testament it is even more of a task to achieve an understanding of what is to be learned. The Hebrew Scriptures are essentially the work of enlightened prophets and used by learned Rabbis to guide and lead the faithful in their daily spiritual unfoldment. It was only in the latter days of the Dispersal that these Biblical episodes became only a recital of actual historical events. Originally they had been allegorical events with some history tacked on.

A large part of the work of Jesus was involved in rescuing Holy Writ from the debasement in which it slumbered. "I came not to destroy the law, but to fulfill it." The reason there are so many people with a preference for a literal translation of Holy Scripture is simple. It allows them to place all of the responsibility for their deeds on an outside source, while continuing in the laziness of their thoughtless activities. The Bible is not for the lazy and the irresponsible. There is no personified Satan to blame.

Our experience changes with a change in our Consciousness. If we maintain a constant state of awareness of our Godliness, our experience will be God Expressive. We can go about our daily life doing all those ordinary things such as working at our job, interacting with our families, sharing with our religious brethren and so on, while remaining totally aware that *we are God* in expression at all times. This is what true salvation is all about.

Chapter 15

Can We Really Know God?

O Lord of Hosts, may my eyes wide open be
To see the Christ in every man I meet.
O Lord of Hosts, may I rise from the small confines of self
To the selfless Light in Thee.
O Lord of Hosts, may I resigned be to speak in love
The love which Thou behold in me.
O Lord of Hosts, may I grasp the hand of my fellow man
In all sincerity and seek no claim of reward
But that of love from Thee.
And with the Christ who in Jesus dwelt may I learn to say
And I, if I be lifted up, shall draw all mankind to me,
A Christlike Christian to ever be
Amen, Amen, Amen

This poem is chosen because it is one of the expressions that when we read them appear to be a paradox. Even though the name of the author escapes me, the poem speaks complete truth as far as the relationship of the I AM and the me is concerned. At first reading it appears as if it is an appeal to some outer or 'far away' divinity, whereas it is actually an invocation from the lower self to the higher or I AM self, present and active in our daily life.

There are three fundamentals that are basic to all spiritual and esoteric understanding and teaching.

Firstly, everyone we know in our lives, including ourselves, is *God existing as individual being*. This be-ingness is not something separate from us, but is an integral part of us all, at all times and in every dimension.

Secondly, we must recognize and accept that from a particular stage of development, this state of awareness is a must if we are to go forward in our spiritual growth. We cannot make progress in spiritual growth unless we accept God as the totality of our individual being and as the source of the totality of the *all*. This means that we as individual personalities cannot ascend any mountain or enter any cave of living with the intent of conducting our own personal and exclusive unfoldment without recourse to the rest of the world around us. A diamond is only polished by being pressed against the abrasive wheel. Spiritual unfoldment is co-existent throughout all of humanity. "No man dies but a part of me dies with him".

The third fundamental is the understanding of the nature of error. There is only one error in the world – the error which presents to our attention, by way of our senses, the illusion or suggestion that there is a real world of permanent material expression out there, which is controlling our life. This is the cardinal error of all humanhood. Contrary to this illusion is the fact that we have created this material world from the consciousness that is eternal and all powerful. The real world is the world of creation, which is the permanent world of spirit matter. The world of illusion and impermanence is the world that is created from the essence of spirit matter.

Reality is not the physical body, which is constantly replaced by our soul being, but the consciousness which replaces this body at the time and place of need for manifestation. Our body is the form which the I AM Self has built for its own purpose while operating on the earth plane. This is the temporal and temporary plane which we have created as part of our earth expression. The real world is the world of everlasting consciousness which exists even when there is no manifestation taking place in the universe, and even no universe in which to manifest. The only real reality is Divine Consciousness. The only temporary expression is the expression of this Consciousness.

If we can catch a glimpse of the fact that any limitations or so-called sins are merely suggestions of the senses that have, over time, achieved world acceptance, we begin to break the continuity of the delusion of being merely human. The mesmerism that maintains the illusion of our separation from God is of long-standing and is also powerfully entrenched. It is also to the advantage of many people in this society to maintain this illusion for their own personal power and control. We must set about realizing that sin, disease (or whatever we wish to call the condition of personal or group disharmony) are suggestions that have been put out by the humanity of the world in its state of separative consciousness. It is that which we have accepted for ourselves on an individual level. When we do realize this, we break the 'power of the world' over our lives. Jesus referred to this when he said: "I AM in the world but not of it".

This means that instead of being a victim, we become a creator. The circumstances out there do not bother us because we have become aware that we are an immortal eternal being, and all that physically exists is that which has been created by us in the recent or more distant past. It is through this recognition that we become what John in his Gospel calls "the Light of the world". This becomes so because this recognition enlightens our entire *beingness*, and changes our total outlook on everything with which we are involved. Even if we are standing by our disabled car on the highway, it does not cause us to be discommoded, for we know that we are still in the Divine Stream of Consciousness even in this situation. More importantly, we know this is the last time this will happen to us, provided we remain in this Consciousness. This is part of the inheritance of the pearl of great price. It is the truth that sets us free, and the truth that sets us free is the recognition of God as *Individual Being.*

If we can look on our friends and see them not as merely human, but see the Christ-Self within them when they speak, then we will listen to them with reverence and attention. Furthermore, we will reply with respect to the dignity of what we have heard. It does not matter if what has been said is total nonsense, we still respond and not simply react. We respond by having the person to whom we speak turn inwards. We ask a simple question, such as how did they come to know this or maybe how did they reach this decision. In this way we have caused the person to reach into their own Divinity to understand their own soul expression. Most likely they will then become aware of their potential for clear expression, and thereby we have joined together in an awareness of our unlimited Consciousness. Whenever any one of us remains actively conscious of our Divinity and recognize that self-same Divinity in those with whom we are currently in communication, we increase the overall awareness of the humanity of which we are a part. In this way we maintain the creative aspect of our Consciousness world.

Being consciously aware of our Divinity is really quite simple. It is remaining constantly aware of it that causes us the difficulty.

We are told in Holy Scripture: "For a while I AM with you and again for a while I AM not with you… …". In the early stages of the spiritual unfoldment process we have long and frequent periods in which we are not fully aware of our Divinity. This is due to the fact that we are part of a long culturized history of separation from the concept of our Individualized Divinity. For generations most of us have been taught that God is a distant and separate Elite Being who is out of touch with us because we have been disobedient and therefore we are imperfect.

This is a total inaccuracy of the condition of humanity upon which we are looking. What we see around us is a collectivity of Individualized Consciousness which, at this stage of expression, is undergoing a state of occlusion regarding its Divine origins. The logic of this situation is quite simple to see. If God is remote and has been disobeyed by us, the now imperfect ones, the level of perfection we previously had could not have been optimum in the first place. Furthermore, it also means that we do not have a God who is omnipotent, omniscient or omnipresent. This is an absurdity that leaves us without any possibility of a personal salvation, now or in the future.

A more sensitive and spiritual scenario would be that the situation we are seeking is one that is an integral part of the Divine Plan, and that we are willing soul-being participators in a creation process that is still in the making. Instead of disobeying, we are expediting the Divine Plan even if at this moment we are doing so at the level of the collective unconscious. At least this way, God does remain omnipotent, omniscient and omnipresent. It also allows us an opportunity to restore our awareness of our Indwelling Divinity.

The whole purpose of meditation is to increase the awareness of our God-centered Consciousness. To increase this awareness is to align our own individualized be-ingness with the Divine. When aligned in Consciousness with the Divine part of our spiritualized nature, we are in the state of 'knowing God'. This is a part of the praying without ceasing spoken of in the Bible. Meditating or praying does not mean being in a constant state of begging or asking God for favors. Nor does it mean asking to be forgiven for some infraction of a church-made code. Praying without ceasing means to be in a state whereby we are continually aware of our Divinity, and also aware that as we pursue our daily activities we are doing so as *God in action*. In order to gain proficiency at this Divine activity it is necessary that we use our meditation periods as stepping-stones to such activity. We can easily do this by simply retaining our state of Divinity Awareness while undertaking the first activity following our meditation. As we progress in our own individual spiritual unfoldment pattern, this continued application of retained Divinity will expand into an extended awareness of God's creative process in the universe.

When we begin to live the life of the Divine we become more consciously Divine. As this awareness grows, we find it easier and easier to maintain our peace and harmony of living without detours into hostility, greed, jealousy, envy, lying or cheating. In effect, we enter the world of which Jesus speaks when he says to Pilate: "My kingdom is not of this world... ...". He is saying that our power in this world stems from our Divinity and not from the confluence of the interacting atoms by which we are surrounded. As long as we accept the concept that we are the outcome of an accidental molecular process over which we have no control, we cannot exercise our Divinity. "He who is not with me is against me". This statement leaves no room for compromise. If we choose not to be Practicing Divinities, we have creatively chosen to be victims or effects of the society in which we spend our daily lives. That is an expression of free will to which, as Divine Beings, we are entitled.

As there is only One Consciousness from which the entire universe is created we are, therefore, an integral part of the Consciousness, and *that Consciousness is God*. That Consciousness is *our* consciousness individualized as soul-being. Everything we express is the expression of this One Consciousness. We have no choice but to be God in expression. To think otherwise is no less than the delusion brought about by ignorant pride. *This is original sin.*

The ignorance comes about because we have occluded our own individual Awareness of our Divinity, and become caught up in the role we have elected to play in a particular incarnation. Each role is an essential part of the ongoing creation process. Each one of us in the body of humanity is an active ray of the creative urge sent forth by Universal Divine Consciousness. We are the point at which God becomes visible in the conscious process of creation. As God is Consciousness and we are visible Consciousness, we become the instruments of continuing creation. The pride arises from the unconscious knowledge that we are a unique ray of divine activity. Because of our occlusion we see that uniqueness as separate independence. In consequence, we are always a step behind the perfection our personality would like to express.

As we go about our daily activities and begin to be consciously aware of who and what we are and the true purpose behind that which we are doing, we enter into the state of Consciousness whereby we become capable of lifting even the most banal effort into an action of joy and beauty. In this way we have begun to accept our primary role in the creation process. We have begun, through this acceptance, to never withdraw from *GOD CONSCIOUSNESS*, the concept referred to in Scripture as "My soul doth magnify the Lord". When used in Scripture, the word Lord means the process whereby the awareness of God's Presence as us enhances every single act we perform or encounter in our daily life. There is no place, time or condition in which God is not present, otherwise omnipotence, omniscience or omnipresence is a contradiction in terms.

Many of us, when faced with responsibility of the co-creation aspect of our consciousness, try to escape into the realm of not knowing what is the Will of God. The simple definition of the Will of God is that which is God's Will. There can be no other source of manifestation in the universe. We are often confused by this matter of our Godliness. When we look at the world in which we live our daily lives and see events of which we do not approve taking place, it becomes difficult for us to be aware of God's Presence in what we see. Although we may be aware of God's Presence at any given moment, others may not be so aware. Ignorance of the Presence of God does not eliminate God from the game of life; it simply keeps the activity in the three-dimensional world. It further means that the full power of creative and enlightened Consciousness is not being applied to the circumstance in question.

We are constantly brought into contact with exhibitions of abuse and cruelty in our daily activities and cannot understand why we are being exposed to such happenings. If we ourselves are consciously pursuing a spiritual path of life, we must ask what is there for us to learn about ourselves so that we no longer experience this form of expression in our life. It is never the responsibility of the other person to change their behavior on our behalf. It is our own responsibility to change ourselves so that we rise to a higher state of Consciousness where we are not exposed to such happenings.

It is the belief in a self-hood apart from God that is the root of all evil. As long as we remain in the consciousness of separation from God and see God as separated from human activity, our own and others, we shall continue to live in the world miasma of good, evil, right, wrong. As long as we attempt to rectify error, ill health, poverty, war or any other personal or social malfunction, we are destined not to succeed. "Unless the Lord build the house, they labor in vain that build it." No-thing can ever be one hundred percent successful when it is deprived of the Consciousness of at-one-ment with Divine Source. It is the lack of such awareness of their Divinity that causes people to lie, cheat, injure, abuse and even kill their fellow humans. No-one who is consciously aware of their Divinity can go out and perpetrate any one of these acts against his neighbor. *God Consciousness is Creative, not Destructive.* Therefore, as our God Consciousness unfolds through our acceptance of ourselves as Individualized Divinity, all of these experiences diminish and eventually disappear from our Life.

When we embark on a spiritual journey to awareness of our Godliness the only real difficulty we experience is that we have culturized ourselves into the belief that we can have everything in our life instantly. We have instant tea, instant coffee, instant credit and instant gratification of every kind. Within spiritual law we have a condition whereby we work chronologically, slowly and incrementally. Each step of Consciousness growth must be implemented before we can go forward and claim the grand prize of living in the state of grace.

There are two fundamental and primary steps we must undergo before we can justifiably expect to share in the benefits that always accompany living in the state of grace. The first of these is to enter into at least an intellectual understanding of the truth of Being. This means to accept mentally the role of being God in action. The second step is to enter into a realization and acceptance of the true nature of error. We *must surrender* our mesmeric belief that there is any condition anywhere in the world which has a source apart from God. These two steps are an essential part of the unfoldment process in the course of spiritual evolution. We have no choice but to be *God*. There is nothing else to be.

These words *could not be written* at this time if humanity were not on the verge of being able to accept this concept of their Godliness. This condition is not one reserved for a limited group of denominational elitists. "Go ye therefore and teach all nations. Behold I AM with you until the consummation of the world." All of humanity is on a spiritually unfolding path, whether they know it or grant it to other people. The destiny of humanity is to enter the Promised Land. This Land is the one in which all of humanhood is transmuted into the Consciousness of their Individualized Godliness. In esoteric circles this is usually referred to as Christ Consciousness. The Consciousness that recognizes itself as God Consciousness is Redeemed Consciousness, and dwells forever in the awareness of its immortality. This is knowing God..

When we live and work in God Consciousness we do not have to strive. If we are striving we are not as yet fully in God-Consciousness, and are functioning partially in the world of averages. Sometimes that striving can be as simple as becoming an uninvited propagandist for spiritual growth. Very often we rush out and attempt to share our new- found joy of awareness with someone who has not asked to be saved. They are at the stage of being quite happy with their current lot. They have no need for us to gain spiritual benefits through their salvation. It is not easy for us to keep silent until asked, but only when we are asked for help or assistance do we come forth, and then we can do so only until the seeker's cup is full. We must never be other than strong in our awareness, but at the same time we must never be aggressive in sharing it with others.

Always we must look to the inner feeling of our own Soul-being. This inner feeling is the God Consciousness in expression. We must exercise care in what we say and do. It must always be what we feel and not what other people expect or demand of us at any time. This inner feeling is the kingdom within of which Jesus speaks when he says: "Seek ye first this kingdom, and all else will be added unto you". We must also have compassion for our own failings as well as for the failings of others. No matter what we have done or failed to do or what others have done or failed to do, all is God's Will in action. There are no ifs, ands or buts; there is only Divine Expression at all times. It is only our occluded personality that does not permit us to see the Hand of God in that which is before us.

When we work in God Consciousness we do not have to strive. But frequently it happens that when we become spiritually alert, we become fervent and reach out to others in far too strong a manner. We seek to proselytize all over the area of our social contacts and community. We do not have to make a big issue of our new-found awareness and bear down on others. We must remember that we are only responsible for our own spiritual growth and can never take anyone with us into the kingdom. Each person has their own spiritual path to pursue, and any interference by us, however well meant, is a form of aggression and a lack of faith in God's awareness of the needs of a single soul.

If we will commit ourselves to remember that anyone with whom we speak at any time is *God*, and only *God* expressing, we will have far less difficulty with this whole process of spiritual fervor. Let us always remember the Hindu salutation on meeting another person: "I salute the Divinity in you". At no time is there anyone who is not expressing Godliness. There is only the state in our mind where we do not recognize Godliness in that which we see before us.

Yes, we *can* really know God.

Chapter 16

Invoke – Don't Beg

There are two words that are commonplace in our society – the word prayer and the word invoke. Frequently they are spoken in the same breath, and just as often confused one with the other. They do not mean the same, and cause great confusion to sincere and honest seekers when reading or hearing esoteric facts being presented for their attention.

Let us begin by defining prayer, the most frequently used of the two. Prayer is the Word of God which comes to us in silence when we are still enough and receptive enough to receive. It is the still small voice within that directs and guides us through our intuition. It is never our own voice asking, demanding or begging for help or a hand-out from the celestial sphere where God is assumed to live and spend His days listening to hymns of praise. To consider prayer as asking God for anything is to separate ourselves from God and enter into the realm of duality. Praying is primarily the clearing of the spiritual airwaves so that God can speak to us on a clear channel. The instruction for this state of awareness is given very clearly in the 46th Psalm – 'Be still and know I AM God'.

The practice of stillness requires a very definite self-directed discipline. It is desirable that we select a time and a place where we can be quietly relaxed and free from noise and interruption as far as is reasonably practical. To develop a state of quiet awareness it is essential in the early stages to go easy on ourselves, and not attempt to relax and be quiet in the middle of a metropolitan airport. This does not mean that God is not around because there are distractive noises, but it does mean that we have more difficulty in focusing our attention as we need in order to become still. It is not the I AM that has the difficulty but the 'me'. The me of all of us, which is the outer expression of our be-ingness, has been so long in a state of separation from its sense of Godliness that it requires gentle persuasion in order to return to the condition of at-one-ment, which is the natural home of personality consciousness.

There are times in which it is not possible to select a place where all distractive sights, sounds and other interruptions are completely absent. In such circumstances we can begin to practice stillness by using the following aphorism: *I accept all sounds, sights, smells, touches, tastes and feelings as being the expression of God*. By doing this we transform a potential disturbance into an integral part of the receptivity we are building. As we begin to do this, we are really putting ourselves in the position of participating in prayer, where we can hear the Voice of God.

Another aspect of the prayer mode is that it is the identification of all that is as being the expression of God in the universe. Not only is the me an expression of God, but so is all that there is, both in earth and beyond.

It is fundamentally important at this stage of our development to understand exactly that the 'me' is that part of ourselves which is normally referred to as the lower self or the personality. This personality is the vehicle used by the soul-being, or higher consciousness, to express in the material or natural world. This lower-self is neither bad, evil or devoid of Divinity in any way. It is, however, always occluded until it is reconnected to the awareness of its origin. It has no power of its own, but relies entirely on the power it is given from above, i.e. the Higher or Divine Consciousness. It is to this that Jesus refers when he says to Pilate: "You have no power were it not given you from above". Jesus is not denying Pilate's earthly power, the power of Caesar, but he is pointing out that this power is bestowed by Divine Consciousness (whenever the word above is used in scripture it always refers to the Divine).

It is most important that we understand the difference between temporal power and eternal power. The former is temporary and relies on eternal power, which is power without end, for its energy and authority. It is because this power is eternal and its outer effects are temporary, that the esoteric teachings claim that the material world is an illusion, as the material world is only a passing effect, temporary by nature, of Universal Divine Consciousness, which is eternal. It is the recognition that the me is an integral part of this eternal consciousness that eliminates the need to pray for something that will only manifest for a limited period in the material world. All that we ever need is already in the making in our consciousness. It is the Father's pleasure to give us the Kingdom. We do not have to strive, we simply have to accept our Divinity as the source of all we need, now or ever.

In this modern era of mind control, psychic readers and all the other so-called New Age activities, it is quite easy to get lost in the worlds of mind and psychic power, and in so doing lose sight of the fact that it is the spiritual power of Divine Consciousness preceding them that provides the energy in all creation. That is one of the most important and fundamental truths of all esoteric teachings.

If at this particular period of our life any of us are wanting anything and are attempting to bring it about by power of mind techniques, we will find that we very soon run out of the energy needed for success. The mere reiteration of affirmations when repeated by someone who is not aware of their indwelling Divine Power, and are relying on their mind power, are due for disappointment. However, when we make the recognition that the me is the *I* in action and that I is God in action, we change the entire foundation of our creative processing.

There is no magic wand that can be waved which will bring about a manifestation in this physical world if we are by-passing the path of the Divine Creative Process. There is only one method of creation in this universe, and that is the one that has brought the whole Cosmos into existence and is continuing to creatively perfect the original Divine urge to manifest. The original Divine Idea is still the dynamic of our ongoing universal manifestation. There is but One Source behind all creation, both then and now, and there can never be another source in the future.

This I AM creative consciousness can only be expressed and utilized after we have expanded our awareness to the level of Christ Consciousness. By definition, Christ Consciousness is that consciousness which realizes and accepts that it is God-in-action at the me level. This is the Saviour, the Messiah which redeems us from the state of occlusion in which we have been dwelling. This Christ Consciousness does not rely on any one unique being nor is it possessed by only one unique being.

This Consciousness is referred to in the Bible quite frequently, but most specifically when we read of the pearl of great price. It is the wisdom that lifts us out of the tomb of our spiritual crucifixion. The whole purpose of meditation is to acquire the state of stillness and receptivity which permits us to enter into our sonship of God. When this happens, the first fact we notice is that outer assertiveness of our ego-self begins to decline. It becomes more mellow and is prepared to give credence to other people's needs. Additionally, we begin to realize that when we make a cup of coffee for someone it is not merely we ourselves who are performing the act, but we become Consciously aware that God is the provider and we are the channel of that provision.

This is the first step in the awareness of the Presence, a sense of feeling that comes over us as we carry out our actions. When we get up in the morning, we realize that the only energy we have is the energy that is God, that there is no other energy and no other Presence; as we speak, we realize there is no other power with which to speak but the Power of God. As this recognition begins to penetrate our mind-self it begins to transmute us from the occluded state to that of the enlightened. This sense is not an intellectual component, but a feeling; not an emotion, it is a spiritual awareness which cannot be mistaken for anything else. Because we are experiencing an effect beyond the range of physical sensation, we cannot adequately define it in material symbols, such as words.

Each and everyone of us will have a certain but different physiological response, which will be a signal that we are plugged into a level of beingness that is quite uncommon compared to our routine daily knowledge and expression. That response is the outer expression of what is known as the still small voice within. It is the causative agent of the physical reaction we are experiencing. Effects in the body are always reactions to input – the body never initiates any act of its own, but always reacts to stimuli presented to it. Many people who set out on a journey of self-unfoldment think that at some stage of the development they are going to be visited by an Angel in white robes, who will guide them to their next assignment. There is little or no evidence of this form of communication, but there is no end to reports of the inner voice of intuition speaking with truth and validity.

What frequently happens in cases of inner awareness is that we are suddenly surrounded by the perfume of jasmine or orange blossom when we know there is none of either of them near where we are at the time. This is a clue. It soon follows that we begin to feel the stillness and the peace that are the heralds of the state of receptivity, which brings with it the condition of detachment from the outer world (not a separation) which allows us to hear that which is for our ears alone. When this kind of thing takes place, we are uplifted to a higher vibratory state where the effects in the outer world no longer interfere with our Individualized Consciousness.

There are many currently incarnated people who are experiencing this level of consciousness. There are some among them who experience this level most of the time throughout their daily activity, and some who only experience it spasmodically. The fact that anyone is experiencing this level of consciousness indicates that it can be achieved by all of us. The evidence for the existence of this consciousness is to be seen in the activities, health, harmony, peace and joy exhibited by those people. They are in the process of becoming what scripture calls 'the Light of the world'.

We have all met these people in the course of our daily activities, in the drug store, gas station, dinner parties and church. We must not make the mistake that it is only in churches these people are to be found. Most likely that is the place where the least number of them are to be found. We must get away from this society's concept that spirituality is only to be discovered within the confines of orthodox religion and its various denominations. God does not rely upon any church or any denomination for the expression of His Presence. Man, both individually and collectively, is the point where God becomes visible in the material world.

And we, as Mankind, do not need doctrine or dogma to open our awareness to this fact. We only need to know and accept that there is nothing else to be but God in action.

The reason we rarely find the level of consciousness we call stillness in orthodox churches is that they are involved in the practice of ritualism. Where ritualism is practiced we usually find the people concerned think of themselves as separated from God, spending their time "begging" and even telling God what to do for them here and now. They never listen, they only beg and think they are praying by so doing.

When we pray or beg in this manner we are saying that God does not know what is already going on and needs to be told by us what should be done. This is a contradiction in terms. It is a paradox which mentally invalidates the whole Christian Divine concept. Either God is Omniscient or He is not. If He is, He does not need help from a group who are already incapable of taking care of themselves. If He is not, He is little better off than we already are in our present state. The fact of the matter is that God is Omnipotent, Omniscient and Omnipresent, and therefore does not need to be begged from or told what to do in any circumstances whatsoever.

As long as we consider ourselves as other or less than God, we are still in our occluded state of awareness, and in this state we must continue to place the responsibility for our welfare upon a power that is alien to ourselves. If we are not connected directly to the Source of the welfare, we can never call upon or utilize that Source on our own behalf. But once we learn that I and the Father are One, we begin the process whereby we can utilize the power of the Source and become responsible for our own wellbeing.

In order to enter into the At-one-ment Consciousness that is the Father, we need to engage in certain disciplines. We need to become disciples of truth and follow the spiritual path that has been laid down for generations. First, we must have a firm conviction and a firm goal of pursuing the state of At-one-ment. Two, we must have a heartfelt desire to surrender our outer personality. Three, we must have a clear-cut statement of intent. An example of this might be: "I surrender body, mind and soul, here, now and hereafter; let there not be me and mine, but Thee and Thine alone. Be Thou me". This is the surrender of the lower self (me) to the higher (I AM) self. This is an invocation calling down the power of Universal Divine Consciousness to be present in all our thoughts, words and actions. This is a statement of our willingness to be an active co-creator and a participating attribute of the Divine Will. From here on, we can no longer place the responsibility for our actions, words or thoughts on any other expression than our own. What will be in our life will have been in our consciousness from the beginning.

When we function outside of the parameters of At-one-ment, we can never be completely successful at anything we do in our lives. "Unless the Lord build the house, they labor in vain who build it." It is not that we have to undertake all sorts of noble projects in our life, but that we have to undertake the ordinary activities of our daily life in the spirit of our Godliness. In other words, the 'me' does all the menial things in the world – digs ditches, cleans toilets, washes dishes and much more – and it continues to be menial until we learn that we are God in action, when it becomes enhanced and uplifted to the realm of creative maintenance, otherwise known as the perfection of creation.

All these menial tasks become debilitating when they are disconnected from their Source energy. They are disconnected when we are unaware of our relationship to Divine Consciousness. Once we have made the connection, they are no longer debilitating and do not rob us of energy. It is for this reason that many spiritual leaders, when engaged in their work, maintain a very high level of output without much energy loss.

There is a fourth aspect to the At-one-ment process. We must give recognition and acceptance to the Power of Invocation. The calling down of Divine Consciousness is the most sacred and sanctified activity we can undertake in all of our life. It must be undertaken only when we are of the most dedicated intent. We are calling on the Power of the Universe.

Let us focus on this Universal residual power that is accessible to us at all times. We cannot call upon this power unless we have completed the steps outlined above. We must recognize and accept the natural laws as being the Law of God. When we use our body we must be aware that we are using the Temple of the Holy Spirit. We must learn not to abuse this body, and attempt to work it beyond its norm of function. The acceptance of natural law as the Law of God enables us to use the natural law. Unless we are prepared to obey the law, we can never apply the law.

When we proclaim "Be still and know I AM God", we are ordering the me of ourselves to be still, so that the I of ourselves can function in its Divine capacity. In this way, we allow receptivity to come into play.

When we enter the stillness and go into a state of receptivity, offering no resistance, all the desires, yearnings, hopes, dreams and wishes come to the surface of our mind. At this stage, it matters not what the impressions are. It is only necessary at this point to recognize that they are there and they have been initiated by us and us alone. This is the first step in taking responsibility for our ideas. These are genuine ideas, and as such they rank with all ideas, which are the Father of all manifestation. These are the things we feel and are constructs of our consciousness, and it is from these constructs that the things and relationships of our life are created.

It is essential at this stage of our moving into the invoking process that we recognize and accept, without reservation, that the longings and desires we feel are none other than the I AM expressing the necessity of manifesting the primary idea of creation. There is no "desire energy" or "wish energy" that can stem from anywhere other than Divine Consciousness. It is absolutely vital to realize there is only one single Source of all thought, word and deed. To hold any other idea is to set up a duality for creation, and thereby separate ourselves from the Divine Stream of Consciousness. We cannot invoke or call upon Divinity if we have broken the connection. It would be like picking up a telephone instrument that was not plugged into the central exchange, and expecting to talk to the people at the auto repair shop.

How then do we set about learning to handle our desires, distinguishing that which is our long-term interest from the merely ephemeral and "self" destructive? To begin with, we write down all the desires we have, without any discrimination for their value. Having done this, we then set about examining them for an order of priority in terms of urgency and importance. We then analyze them for contradictory or canceling qualities. As we do this, keeping in mind who *we* are and the Source of all thought and action, we soon find that we are beginning to eliminate many of the desires we first set out. Once we begin to enlist the power of the Inner Consciousness, our capacity for more optimum selectivity takes over from our personality's emotionally driven urges. We must be aware that we are not going to be experts overnight, as we have a long history of irrationality to overcome in our journey to spiritual self- hood.

What we have done with this procedure is to hone the instrument of desire of God's creation. Instead of 'me' desiring it, 'me' is now allowing the I AM to use the apparatus, which is the desire. It is what is done with desire that causes the problems in our society. It is what 'me' does with desire, while not permitting the I to utilize the apparatus, that brings about all of the disasters in our lives. There never has been anything wrong with desire, other than its lacking guidance from the Higher or Inner Self. We have to clear away the occlusion under which we have operated for many generations. Once we have cleared the debris in the manner indicated above, we are in a much better position to use our Inner Self to achieve those things and relationships we all seek. It must be clearly understood that there are several methods by which this can be done, but they all must include the idea of the One Source.

Having made our list of those things we desire and cleaned it of all conflicts, we can now give our attention to that part of our process which requires us to recognize that all we have in our lives at this time has been created by ourselves, even if we are no longer aware of having done so. Until we accept and take responsibility for our thoughts, words and deeds and the effects they create, we cannot move forward in our growth. We must look at that which is in our life and realize it is ours, bless it and pronounce it good. This is what the first chapter of Genesis is telling us. In order to proceed to the next step in the creation process, we must recognize that all we have now brought forth is good.

Unless we are prepared to accept that we are the creator and pronounce our kingdom good, we are limited in what we can expect to do with our new-found knowledge. This is so, because the process by which we have created this level is the same process by which we would expect to create our new environment in the future. We cannot condemn the outcome of the process and at the same time hope to use it effectively. So, cleanse the chalice of the lower nature in order to receive the wine of the Higher Nature. In this way we can enter the Holy of Holies, the state of receptivity.

Many of us are concerned about the present state of the world in which we live. We have concerns about war, nuclear armament, pollution, global warming or even an inhuman boss, but we must remain aware that all of these things and situations are stemming from the same source. It is only because people are unaware of their Divinity that they can behave in the non-optimum manner they frequently do. We usually find that these people are operating in a world that has a duality of power in their thinking and philosophy. No-one who has come to accept God as the only Source of all manifestation can ever be seen to behave in this manner. It is true that we do not see many such people in our normal daily activity. There are, however, a great number of such people on our planet at this time who are currently working to raise the level of consciousness of all of us to the place where we can function within the understanding of there being only One Source of all manifestation.

When we are faced with a situation in which it seems that the effect is not optimum to us, it becomes our opportunity to rise above the condition by recognizing that we are faced by an unredeemed body of energy, which we can transmute to a higher level of expression. This we do by using a simple affirmation with a complete sense of commitment and faith in our belief that there is only One Source: "… …So now you did not bring me hither, but God".

This statement is a declaration that all that has happened in our life up to this very moment has always been an expression of the Divine in action, and could not be other than the Divine, for there is nothing else to be in action. There is no power in the universe that is not the Power of God, and therefore all by which we are confronted is that Power. A claim that there is an evil or satanic power in the world can only be made by those who have not accepted the Omniscience, Omnipotence and Omnipresence of God. They, in fact, deny what Divinity truly and always is: "He who is not with me is against me".

Once we recognize who we are we can no longer be destructive, angry, jealous or fearful. We can be none of these things from the day we accept and begin to live our Divinity. There is no other power to fear and none to compete with our Divinity. Until the leaders of the world learn this and begin to practice the Presence, there is little or no point in having peace conferences or any other form of international treaty arrangements. Any group of well-meaning humans who foregather to arrange a new social structure for the world can only do so with all the limitations of being "merely human". Any group of people acting through assertiveness and fear are doomed to failure. That is why all the peace treaties of the past have always failed. Sincere human intentions are never enough to complete the endeavor. "Unless the Lord build the house, they labor in vain who build it."

The main task of all of us on this planet is to raise our consciousness to a level where we have no need of peace conferences or treaty arrangements. Above a certain level of consciousness, behavior becomes peaceful and does not have to be legislated. When we feel the sense of God within, we have no need or urge to express other than in a manner that is compatible with Divine Will.

The earlier reference to clearing our lives of the blocks and hang-ups of hostility, greed and jealousy, together with all of the other attributes we no longer wish to hold us back in our spiritual growth, is not just a pipe dream; we can do it if we are sincere in our efforts. By actively focusing upon our Divinity in its individualized form as our soul-being, we immediately begin the process of our resurrection from the state of occlusion. When our attention is focused upon Divinity, the attention of Divinity is focused upon the me of the personality, which can then be transmuted to a higher level of consciousness expression in our daily life.

Not too long after we begin this process, we find that many of the things we thought we wanted are no longer desired by us. This is because they were most likely wants of the unenlightened personality, which have nothing to commend them to soul growth. As soon as we make this realization, we can be fairly sure we have begun to truly follow the path of spiritual unfoldment. It does not mean that we have now come all the way into living in the state of grace on a continuous basis. It does mean that we can take encouragement from what we have achieved so far. It means that our channel is opening up so that the Divine Stream of Consciousness can flow through more freely in all that we do in our daily life. Now we no longer need to beg or to pray to some distant and separated entity, for we are in the Divine Stream of Consciousness. For this we came to the Earth planet – to further the perfectability of creation.

It is more than conceivably possible that someone pursuing this path of spiritual unfoldment will resolve the greater number of their emotional problems in six months or less. The water of spirit wears away the rock of resistance to growth. A clue to this growth is that we find ourselves with far more energy than formerly; it is no longer held in our blocks and hang-ups. The moments of our lives become shining lights that guide us even further along the path we are pursuing. Eternity is the necklace of moments in our lives.

Chapter 17

Becoming a Whole Person

When we wish to speak of a "whole person", it is only fair that we give some sort of definition. In order to give a definition, it is desirable to first look at ourselves in order to see if we are whole already. If we were a whole person there would be nothing in our life with which we would not be pleased, because we would be aware that all of life is the expression of I AM.

Let us, therefore, look at our life, at the things with which we are not pleased. We then immediately know the areas in which we have to grow and extend our field of responsibility. We are constantly saying that it is *their* fault, *they* are to blame, it is *their* responsibility, it is this, that and the other. This is simply our indication of the areas at which we have to look, which makes it very easy to see where we need to grow. It is not so much a definition as a description of what needs doing. Definitions are limiting, descriptions are open-ended in the sense that they encompass more.

It is a generally conceived and accepted idea in the world in which we live, irrespective of whether our denominational approach is Islamic, Hindu, Judaic, Christian or any other spiritual path, that Man is created in the image of God. In the Western world it is generally accept that Man *is* created in God's image and in one specific way more than any other, namely in the *image and beingness* of creativeness. What does this mean?

If we are creative beings, what do we create and how do we create? We can see what we create and do, if we but choose. We may not always like what we do, we may not always be prepared to change what we do, but the first step to becoming a whole person is to recognize that we *are the doer*. To just recognize that we are the doer and not regret what we have done is not what we are talking about here. The point is to recognize that we *have done it*. As long as we are not prepared to be or recognize ourselves as a causative agent, we *cannot* be a whole person. While we see ourselves as an effect, while we see ourselves as only one of the mob, as one of the crowd, as one of the crew, having no responsibility for the conditions at any given moment, we *cannot* be a whole person.

This is the very basis and essence of wholeness, and there is not one person reading these words at this particular time who has their life under total control. If we are really sincere, we will pull the chalkboard out and list the 5,000 areas we have not yet tackled. We know about them, but we have not tackled them.

What is this creative aspect of which we speak? What is the key, what is it we can get in touch with in relation to a creative ability? The most immediate and recognizably accessible element is our imagination. *Our imagination is the technological tool of creation.* There is a clue right here for those who are metaphysically inclined and have been wandering around in the spiritual unfoldment field for a long time. This clue is in the first line of the Great Invocation, which says "From the point of Light within the Mind of God let Light stream forth into the mind of Man". Where does imagination function? It does not function in our left big toe, nor does it function in our right ear or our left nostril. The imagination functions in the mind. That is step one- it functions in the mind.

The imaginative or intuitive quality functions through the mind. Some will say "That's great, but how do I get in touch with it?" In order to get in touch with the creative aspect of our beingness, with our imagination we must accept imagination as the instrument to *image into action* – to bring forth into action, and there can be no variation on this.

To be capable of using our imagination, our creative ability, the first thing we must do is *focus our attention* upon it. Attention *is* Divinity in action, which is a little hard for some people to believe. Whatever we have our attention on, Divinity *is* focusing. The difficulty for most of us, if not all of us, most of the time, is that we are not prepared to accept there is *only* God. Most of us want it to be God *and* me.

Because most of us are not prepared to accept that there is only God, we say "Please God, help me; please God, help me to overcome my foul temper; please God, help me to overcome my jealousy, my resentment". If we are resentful, God is being resentful. If we are angry, God is being angry. This is the clue. This is why it says in the 46th Psalm "Be still and know I AM God".

If we were to go to our mirror when we awaken each morning and, as we stand and look at the image of the body we have created, repeat quietly within "I *AM* the Lord the God, and all that I do this day I accept and bless", we would begin to change our life. This includes screaming at our husband or our wife, our children, our neighbors, our employee, our employer, some city official, some cop on the beat. If we were to accept all of our actions, all of our words and all of our thoughts as being the expression of God, we would be capable of changing more of those habit patterns and more of those actions than in any other way, and doing it more quickly. There is only One Source and only one Power in the Universe.

We must relinquish regretting what we say or do. We must make no apology for it. We must make no excuses for it, but we must consciously resolve to change our behavior in future. If it was not the Will of God, it could not have happened.

If we wish to become a whole person, we have to accept the entire expression of our beingness as the total expression of *our* Godliness. This does not mean that the totality of Godliness is in full expression. It does mean that at the time of expression all that ever expresses here, now or in the future *is* God. There is but one Power. There is but One Will. There is but One Law. *"I AM the Lord the God. I shall not have strange gods before me."*

Who do we think is speaking at this moment? Who do we think is listening at this moment? There is no 'Becky' listening. There is no 'Norman' speaking. There is no separate personality speaking or listening.

The second factor involved in becoming a whole person is a conscious and deliberate decision to allow the *old* expression of consciousness to die. A deliberate preparedness and decision to allow the old consciousness to die is essential. We cannot take it with us. There are four aspects of our beingness, which are our Cosmic Beingness, which is a non-material aspect of beingness (meaning it does not express visually in the sensory world); a Monadic or Angelic level of Beingness, also non-material; our Higher Self, and last but by no means least, our Lower Self or our personality.

If we are prepared to relinquish or change our personality, we can begin to change towards wholeness. It is the personality that screams "It is not my fault, it is not my responsibility". It is the Cosmic Godself's responsibility, and God does not goof!

If our personality is expressing in a particular way, that personality cannot express in that way *in spite* of God. It is even possible we might describe what it leads to as "stinking thinking". We must stop blaming ourselves or others. There is a difference between blaming and accepting responsibility.

One of the biggest problems in our society at this time is what is called the conflict between the younger and older generations. One of these problems is that the younger generation wants to throw off authority, but for the most part only at the level of the personality. The problem with the older generation is that they want to impose the authority, but only at the personality level. Most of us, young or old, are guilty of the same thing.

We have a system in which we flip-flop between compensating for rejecting others and seeking compensation for the rejection we receive. The only reason we can get into this situation is because we are not accepting the fact that all we are and all we do is the expression of God in this Universe. There was not and never will be a time when we go into action with Godliness at the forefront of our consciousness, in which the outcome is not perfect. If we approach someone wishing to speak to them, and are consciously aware of our mutual Godliness before we speak, the message passes from one to the other in total accuracy.

We must get it into our heads, once and for all, what the Presence of God is. It is not an old man sitting on the side of a cloud playing a harp. It is not a man struggling up a hill with a great trunk of cypress on his shoulder. Most of us in this Western world, whether we are orthodox Christians, orthodox Jews or orthodox Muslims, have been inculcated into accepting the belief that we are not responsible. As long as we accept that belief in one area, we can be controlled in all areas. If we really understand what totalitarianism is in a society, we will know it is when the population as a whole surrenders its philosophical or political rights to sectarianism. And this is a population that surrenders its Godliness to a group that has already abandoned theirs.

This can only happen in a society whose individuals do not accept their Divinity. Does that sound a little frightening? I hope so. We may think it could not happen here, but we had better believe it could – here or anywhere. How many times have we compromised, for whatever reason, our Godliness. This is what "Unless the Lord builds the house, they labor in vain that build it" means.

We must take active steps to become conscious of and consciously express our Godliness. This is why the Master Jesus said: "He that seeth me, seeth the Father". He was not speaking about the exclusive personality of Jesus, but of the Divinity of expression of I AM at that particular moment. He repeated the same concept on other occasions, such as when he said: "I and the Father are One". "I". This is why if, when we look at ourselves in a mirror, we consciously state: "I AM the Lord the God. I accept and bless my thoughts, my words and my actions this day", we have taken a beginning step, ensuring us of a more harmonious day. We then begin to find all the areas in our life where our Godliness is not quite perfected. Now we can really work on them because we now have the spiritual tool to do the job.

Most people go through life in what we might call a state of apathy or, as Gurdjieff says, "in a state of sleep". Most people have not yet wakened up. There are people walking down the street who are not yet awake. They do not even know what is going on with themselves, let alone what is happening around them. They see themselves in the role of victim – victim of every crisis, victim of age, the victim constantly, and they do not even know that they set up the system. When we do begin to realize that we set up the system to begin with, we become capable of changing it. Until we recognize that we are the designer and builder, how can we be the changer?

It is very clear. It is a simple choice. It is a simple choice if we wish to be a whole person. In order to have holistic being-ness, we must accept the fact that we are *not* merely humans. We must relinquish this concept with which we wander around and to which we give authority. "Oh be patient with me, I am only human". We are *not* only human. No one of us is only human. Our humanness is only one small part of our expression, expressed in a very, very limited period of time within eternity. Are we aware we have only been physically manifesting for the past 18 million years? A mere 18 million years we have been physical – that is all. Compare that to eternity.

All ideas of perfection are correct. They are different facets of the same diamond, the diamond of perfection. So many people think that perfection has only one facet and one facet alone. Perfection is a multi-faceted expression. The exercise that follows brings success to each of us in our own particular way. It brings us toward perfection because we could not have done any different at the time of our doing so.

> *Place your feet flat on the floor and rest your hands comfortably on your lap. Close your eyes and focus your attention on your breathing for a few moments. Now think of your left nostril as you breathe in and your right nostril as you breathe out. Make no physical effort whatsoever. Just think of your left nostril as you breathe in and your right nostril as you breathe out. Be aware in this moment that the attention you are applying as you put your attention on your left and right*

nostril, **is** Divinity in action. Take this same attention and transfer it to a time in the past before you ever existed. Then put this attention on a time in the future when you shall no longer exist. Bring your attention back to your breathing just for a moment, and think of your left nostril when you breathe in and your right when you breathe out. Now count to five and refocus to a point of your own choice.

Each part of this exercise should be maintained for thirty seconds.

Some of you will have done this exercise before, and it is, therefore, not a new idea to you. When you do the exercise you will find that you cannot visualize a time in the past when you did not exist, and you cannot visualize a time in the future when you will no longer exist. *The reason for this is that attention – Divinity – is immortal.* Attention ever began and attention will never cease. We must become aware of the validity, the power and the significance of what attention actually is. It does not matter whether we are looking at a handsome man running on the beach or a beautiful woman lying on the beach or a gorgeous German Shepherd running on the beach. It is the same attention that is doing all three. It is the same attention that makes up the marketing list. It is the same attention that picks up the marketing in the market. There is but *one attention*. When we begin to realize that attention is the I AM – not only realize it, but begin to implement it, to actualize it – we move toward wholeness.

This is Christ Consciousness. "None may come unto the Father, but through *me*." What do you think is being said? It is simply a matter of grammar in this instance. We do not say: "Nothing can come unto the Father, other than through I". *We can only come into God Consciousness by recognizing the Godliness of the I.*

"Unless thine 'I' be single, thou canst not enter into the kingdom of heaven." Not "eye". It has nothing to do with being a cyclops. It has to do with becoming totally and completely aware and functioning and implementing the attention as the I AM.

The first step is to stop blaming and condemning ourselves for what we have done, which does not mean we have to continue to do the same thing next time around. This is where people get very confused. The fact that we have beaten our wife on Saturday night for the last thirty years, does not mean we have to beat her next Saturday night. *We are not locked into our own pattern.* We are a Divine creative being. We can change the game.

We are raised in a society of strictures and rules, which are stagnant. At the time when most of them were made, they were totally and completely valid, but at this point in our development sixty percent of them are now garbage and should be thrown in the trash can. And rule number one to go in the trash can is: "I was to blame". We have never been to blame.

Most of us refuse to accept the fact that we can be an instrument of reminding or chastising for other people, and that is spiritual arrogance. Why do we consider ourselves so great that we should not be an instrument of God's chastisement and teaching? What do we think of the story of Jesus driving the money-changers from the temple? What do we think is being taught? Even if we accept the orthodox establishment concept of what Jesus actually was, how could a magnificent, sublime being like this beat the "living daylights" out of fifty or sixty people? Does it not cause us to think again? This magnificent, sublime being was humble enough to be the instrument of chastisement. This is the key to the whole thing – was *humble* enough. It takes humility for us to be an instrument of Divine Expression.

We have to stop saying: "I can't do that". It is true our personality cannot; our personality is inadequate. It is said: "Without *me* you can do nothing", the me in this instance being the I AM Cosmic Self. No, we are not a whole person when we condemn ourselves. No, we are not a whole person when we accept blame as distinct from accepting responsibility. No, we are not a whole person when we apologize for what we have done. If it did not need to be done, we would not have had the power to do it. What makes us so egotistical as to think that there is a Source other than God from which we can receive power? We cannot walk up to someone and slap them on the face using an alternative power. The only power that hand has is the Power of God, therefore someone's face cannot be slapped with anything else other than the Power of God. When we *know* this, we will have no urge to slap a face.

Either God is omnipresent, omnipotent and omniscient or He is not, so let us stop this theological absurdity we listen to and practice. If we think God is all three, then we must accept that it is God in action, and not another force. We must deal in realities.

If we do believe in immortality, what we have just glimpsed is a pinhole view into this immortality and eternity, therefore we must behave as immortals. This is why we could not visualize a time in the past when we did not exist. There are none who are capable of doing so, none of us. We cannot do it because we are immortal. The one thing we *cannot* do is make ourselves mortal, because we are God in Expression. So is the "punk kid" who rides his motorcycle at breakneck speed down the highway. So is the professional misfit who is carried into the hospital emergency room with his arm looking like a pegboard from needle holes, all of which are self-administered.

"Judge not lest ye shall be judged." When we judge something, we are seeing it as being separate from God. This means that we have now separated ourselves from God by the very judgment. As soon as we look at an adversary or a friend and make a judgment that they are not a 'good' person we have separated ourselves from God. We are saying *that* Expression of God is not good. At that moment in Consciousness we have separated ourselves from God.

We have judged someone to be other than God Expression, therefore, we ourselves, in that instance of time, become other than God Expression. In this moment our thoughts, words and actions become spiritually sterile.

There is only one way to become a whole person. People like to think there are other choices, but there are not. There is but One Source. There is but One Power. There is but One Will. There is but One Consciousness and there is but One Mind with a multiplicity of Expressions. We do not have a separate mind in this realm. This is what it means when it says: "There is no separation in Divine Mind". We cannot advance spirituality by kneeling and going around the beads and praying to something abstract. We can go around the beads being aware as we do so of our own Indwelling Divine Consciousness, together with its limitless Expressions. Unfortunately, a great many religious denominations have totally lost the connection to an Indwelling Divinity in their ritualistic expressions, and thereby separated themselves from the Father in Heaven.

There is nothing wrong with the ritualistic practices of any denomination, if the practitioners would not see themselves as separate and better than others. "In My Father's House are many mansions." But notice, all the time we come back to the same thing – always to the one single source. Each one reading these words is at this very moment as Divine as they are ever going to be. None of us is ever going to become more Divine. We are never going to be less Divine. All we can do is become more aware of our Divinity. We cannot expand our consciousness because it is already expanded to the uttermost limits; it is boundless; all we can do is increase our awareness of our unlimited consciousness.

Remember what we say to ourselves from time to time: "I will do this, I will do that or I will do the other, *but*...". What we have done with the "but" is very simple. When we say "I will do this...", we have a creative thought. The "but" is a second creative thought laid straight across the path of the first creative thought. In so doing we have intercepted, even blocked, the flow of creative energy.

The first recognizable and immediate advantage, in terms of benefits, is peace for self. No regrets. No fears of the future – the future being tomorrow or a half-hour hence, as the case might be. No fears, no regrets. Peace. And that reflects itself in improved physical health.

Let us be honest with ourselves at this point, and I want to make this very clear, because people sometimes tend to run ahead of themselves, grabbing the torch and running towards Olympus, a very long way. Increasing our awareness in this way does not mean that as we move into this Consciousness today, we are going to rectify all the psychological and physiological ailments and ills of our mind and body overnight. It *does* mean, because of the new process and pattern of thinking, the body we will build next time around will have much fewer of the ailments our current body is heir to, and the reason is very simple. It is because of what is said when referring to the sins of the fathers: "the sins of the fathers are visited even unto the fourth generation". In our current incarnation we are the father of the incarnation that is four incarnations ahead. In terms of 18 million years, four incarnations is a mere blink of an eye.

Far too many of us want to plant our spiritual seed and turn around the following day to collect our spiritual crop. If we do not go that far, we get up the next day and pull the seed out of our spiritual soil to see if it is growing yet. As we put it back we complain that it is not doing too well.

How do we become a whole person? There is only one way – to reject the limitation of merely being human. To accept our Godliness. There is no other way. This is what is known as spiritual alchemy. It is the transmutation of base matter into spiritual gold. So, let us resolve at this time and place that one of our 'bad habits' goes, as of now. *"I relinquish from my Consciousness the concept that I am not God"*. To think that we are not God is the foulest of all bad habits and the greatest limitation on our spiritual, mental and physical growth. It is essential that we use this proclamation as often as we can until we have erased the concept "I am not God" from our mind. Very good times to use this proclamation is last thing before we go to sleep and on first awakening in the morning. There is one most beautiful and inspiring thing that comes to us from India – it is the salutation used by Hindus, which is "I salute the Divinity within you". This is uttered while the greeter's hands are held together in front of the heart chakra. It is a recognition by the one who salutes of the Presence within the person whom they have encountered, and is also used at the time of parting. Just think how we can change our outlook and our life if we become aware of the Divinity in all those we encounter in our daily activities. If we are to be a whole person, we must consciously be a whole person and also see the whole person in those we meet throughout our day. This awareness can only bring the ultimate in peace and harmony, for then we no longer have enemies or competitors, we have only soul-mates. By being consciously aware that the person before us is the same Expression of Godliness as ourselves, we are on the path towards the restoration of our unity of which the song *Amazing Grace* so eloquently speaks.

Chapter 18

Truth Develops Awareness

The very heart and soul of the mystical life is the *inner experience*. It is essential that we do not confuse an inner experience with a need for an outer expression. Matthew's Gospel relates to this very point when we are told that Jesus tells a person he has healed: "Go thy way and tell no man". What we are being taught here is that the healing in question is an inner experience which does not have to be spoken of to anyone at any time or place. It does not have to be expressed in the outer material, concrete world within any time frame or sequence.

Society today puts tremendous pressure on those who are seeking self-development, by expecting them to demonstrate their growth immediately. We learn that a friend is attending self-development classes, reading the appropriate literature and practicing yoga, so we expect he or she to behave like a super-being in our company. Our misconception here is that the person in question *has to express* to us what they are feeling or thinking on the inside. The time to do this, if at all, may lie in the future and in different circumstances. We have no right to demand that *God ever performs in any particular way in our presence.*

This aspect of development is referred to only in Ephesians, when St. Paul says: "By their works you shall know them". Yes, we will know them when *we* have reached the time and place in our own consciousness where we can receive the level of expression involved in this new dimension of consciousness. It will manifest for us when we are ready. "When the student is ready, the teacher appears." It is never the obligation of the other person to meet our standards. It is always our opportunity to rise to the occasion. An inner or mystical realization may need a whole incarnation to grow and manifest.

For the person who has made the realization, there is a comparable aspect to the question of manifestation. As long as we are trying to experience our inner change on the outside, we limit the opportunity of that growth. Once we begin to make demands on ourselves, we are attempting to have God do the bidding of our personality. All that we have to do is remain aware that in all good time our realization will come to pass.

At our present stage of development we are hardly capable of setting any structure of spiritual energy in its appropriate synchronization. At this stage of our growth it is not uncommon for us to assume that we have reached the "ultimate", when in fact we have only just begun. Our enthusiasm carries us far afield in our expectations. We must not make demands on ourselves or on others, but must allow the tempo of action to come about at the natural pace of Divine Order. Our difficulty always is that we perform according to the dictates of the personality, which has no awareness of its Divine origin.

There is no need for us to set a goal of manifesting time limitation on this earth plane. We do not have to say that because we have had a wonderful mystical experience, we will no longer be telling lies or stealing by the end of the month. Let us drop this concept of goals in relation to our spiritual development. Let us make the goal to stop lying and stealing, but let us keep the time reference completely out of it. We need to make the decision that it is no longer what *we* want that needs to be expressed, but what *God wants to express* of His idea of creation. We do not have to excuse or condemn ourselves for our so-called failures, nor even praise ourselves for our successes. When we can do this in comfort, we are on our way toward truth consciousness.

In spiritual unfoldment, the position that is the most desirable to occupy is that of the observer of the scene by which we are surrounded. It is taking the viewpoint of seeing the world "as is" at all times. In this way we are accepting that what is before us is the Presence of God at all times. What we normally do and expect, having made an advance in our spiritual growth, is demand, for example, not to have the common cold ever again. In doing this we are, in actual fact, trying to tell God what the benefits of spiritual growth ought to be for us, rather than accepting the benefits God has to give us.

This is still the personality, the unenlightened "me", attempting to run the show just as it always has. We need to be very careful at this point not to enter into a land of delusion in our spiritual work and unfoldment. Just because we have had an input of Divine awareness does not necessarily mean that everyone around us has to notice and pay attention to our words of "wisdom". It is at this stage of growth that we must exercise the greatest care that we do not become victims of spiritual arrogance, thereby losing all we have recently gained.

Growing in true spiritual awareness allows us to be sensitive to the fact that other people are not obligated to be aware of our growth, and therefore do not have to respond to us and the world at large. We sometimes make the mistake of expecting other people to be in their consciousness level where we would like to be, but have not yet reached. When we can see these aspects in ourselves and begin to align our words and actions accordingly, we will have made a good start on our understanding of what *truth* really is and how Divinity actually functions in this earth plane. We may be seen to be withdrawn and aloof, whereas we are merely being detached and accepting the world as it is. This is our opportunity to be at peace with all mankind, most particularly with the section of it with which we are interacting at the very moment.

We must bear in mind that all earthly relationships are temporal and temporary. Therefore, we have to be prepared to relinquish all attachments to earthly connections on our journey to our ultimate state of spiritual being. It is to this that scripture refers when speaking of the young man who is told to sell all his goods. These goods are the conditions we have in our life at this very time, and we must be prepared to relinquish our dependence on all of the things and people upon whom we currently depend. This is the time to enter the state of consciousness where we sincerely say: "Not my will, but Thine be done". What this means, in fact, is that we must be prepared to accept the very next thing that occurs in our life, no matter how unacceptable it has been before. Surrender must be total if we are to enter into truth consciousness.

We must be prepared to relinquish our peeves, likes, dislikes and, most of all, that which we love in the material world. This could be praise, approval, reward, fame or indeed all of the assets we possess. The key here is our *preparedness* to relinquish, not that it ever has to take place.

When we set out on the path of the mystical life, we must make very sure that we are not seeking some specialized concept or attribute called God-power. Many people, upon getting involved in self-development processes, begin looking for some unique or abstract specialty, which they designate as God-power. This is usually expressed as a desire and a need to bypass natural law. They demand miracles in support of their personality-granted status.

We cannot contravene the laws of nature for the simple reason that they are the Law of God. When we attempt to bypass these laws, we are asking God to work against His own system. The attempt to achieve and utilize specialized and unique God-power is no less than spiritual arrogance. As we are already God-in-action, we would be trying to limit Divinity to a single line of expression, which cannot work since Divinity is universal.

In St. Paul's letter to the Corinthians (Chapter 2, vv.3-6), we are told: "The natural man receiveth not the things of the Spirit of God". Paul is saying that if we act without an awareness of our God-self, we are going to fall short of our goal. By attempting to personalize our activity and our achievements, we eliminate the main element of power in our lives. Yes, we are individual in our expression, but we are not unique in our creative ability.

Paul is saying that we cannot reach God or God Consciousness through our normal extrapolative mental process. We cannot reach God-sense within us through the norm of logical sequentialness of intellectualism. We can go to all the classes and read all the books, but they are all words. Words do not become a part of our active experience. God awareness must be experiential and must be practiced.

Joel Goldsmith speaks of practicing the Presence. This is the very kernel of awareness of the God-self. There is a tendency in this Western world to think of meditation as something to do with the gurus of the East, who sit on top of a mountain in an ashram and meditate, hour after hour, and then give benedictions to the lowly faithful. If we hold this illusion, we have to move from it to a simple recognition, namely you and I as individuals need to sit down and use the Psalmist's words: "Be still and know I AM God". We also need to become aware of what it is that is being asked to be still – our occluded personality and thinking, which is being silenced. We are not demanding that our right big toe does not itch or our left eyelid does not flicker. We are pausing for a while to allow the feeling of God's Presence to emerge in our awareness. As soon as we feel this Presence, we decide to hold it in our Consciousness, and set about doing whatever is next on our personal schedule. By so doing we are carrying the Presence into our active daily life, where we need it to operate. We are not allowing the 'high' to dissipate before we go into action. We do the very next action, however lowly – even loading the dishwasher – while still in active God Consciousness. What now happens is that the 'high' becomes perpetuated. This is the one and only 'high' you and I will ever experience. It becomes manifested on the outside, but not necessarily to others. We do not have to prove it to anyone, only to ourselves. In fact, we only have to do it. It really does not matter what we do. There is no such thing as "spiritual work", because everything we do is spiritual work.

The moment at which we cease to think is the closest we get to God in our normal humanhood condition. We are no longer thinking about our children, the office, our mate, the mortgage payment. Once the feeling comes, and we are no longer thinking, we must not make the mistake of attempting to hold on to the feeling. As soon as we try to hold on to it, it vanishes. We must take that feeling and go into action with it. If you are a cook, go cook; if you are a typist, go type. We use that higher state of consciousness in the process of creation and implementation. We can cook our meal, write our song, type our novel.

This is what Joel Goldsmith is really talking about: we must practice the Presence, otherwise we are empty vessels full of noise, as St. Paul calls the personalities. Once we begin to practice the Presence, we will be amazed with our progress. Our life will be changed.

A lot of us have a great deal of difficulty in dealing with things that happen in our presence. We get involved with the emotion and the affairs of what is taking place around us. A change on the inside brings us to the state or condition where we are not indifferent or unaware of the circumstances around us, but are not reacting to them in the old way.

The change in question is of an interior character, and removes the need to get involved at a personality level, while continuing to be aware as an observer. It also includes the ability to see and understand the connections between an inner state and an outer expression of that state. It is to this connection that scripture refers in the words: "Blessed are the meek, for they shall inherit the Earth". The Earth in this instance is *DIVINE UNDERSTANDING*. We can use any spiritually psychological technique we choose, provided that technology is oriented toward the concept of our own Indwelling Divine Consciousness.

The whole purpose of expanding our awareness is so that we can come to know who we are. To be aware of who it is that thinks, speaks and acts when we do, is to become spiritually enlightened on an individualized level of beingness. This is God Consciousness, individualized in expression on the earth plane. When we begin to recognize and accept who we are at the individualized level, we also become aware that when we utter the name-word I, we are God speaking. As such we can no longer lie, cheat, belittle or denigrate another human being. We come to realize that not only ourselves, but all humans are God-in-action. This is the at-one-ment which we all seek and call salvation.

As we move into this level of conscious expression, we become aware that all by which we are confronted stems from one single Source. As all stems from the same identical Source, there is no-thing to threaten us and no-thing to fear. Whatever exists has a need of expression. This realization is the beginning of living in a state of perpetual spiritual knowledge. This *is* Individualized Divinity.

There is never a time or place where Divinity is not expressing, and there is never a moment in our lives when we are not expressing Divinity.

Every spiritual book we have ever read, every class and lecture in the area of self-development we have attended, we have taken into Consciousness, even if we do not seem to remember. The facts and principles have impacted according to our sequential spiritual need. Frequently we might say: "I wish I could remember what Dr. Robertson said about that", but later, when the time is appropriate, it will emerge without us even needing to remember that it was Dr. Robertson who said it in the first place. It may even appear to us that it is our very own intuition, and it is our own intuition in the sense that the idea stems from the One Source. We had taken it in and stored it in the intuitional level for use at a future appropriate time. We have taken the seed into our individualized beingness, where it has germinated, bloomed and borne fruit at the precise time and place needed. At no time did this idea ever belong to Dr. Robertson, nor does it ever belong to ourselves at any time. It is a focal point in the Mind of God. There is only One Thinker and One Mind. This is the first fundamental truth that we must understand in the field of self-development. This means that we have never once wasted our energy and time, that we have never missed anything that we need. This means that we should never regret not having attended somebody's class or bought somebody's book or listened to somebody on television or radio. We cannot miss what our soul needs at any given moment. So we went to the beach and played beach ball. Wonderful. We stayed home. Marvelous. That is where we should have been. No, we should not have been at the religious service, the lecture, the seminar or whatever. These points are important to understand because we do convolute energy when we spend time in regret. "I wish I hadn't wasted my time going to hear that guy." We did not waste our time, because somewhere in the smorgasbord there was maybe one leaf of lettuce that was ours, that we needed, and we got it.

Joel Goldsmith tells us that all of the experience we encounter leads to "that act of grace bestowed on individuals at a certain time in their unfoldment, lifting them into the Master state of consciousness" (*Parenthesis in Eternity*). Goldsmith is actually saying that everything we need at any given moment in our life is constantly available to lift us to Mastership, because Mastership is the inevitable outcome of spiritual evolution. We always receive what we need at any given moment, and everything we receive we have need of in our growth. We walk into a bookstore and a book falls from a shelf, right at our feet. Is this just a mere accident? Many will say it is, but they have not yet come to realize that there is but One Source for all happenings in the universe.

Along the path of truth there are a great many steps, all of which lead us to spiritual awareness. Many among them, although simple enough, are overlooked. One of the most obvious is learning to dispose of the material objects we posses but no longer have a use for. A great number of us retain objects in case we have the need of them in some far-off and unspecified future. We must learn that: "It is our Father's pleasure to give us the kingdom". There is no need to fear scarcity in spiritual life. That which we fear is that which we attract.

One of the most important steps to be learned is letting go of concepts that never had or no longer have validity, such as all Germans are warlike, Scots are tight-fisted, and other such unfounded and sweeping generalities. We can never enter into the domain of charitable thinking and behavior as long as our consciousness is anchored to these or similar concepts. Any less-than-benign judgment we make of our spiritual environment retards our growth towards spiritual salvation.

Many who are pursuing a self-unfoldment path would seem to think that the repeating of inspirational affirmations is all that is needed to achieve spiritual ascension. We all must learn that it is the active implementation and practice of enlightened and exalted activity that brings us into the Promised Land. This land is that condition of consciousness in which we live our life in harmony, peace and grace.

Truth is not mere knowledge of esoteric facts. It is the understanding and wisdom that comes from the daily practice of applied Divinity. We must actively implement love, compassion, pardon, charitable evaluation, and all the virtues that opportunity presents. There are no complimentary tickets to the arena of spiritual evolution.

One of the most profound steps we must take is to relinquish our long held belief that we are merely human. This is one of the most false statements we ever make. We *must* shed this concept, for it limits every single thing we do in our lives. The limitation we put forth in this mental process becomes a brake upon every department of our life. With this concept, we actively *create* the condition of limitation. Material man is not a creative being, only Divine man is. When we come to accept our Divinity, it is this truth that develops our awareness.

It was on the mountain that Moses realized the I AM. Whenever we hear or read the word mountain in scripture, it always refers to a high or higher place in consciousness. So Moses realized the I AM at a point of high consciousness. When we make any spiritual recognition, we make it at a point of high consciousness. Not intellectual acceptance – knowing about it – but a living recognition. When we make that recognition, we no longer have to be concerned about being able to reach a high level of Consciousness, because we *HAVE* reached it. Where we have once reached, we can always reach again. We can take all of our expressions of Consciousness with us to that high point. This is what Jesus meant when he said: "I go that you may follow". When we make the recognition that "I AM the Lord the God", we can take anger and transmute it into love; we can take our envy and transmute it into generosity. We do not have to aim at giving up smoking, drinking or anything else for that matter. They will automatically fall away at the right and appropriate moment.

As a Master, Jesus entered into the full relationship of the I AM, and in so doing, became the Truth. He stated it: "I AM the Way, the Truth and the Life". Moses took the first step; Jesus took the second step. "I AM the Way, the Truth and the Life, and none come unto the Father but through me." Here is the Truth which separates the sheep from the goats. Jesus definitely was not saying we have to come through him personally. All the things we say, all the things that happen to us, happen to the 'me'. 'Me' is the expression of the I AM, and everything that enters into our life enters the 'me'. This is what Jesus is talking about. We have to transmute the experience of the 'me' into the Divine Recognition of the 'I'. When we have learned to do this, and only then, we enter the Promised Land. The I is in total charge of the 'me'. We assume the responsibility for our thoughts, words and actions, and we become totally responsible for everything that is received by the 'me'. And at this particular point the I decides what the 'me' receives.

This is the Pearl of Great Price. This is the Truth that sets us free.

Chapter 19

Can Consciousness Be Individualized

As already stated in earlier pages of this work, we humans are Divine beings. At this stage of our incarnated life we have little if any memory of our Divine origin. Having descended into human form, we have become occluded as to our true identity. This occlusion is not an accident, nor is it a punishment for some deed committed by us in a former state of angelic beingness. It is an essential part of our mission on this planet. We are here to uplift and spiritualize the earth plane. We are implementing the expression of the original *God Idea*.

Because we have occluded the memory of our former angelic state we do not focus our attention on that aspect of our being. This does not mean that our angelic state does not continue to exist. It not only exists, but is functioning at what psychology calls the unconscious level. It continues to operate as the collective or super-conscious. This condition has been functioning in this manner for several thousand years, and has given rise to the idea that mankind descended from the animal kingdom. *There is no concrete scientific evidence for such an idea,* there is only a postulate and a working theory.

There cannot be anyone reading these words who would deny the existence of their own consciousness. To even attempt to do so requires an expression of consciousness. The most likely area of dispute would be as to where consciousness originates. It is the contention of the writer that consciousness is the *essence* from which the whole universe is constructed. It is further contended that this essence is currently involved in the maintenance of the universe and is continuing to augment that which is already in existence. In addition to this, consciousness (*God, Source, Divinity*) will continue so to do until the original idea is fully and perfectly expressed. At this stage, humanity is carrying out the idea, but not as yet on a fully conscious level of awareness.

It is only in the very recent past that any recognition has been given to the idea of an attribute of consciousness other than the immediate focused present. Not too many people have been aware that the teachings of the Old Testament and the Greek Myths were none other than expositions of the workings of consciousness. These are expressed in spiritually psychological terms, which remain a mystery for the uninitiated. It is not until we reach a certain stage of evolutionary growth that we become capable of focusing our attention on matters of a Cosmic nature.

It is not only the Greek Myths and the Old Testament that are the repository of the Cosmic teachings. All the Myths of the major cultures throughout the earth have to be included. For us in the Western world the most important of all are those teachings which are expounded in the New Testament. We are told by the Master Jesus: "I came not to destroy the Law (of Moses), but to fulfill it".

The Law of Moses rests firmly within the Ten Commandments, the first five of which are subjective, the second five being objective. The first commandment is pre-eminent, both by numerical position and by content, in which the first law of human personal life is clearly expressed: "I AM the Lord the God; I shall not have strange gods before Me".

This Pre-eminent declarative statement, Divine in origin and in subsequent expression, is the foundation of the structure of individualized consciousness. This consciousness is, in essence, a state of at-one-ment, and in its individuated function is the prime creator of the universe.

The prime requisite for bringing about the manifestation of individualized consciousness is the attainment of conscious awareness of God. This can only be done through regular and constantly active focalization on God, in order to actively relinquish our membership in the great clan of the occluded. God by definition is the sum total of all that there is, the Infinite Invisible, the Single Source of the All.

The first step along this path of focalization is the surrender of the idea that we as individual humans are capable of thinking. We must come to the realization that, as an outcome of our occlusion, we only think that we "think". The intellect is not capable of thinking. It was only designed to be the vehicle of the thinking done by consciousness.

In scripture, this occlusion is referred to as the veil. In the New Testament we are told that at the death of Jesus "the veil of the temple was rent". This is a reference to the death and disappearance of the occluded state of consciousness. This occurs at the moment of realization of our at-one-ment with Universal Divine Consciousness. We no longer see ourselves as limited separate material entities, but have come into the awareness of our individuated but integrated Divine Expression. We become aware of our individual role in the expression of the original Divine Idea.

In order that we may achieve this individualized level of consciousness we need to *actively* focus our attention at regular intervals on our already existing Divine attributes. Of all the ways of achieving this sense of awareness of Divine Presence, none is better than that of meditation. As stated earlier in this work, meditation is not a process whereby we spend our time asking or begging God for favors, nor is it a time where we tell God what to do. God already knows what to do in all circumstances. Meditation is the time set aside to sit in silence and listen for the small voice within, telling *us* what *we* need to be doing as part of carrying out God's Plan for His Universe. Let us remember that all days belong to God.

All life is spiritual, and there is a fundamental fact of that spiritual life that must be learned by us all. We cannot have anything until we first have an especially focused consciousness of it. It is necessary to isolate a specific aspect of consciousness and pass it through the mold of the mind before we can experience effect. We must also have a fully developed sense of responsibility for that specific of consciousness. Many of the things we experience in our current incarnation were inaugurated in previous incarnations. "The sins of the fathers are visited upon the children until the fourth generation."

In order to have many of the things we wish for in life, we have to develop the optimum conditions in our life so as to provide the right setting for their use. A diamond of beauty needs a fitting setting to express its exalted life. As long as we remain in the state of unawareness of the presence and activity of the I AM in our daily life, we are unable to consciously think and thereby consciously create.

We cannot reasonably expect to function at a fairly high creative level in our lives, a Godly level, if our attention is constantly fixed on the effects of creativity, rather than on the cause. All things and all effects in our lives are preceded by a cause. If we are not aware of or in touch with the cause, we can have no direct influence on the things and effects in our lives. All of us need to find a door to the realm of cause if we are ever to live peaceful, harmonious and fulfilling lives.

It is for this reason that meditation plays the vital role it does in our ongoing spiritual development. Through the constant practice of "I am centered" meditation consciousness becomes particularized and individualized. St. Paul makes this abundantly clear in his statement: "I live, yet not I, but Christ liveth in me" (Galatians 2-20). Christ or Christ Consciousness is that consciousness which is individually and actively aware of its at-one-ment with the Divine.

We must work to gain this conscious awareness of our Godliness in order to enter the state of Spiritualized Beingness, where all created expression is conceived. There is little or no value in a mere intellectual acceptance of St. Paul's statement.

The need of personal commitment and self-directed activity is clearly indicated to us in the scriptural statement: "By the sweat of thy brow thou shalt eat". What we eat is manna or the reward of spiritual consciousness. Each one of us must pursue a path by which we can attune our already "separate" consciousness so that it becomes the vehicle of our own spiritualized expression on an individualized basis throughout our entire activity.

We cannot enter into this consciousness by simply reading of it or getting to know of it, nor can we do so vicariously by being around other people who have done so by engaging in self-development disciplines. Only through an individual conscious decision on our part can we enter into Divine Consciousness.

And again, only through personal endeavor can we arrive at this state of consciousness and be capable of individually expressing conscious Divinity in our daily activities. We cannot achieve vicarious atonement for past undertakings.

Once we begin to feel the presence of at-one-ment, we are on our way. At first the sense of the Presence may be vague and fleeting, but gradually it becomes stronger and lasts longer. So that we do not delude ourselves at this stage of our development, we should adopt an observer's posture about what is happening. We can await with calm assurance and patience the next stage of our development. This is the stage at which we "tell no man". It is also the stage at which we avoid, at all costs, any form of intellectual assessment. Spiritual truth cannot be assessed by the intellect. The intellect is far too low in vibratory frequency to assess the much higher vibration of Spiritual Consciousness.

We need have no concern about recognizing the feeling when we first experience that initial fleeting Presence. It is unique. It *cannot* be confused with any material experience we have undergone previously.

Once we get the feeling of the Presence of the I AM of God and the I AM of 'me' being One and the Same, we have begun to express the Eternal Presence of God, in a very specific and *individualized* manner. No two people ever express Divinity in exactly the same way. What is being expressed is Divine Consciousness that has become Individualized. It is for this purpose that we have come to dwell on the Earth plane. It is in this manner that God is glorified.

The use of the spiritual exercise which follows will assist in the development of this awareness. To use it to the best advantage, it should be repeated at least twice daily, morning and evening. The more often it is repeated, the better the result.

NUK PE NUK *(Egyptian)*
I AM THAT I AM *(Translation)*

I have at last reached my goal, and solved the secret of my soul.
I am "that" to whom I prayed, "that" to whom I looked for aid.
I am "that" whom I did seek, I am my own mountain peak.

I upon creation look as a page from my own book,
For I am the "one" the many make of substance which from
    "Me" I take;
For all is "Me"; there are not two; creation is myself all through.

What I grant unto myself I just take from myself,
And give to me, the only One; for I am the Father and the Son.
What I want I do but see my wishes flowing forth from me,
For I am the Knower and the Known, subject, ruler and the throne.

The three in one is what I am, and hell itself is but a dam
That I did put in my own stream when in a nightmare I did dream
That I was not the only One; and thus by me was doubt begun,
Which ran its course till I awoke, and found that I with me did joke.

So now that I do stand awake, my Throne I do surely take,
And rule my kingdom, which is me, the Master through eternity.

Chapter 20

From Individual to Collective Consciousness

The first thing we need to know about individual Consciousness is that there is a fundamental rule which applies to all of life's expression, a rule that all of us must learn and practice if we are to come into the fulfillment of our own Divinity. *We will never individually manifest anything in our life until we have this rule in our Consciousness. If there is something we want, object or condition, we must have a clear image of it.* It must be precisely and clearly defined. We must also make certain that it does not conflict with something else we are imaging. It must be clearly distinguished from all of our vague desires.

Some years ago a lady wished to have a new car. As the result of attending a seminar she learned of creative visualization, so she began visualizing a new car sitting in the garage alongside her husband's. A short while later she and her mother went on a vacation. On returning in the middle of the afternoon two weeks later, she went into the garage to use the washer and dryer. To her great surprise and joy she found a new car sitting in the space her old car normally occupied. She immediately rushed indoors to phone her husband and thank him for his generous gift. To her further surprise, he told her it was not their car, but belonged to a neighbor who was having work done on his garage. Her husband had helped by loaning the parking space.

There are some things we need to clearly understand if we are getting involved with the realm of visualization. First, as already indicated, we must be very precise in our visualization. Secondly, we must also understand that our wish for a new object or condition must stem from our Higher Self and be free of greed, lust, envy or pride. Also we must be prepared to accept the fact that our creative power may be a little weak due to lack of recent conscious use. Just learning the technique is not sufficient to bring about proficiency of application. Until we have the 'me' totally under the control of the I AM we have a low level of generating power. Before we can light a city we must learn to light our own room. The impossible we may do immediately, but miracles take a little longer.

We have to clearly visualize. We have to be clear in our Consciousness what it is we want to bring into manifestation. We cannot succeed until we have a distinct form of it in our Mind. Some people will try to tell us that they are constantly getting surprises in the things they get. If they stop and think for a moment, they will remember that some time ago they really desired to have this very thing, but in the meantime they have been focusing on different things. It is the desire element in the creative process that is the generative instrument. However weak the lower-self, the personality, may be, it does retain some power of manifestation, even if it is erratic and not under control. Creation is never totally absent.

This brings us to another aspect. Often there is something we want ardently. We have a tremendous desire to have it and have it now. Desire, being the engine of creation, causes the idea to begin to oscillate in our individual energy field. We would really like to have it this very week. It is an urgent 'want'. But we may not get it this week or month, and by the time we do receive it we may have completely forgotten we ever asked for it. We then ask where it has come from, because when we wanted one, we could not find it anywhere. We make the mistake of trying to fit the creative process into a time span. This is a common occurrence in Consciousness development.

Every single thing and every single experience we have or have ever had was first a part of our Consciousness some time in the past, even if it has not been active in our Mind in this incarnation. We may desire something in one incarnation, and not receive it until one or two incarnations later. The reason for this situation is that at the time of the request, the conditions and ambience of our personal and societal life were not aligned sufficiently to allow that manifestation. But in the later incarnation all is now synchronized and manifestation comes forth.

As an example, if we live in a rat infested low-rent apartment somewhere in the slums and desire to have a Rolls Royce, it is not really in keeping. When, in a later incarnation, we have become a professional in "Middlesville, a Rolls or its equivalent is much more in keeping with our environment.

In order to have anything, it must be inaugurated in personal consciousness. Therefore, if we wish to change the experience we are having in our life, we first of all have to change our "daydream". It has to be an integral part of our own on-going daily consciousness, because the only person who is going to feed it for us is ourselves. It cannot be simply a spasmodic image. The amount of spasmodic nourishment we give to an image is frequently incapable of making it produce as a reality in our normal daily life. Therefore, when we note whatever it is we want, it must be constantly fed – not wondering how we are going to get it, not wondering how the money will come nor when it will come. None of these things must be projected. For example, we must never say that we will have to moonlight on jobs or we will have to borrow from our parents. That is not what we do. We are not concerned with how it arrives in our possession. All we are concerned with is retaining the image of it. And to retain anything, we must maintain it in our consciousness. We must not forget to put gas in the car. We must not forget the maintenance of our home, or whatever else it may be.

It is an interesting thing about rich people. They have a good metaphysical process. They pay to keep everything they have in good order. That is why they get richer. This is what is meant when it says in scripture: "To those who have it shall be given, and from those who have not it shall be taken". What this is really saying is that for those who have the consciousness of it, it shall given, and from those who do not have the consciousness of it, it shall be taken.

A very practical example of this concerns a lady who was probably worth fifty million dollars. When she called in a workman to take care of something, she would ask how much it would cost. On being told it would cost fifteen dollars, she would say: "$15.00! Couldn't you do it for $7.00?". The workman would refuse to do it for the smaller amount, so she would send him away because she could not afford to have it done. Eventually the situation became a total emergency, and she had to send for a workman at two o'clock in the morning. The workman spent an hour-and-a-half taking care of the problem, charging her $450.00. It was taken away from her – $450.00 instead of $15.00. The case of people who take no care of their clothing is the same thing, producing the same result.

We must be consciously aware that we are conscious, so that the consciousness we are using becomes the guardian of that with which we are dealing. For example, we are given a gift. When we receive the object, not only do we thank the giver in recognition that they are God in action, but at the same time we are inwardly saying "Thank you, Father, for this bounty of the kingdom". What we are actually saying at that moment is that this is the 'me' thanking the I of both of us – the giver and the receiver. This is keeping the consciousness active, alive and functioning. We do not say: "Thank you. It is very nice of you, but you should not have". We *never* say to a person who offers a gift that they should not have done so. This is one of the ways in which we begin to turn off the kingdom. When you tell a giver that they should not have, you are telling them that you are not worth it, that you are not capable of taking care of this very valuable tray, for example, and they should have given you a plastic one instead. This response has started to degrade Spirit or Consciousness, forgetting that the gift is an outer expression of Divinity. Materiality is the lowest or densest level of Divine Expression. We are experiencing it every day. No matter what we are given, we must recognize that it is the outcome of Consciousness. We must also make the recognition that the Consciousness which it is, is the outcome of Individualized Consciousness. With this recognition and acceptance we begin to get in touch with Collective Consciousness. If we are given a gift, the Individual Consciousness giving the gift is really the Consciousness of Collective Consciousness functioning on a precise lesser being level. In fact, another name for this presence of Consciousness is God.

The simple way to go about this is to fix our attention on the object, experience or condition, together with our awareness of our own personal Godliness. This applies whether we are dealing with our attitude in the past or in the future. We focus attention, because where attention goes energy follows. The understanding of the meaning of attention and its relation to energy is vital to our own development.

As of this time, not too much attention has been given to the concept of attention itself. As an attribute of human activity it has not been considered worthy of much study. However, if we pause briefly and focus on this attribute, we notice that it has the quality of alternation or movement. We will further notice that this movement is the result of decision. We already know that decisions are made by consciousness and communicated to the external world through the vehicle of the mind. It is also known that decisions relating to attention that is directed outwards produces an energy transfer that can be monitored on feedback equipment.

The source of this energy is not located in the cell structure of the human body. We already know that our bodies are forms constructed of the energy to which we refer here. This means that our body is an effect of an energy field. This energy field stems from and is directed by consciousness. As an individualized structure and functioning system, this consciousness is an integral part of a greater or universal consciousness.

When universal consciousness focuses through a particularized attribute of itself, there is a direct energy transfer that takes place at a sub-atomic level. Everything by which we are surrounded on this planet is the outcome or effect of an idea in universal consciousness, and has been particularized and transmuted through individualized consciousness. We, all of us throughout all history, are those individualized attributes of consciousness. We bring all material things into manifestation.

Through our recognition, awareness and acceptance of this creative process we enter into the be-ing-ness of Collective Consciousness.

We must practice this. It is like playing the piano. We are not going to be in touch with Collective Consciousness while *not* practicing the utilization of individual consciousness. The practice and utilization of individual consciousness is what brings us into contact with Collective Consciousness (God).

When we go into the creative mode, expressing a desire to manifest a particular thing or condition, we do so by focusing our attention on that which is desired. Sometimes this is done through the use of a particular image and sometimes through the use of a concept. Whichever system is used, there is always an energy transfer initiated.

Having established the image or concept, it is highly important that we realize it is our own Individualized Divine Consciousness, as the vehicle of Universal Divine Consciousness, which is the nourishment for the manifestation of our desire. We must constantly remind ourselves of our Divinity and of its power to create and maintain the outer world. It is of this process that St. Paul speaks when he says: "Pray without ceasing". We need to remind ourselves, at least several times a day, of who we really are. By focusing our attention on God – our Divinity – we begin to diminish the separation in awareness that limits our creative capability.

As I have already said, there is a simple way to set about this entire process, which is *to fix our attention upon it*, in other words, *to meditate*. Once we begin to meditate, we do not fix our attention on the object or desire. We learn to fix our attention so that it will become more powerful when we focus it. Prayer or meditation is not thinking about ourselves or our problems, but rather the contemplation of God. It is becoming aware that our individual consciousness is part of universal or Collective Consciousness. When we feed this and when we use it to put out for anything, it has become more powerful. We are becoming aware of and enhancing the source of the energy which came down to earth in the first place. Therefore, the more powerful individual consciousness becomes, the more quickly and easily it can manifest what it needs to manifest. Often we find when we meditate there were things at age twenty we thought we could not live without; at age thirty we are not so sure, and by age fifty we find we were lucky not to get them. We begin to find that instead of wanting this, this, this and this, and dispersing energy over a myriad of things, we want relatively few ones. The first of these few things will probably be peace and harmony. The second will probably be the conscious awareness of Godliness in all we do, and thirdly, that we be consciously aware of our Godliness as we reach out and help other people. So we become consciously aware that what we are doing *is* God in action – not that we will be or hope to be. Where we originally started out with twenty or thirty things we wanted, we have now come down to three things, and eventually even they disappear. This is basically what happens with meditation over a long period of practice, and then what we find happening is that the things we really need arrive for us anyway, because way back in time we set up that we wanted them without knowing why. Now the time and conditions for their existence are in synchronicity, and what is necessary for 'the doing of the work' has arrived.

This whole process – this contemplation – must include the Nature of God, God activities and the nature of the world that God Consciousness has created and continues to maintain. *The Nature of God is to Create.* God activity is to Create and to maintain that Creation in the world we know. The seasons on our earth are maintained and come year after year, always in the correct and needed sequence. If we do not open our own Individual Consciousness on a deliberate and active level, we will not begin to experience God Consciousness. There is no being going to come along in a golden chariot, waving a magic wand, while saying: "You are a Son of Light". It is not going to happen that way. It is we ourselves who must do the work. We ourselves must take the steps to raise ourselves to the condition of Consciousness that links us to Universal Divine Consciousness. Initiation always follows the work, never precedes it. This is why begging prayer is not going to do it for us. Psalm 46:10 says: "Be still and know I AM God. *This* is realizing and accepting the power of Universal Divine Consciousness.

Through this means, and this means alone, can we enter into Universal Divine Consciousness. This Consciousness never was and never will be separated from us. We have simply been unaware of Its Expression.

Chapter 21

Becoming Universal Mind

When we enter into the life of Spiritual Understanding, we then know all that we know with our fourth dimensional Consciousness. Let us be clear what is postulated here. Many of us collect data continuously and now have so much we become repositories for a tremendous quantity of disconnected and unrelated information. This condition allows us to be very well-informed, and at the same time to behave as a psychopath or a neurotic. Either of these makes it a certainty that our relationship with other people cannot be harmonious, and is frequently mildly combative.

Entering into Spiritual Understanding is the point at which we become capable of interpreting that to which we are exposed, together with that we already know, with a total and ongoing comprehension of what *we are doing* with what we know, without infringement of emotional judgment.

When we read something in a book or are told something by someone else, which belongs in the category of fourth dimensional

Consciousness, we shall not be able to accept or understand it if we ourselves are not yet in that same vibration. Spiritual Consciousness cannot be attained intellectually. Later we may be able to understand because we have made a shift in Individualized Spiritual Consciousness.

The word understanding has nothing to do with the quantity of data involved at any one time, or its arrangement in our mind. This is why we can load a computer with an enormous quantity of data and all it can do is provide us with answers which are extrapolations or analysis. The computer does not understand, simply because it is not a vital living entity. All of the data in the world cannot give us understanding, for understanding is an attribute of soul life. When we attempt to convey the things that we understand at this fourth dimensional level of our Soul Consciousness to those who have not yet developed Soul Consciousness awareness, we just do not communicate. This is why Jesus advised: "Go thy way and tell no man". The word man when used in scripture always refers to those who have no awareness of their own Indwelling Divinity. Without this awareness we cannot *understand*.

The third dimensional Consciousness is limited to recognition within the third dimensional world. When we try to talk to third dimensional people about vibrations of the fourth dimensional world, the non-visible spectrum, they have the greatest difficulty comprehending or relating to what is being communicated to them. Such things as auras, devas, precognition or other aspects of the non-material vibratory world are totally foreign to their reality. As long as we believe solely in a three dimensional world, we are confined to the limitations of that vibration, but once we open our perceptions we ignite our *understanding*.

One of the ways we can know with certainty that we are moving into fourth dimensional Consciousness is when we begin to realize that *evil is not a power* and has no power over us. Death, disease or lack are not powers because there is but One Power, Source or Cause. As long as we reside in three dimensional consciousness we cannot comprehend this factor. As long as we refuse to take total responsibility for our lives, we have not yet crossed the bridge into Spiritual Understanding.

We cannot know God when we are limited to three dimensional consciousness. Unfortunately, most of us do not even know *about* God, let alone *know* God. What we do know about God, we know only through our carnal or intellectual mind. This carnal mind is third dimensional, and does not have the capacity to understand the invisible aspects of God. So, in the circumstances, we 'make God in our image'. We endow God with all the emotions we undergo in our third dimensional world, such as anger, discrimination and a great number of our other weaknesses. It is true that we do allow Him at least be Superhuman.

When we talk about Spiritual Understanding we are talking about Consciousness actively operating together with Divine Infusion. Until we enter into fourth dimensional Consciousness, Spiritual Understanding does not enter into our mental processes. We simply could not handle the vibratory rate involved. It would be like changing from a bi-plane to the Concorde in mid-air.

To have any awareness of God, as distinct from knowledge about God, means that we have come through the level of the mental or thought barrier of unfolding consciousness. We now do not have to think to resolve situations. By remaining aware of the Source of all situations, we gain instantaneous Spiritual Understanding or knowingness. We know how to deal with a situation without the use of extrapolation, without weighing the pros and cons. We do not apply the positive and negative criteria to the fourth dimensional world situations because there is no need. In coming through the thought barrier or earth mind limitation, we are raised up through the medium of *resurrection*.

The following example is an easy way to follow this. Two families decide to go on a trip to the mountains together, using separate cars. They get into their vehicles and head for Mount Olympus. Having traveled for some time, they decide to stop for a coffee break. On emerging from the restaurant, it seems as if it might rain, so one family decides to return home, while the other elects to continue their journey. On arriving at the mountain camp-site the children scatter in all directions, while the parents set about preparing and setting out the lunch they brought along. The parents know that their friends have gone home, so do not include them in the place settings. At this point in the story there is something the parents do not know. One of their boys has climbed to a higher altitude, and from that point has observed the other family's car making its way up the mountainside. On returning to the lunch site, he tells his mother to put out more food because their friends are coming, but she refuses to do so because she knows they have gone home. The son, who has climbed to a higher level, has the information because of his higher perspective, and understands the other family will soon be at the lunch site. His mother does not so understand because she has not engaged in the climb to the higher altitude.

In this case the son understands but the parents do not, because they are limited by the restrictions of their own perspective. So in this analogy we have a couple who have not yet ascended sufficiently in consciousness to understand what is being presented to them by their son. We all experience many 'sons' in our growth life. In many cases the information we have at any one time is far short of that which we need in order to arrive at an optimum decision or understanding.

Anything that takes place on or below the line of effects is caused by an expression of consciousness above that line. In this life we go on experiencing lessons at the effect level until we learn that we are our own causative agent, and learn to stop seeing ourselves as the effect of what happens.

Change is going on all the time in the universe, but because we are below the line, in earth consciousness, we become the effect of the change, and it frequently seems like a disaster or heart-rending experience to us. The whole of the kingdom of earth, the separative kingdom, is in a constant state of change. It is only at the level of the Source that there is no change. Once the separation process begins, we have the condition of positive and negative manifestation. In fact, we cannot have an expression in the material world that does not involve aspects of positive and negative. They are the constituents of all phenomena.

We are in the presence of change when we experience an earthquake or a hurricane. This does not mean we are pleased our house is falling down; that is not what understanding change is about. It is about having the understanding to discern the difference between being shattered by the experience and understanding what it is we are experiencing.

The process that takes place in the material area of earth living (earthquakes, hurricanes, etc.) is identical with the process in the world of relationships, as in marriages, divorces, families or friends separating. They are all changes and are an integral part of the evolution of human consciousness. Adaptation is the dynamic of spiritual progress toward the state of at-one-ment. "No cross, no crown".

Once we enter fourth dimensional Consciousness, the Presence within that Consciousness is active Divine Consciousness. This level of Consciousness is that which pours forth into forms and effects necessary for our daily experience. The daily experience with which we are primarily concerned is that which is necessary along the path of our spiritual evolution, together with the material aspects of expression. Spiritual growth and evolution must come first. "Seek ye first the Kingdom of Heaven, and all these other things will be added unto you." If we attain the spiritual first, the material things must of necessity follow. We must always seek fourth dimensional Consciousness first. That Consciousness level will then show us very clearly what to do in the three dimensional world. This is Creation in action.

If we first try to seek things or success in the three dimensional world, we are proceeding from a position of ignorance. We do not know where things 'come from' because we are not connected to the causative level of Creative Evolution. The *substance* of which things are made is always available, but frequently we are not yet ready, through ignorance, to express them. What do we do when we seem to hit an impasse? This is the time when the personality is most primed to spiritual urging and help. It is the opportunity to learn and practice the technique of directing a question to our own Higher Indwelling Consciousness. The exercise of belief in this Consciousness will advance our own spiritual growth and evolution.

Many people have great difficulty in understanding why it is they do not get what they ask for in life. For the most part they fail to receive their requests because they have not been directing them to the right Source. Their requests are directed to their three dimensional consciousness, which does not have delivery capacity. All we ever need is always made available to us at the time we need it. Frequently, however, when in three dimensional consciousness, we confuse need with want. God has a habit of answering prayers five minutes before deadline.

One thing we can be sure of – all *needs* are always met, but most wants are passed over. We must come to the realization that we do not have to give God instructions or directions as to when we need something in our life. As God is omnipotent and omnipresent, He already knows about our needs. Probably, the prime thing we need to learn in our present incarnation is patience. When we have learned patience we have gained the foothills of faith in God. Unfortunately, one of the desires of those seeking to become spiritually aware is wanting to see conditions manifest sooner than they usually do in the earth kingdom. We really do try to push God along. The early stages of spiritual understanding do at least allow us to recognize God's Presence in our daily life.

As we move into fourth dimensional Consciousness, beginning to feel our Divinity, we gain the capability of discerning more clearly what our needs really are, as distinct from the multitude of unclear wants. We learn to address the right questions to this ever-present Divinity, and to adopt the optimum valence necessary to receive answers. Primarily, what we do is become still and listen. We focus our mind on a single concept – "Be still and know I AM God". This is an active command to the body and to the mind to respond to the sovereignty of the soul.

This is what Spiritual Understanding actually is – recognizing and accepting the Presence of God in our activity, however seemingly banal or unimportant the activity may appear. We make sure to be still and receptive, and again, if we do not get an answer immediately, we continue with our regular activities, knowing full well the answer will be provided to us at the right time.

The entry into fourth dimensional impersonalized Consciousness is the entry into what esoteric teachings call Christ Consciousness. This is the level of Consciousness from which all blessings flow, all effects are dispatched. Entering into this state of Consciousness relieves us for all time from the need to be concerned about our welfare. We need no longer worry about our retirement benefits, medical bills or those whom we have made dependent upon us. As we enter into fourth dimensional Consciousness, we not only cease to worry about our retirement or our health benefits, we begin to understand there is no thing or condition of any sort to worry about.

There is a dawning realization of our own personal eternal existence. This means that as we approach our senior years, we do so without the fear of death that formerly dominated our thinking. As we begin to understand the indestructibility of our individual consciousness, we slowly come to realize that what society calls dying is simply a process of altered consciousness. We simply release the use of our current body, since we have no further need of it at this stage of our development.

Those who have reached the stage of development in which they realize and *accept* their immortality of soul-being, move towards this transition of mortal life with ease and quietude. By this stage of unfoldment we will have come to realize that this particular incarnation is just one among many that we have traversed. Some among us may even have been planning their next incarnation during the latter days of the current one. Part of the realization of fourth dimensional Consciousness is being aware of the limited role of any single physical body or of our need to depend upon it for our ongoing existence.

Pope John XXIII expressed this as well and as simply as any, when he said: "My bags are packed and I am ready to go", This is understanding and dignity par excellence.

When we enter into this state of Spiritual Understanding, we no longer need to attempt to be clairvoyant in order to deal with life. In this state of consciousness we become instantaneously responsive to Spiritual urging. Instead of sitting in our living room trying to project where we will be on Friday next, we remain focused on the *now*, with the realization that the now is eternity. Furthermore, we know that we will always be expressing what we need to express on Friday afternoon or at any other time. We *know* what to do next.

If we need to put something in a mental image, we are still operating in the three-dimensional consciousness. The mind science people of our society have been trying to present the mind as something that is the primary causative agent, when it is not. The mind belongs, quite rightly, to the domain of the earth plane vibration. It is the instrument or mold used by the soul-being to express in material form the conditions or objects of its ideas. What is beyond earth vibration is also beyond the power of the mind. The mind is not a creative instrument in its own right. It is a replicating tool which reflects the ideas of the soul-being. "Have ye no thought for the morrow, what ye shall eat or what ye shall put on, for your Heavenly Father hath knowledge of thy needs…". When we arrive at this state of acceptance, we can be sure that we have entered the state of fourth dimensional Consciousness.

During our sojourn in three dimensional consciousness we are, for the most part, the effect of unseen forces of which we have little or no awareness. It is as if we were sitting on a chair with only three legs and trying to keep our balance. We know we must remain upright or else we will tumble, and we most often do tumble. The worst part of the situation is that we know, instinctively, that there is a fourth leg somewhere, but we cannot seem to find it anywhere. This kind of situation becomes very personalized and stressful for us. The more we personalize it, the more difficult and stressful it becomes. Whenever we personalize any situation we erect a veil between the Divinity of our Consciousness and our thoughts, words and deeds. It is to this condition that scripture refers when it speaks of the 'veil of the temple being rent'. When the veil is rent, the personality is dissipated and its energy melded into the Higher Self or Christ Consciousness, which is the spiritual name for the fourth dimensional Consciousness. This is the beginning of our living in the realm of *grace*.

For many people the concept of living in the state of grace means being pious and sanctimonious, with a degree of religious mania. In actual fact, living in the state of grace means being consciously aware of our own Indwelling Divinity, and that this Divinity is the Source of all we express in our lives. It also means, sinning no more, not missing the mark.

The word sin has caused more difficulty for the spiritual seeker than any other word in the entire lexicon of religious literature. This difficulty is a fairly modern situation. It has only come into maturity with modern Christianity. Because of the great number of the followers of Jesus who are unable to understand the esoteric or inner meanings of his teachings, they have opted for the lesser or limited meaning. When Jesus said: "Go thy way and sin no more", he was advising his listeners to desist from separating their Individualized Consciousness from Universal Divine Consciousness. Sin is failing to recognize that our thoughts, words and deeds are *Divine Expression*. They cannot be other than Divine Expression since God is omnipresent, omniscient and omnipotent. Since we know that consciousness does exist, we must of necessity agree that there can be only One Consciousness. And, as there is only One Consciousness, it must be Divine Consciousness.

There is only one truth in all of spiritual law, and that truth is that *God is the only Presence in the entire universe*. If we proclaim anything other than that truth, we are sinning. The realization and acceptance of this concept, *God Consciousness, the Only*

Consciousness, is the essential requirement for entering into Universal Divine Consciousness, called in scripture the Kingdom of Heaven.

By realizing, accepting and retaining this concept of our own consciousness and of Divine Universal Consciousness, we have taken the essential step towards the state of becoming Universal Divine Mind. Universal Mind is the instrument used by Divine Consciousness in the process of creative evolution. When we actively and consciously participate in this undertaking, we fulfill our destiny as Sons of God.

There is no greater joy than entering into and living in our heavenly home.

Chapter 22

The Mind Is a Broad Avenue

Lord, make me an instrument of Thy Peace.
Where there is hatred, let me sow Love,
Where there is injury, Pardon,
Where there is doubt, Faith,
Where there is despair, Hope,
Where there is darkness, Light,
And where there is sadness, Joy.
Divine Master, grant that I may not so much seek to be consoled as to console; to be understood as to understand, to be loved as to love;
For it is in giving that we receive,
It is in pardoning that we are pardoned,
And it is in dying that we are born to Eternal Life.

This, as most people will know, is the Prayer of St. Francis. It is probably the only prayer in the whole of Christendom with true spiritual and psychological significance.

The psychological kernel of this prayer is that the 'me' is being exhorted to come into alignment with the I AM God-self. During the greater part of our daily life we experience frequent conflict and deep anguish because of our ignorance of the true nature of the "I" and the 'me'. Our occlusion prevents us from realizing the at-one-ment of the "I", the 'me' and the Divinity of their union. This separation is what brings about our identity problems.

The main purpose of every incarnation is to bring forth our true spiritual identity, which is no more and no less than God made manifest. This must be expressed, not merely collectively, but individually; not merely expressed infrequently, but constantly; not merely expressed imperfectly, but perfectly. It is to be expressed in all of life's aspects, for this is what God expression is when incarnate in Man. This opens up an enormous door and a broad unfoldment channel to the Inner Self for people on the self-unfoldment path. If there is but One Source of all manifestation, whatever you and I are manifesting at any given moment must be an expression of that Source.

The main reason many of us have difficulties in our life is that we do not accept the perfection of our own expression. Whatever we are expressing at any time is the expression of our 'now' consciousness. That consciousness is at all times Divine Consciousness. There are *no ifs, ands or buts* to this. If there is but One Consciousness, then our individual consciousness is at the very least a cell in that body of Divine Consciousness.

Merely improving the level of our humanhood is only a beginning, but a beginning not to be discounted, not to be made light of in our efforts. When we start on the path of improving our humanhood, it is usually the beginning of the path of discovery of our spiritual beingness or spiritual self. Our primary function in any incarnation, but even more particularly one in which we make this recognition, is to reveal God as Individual Being, and therefore illustrate there is not God and Man, but *only* God. For many people this does not come easily, as they are still firmly encased in their less mature understanding of their God relationships.

There is an old Chinese proverb which says "When rape is inevitable, lie back and enjoy it". The rape spoken of here is the process whereby Spiritual Consciousness totally takes over and absorbs the personality. In this situation the personality is undergoing a total change, to the extent that it will no longer exist as an occluded, conflicted and dominant ruler of the human soul.

If we can accept, in this very moment, that we are the perfect expression of the particular manifestation that God wishes to display, we will have no fears, doubts or guilt. It is only occluded humans who keep saying that God's Plan is not the same as ours. In fact, we have made no plans, we have no needs, we have no other function than the manifestation of God on this earth, which is part of a multi-faceted Created Universe.

The difficulties we experience when we do not live in this Consciousness is God's way of telling us we need to get in tune with Universal rhythm. One of the simplest signals in this category is the experience instanced in the statement: "You know, I knew in the beginning I should not have done that". We have all had this experience in our lives, we have all had the intuitive flash, pause or psychic urge, yet we have ignored the signal. Many times the signal is given by other people, for the Voice of God speaks through all of us, all the time, and not just in times of stress or emergency.

There is a very wonderful story told in India about a spiritual student who departed from the home of his guru, and set out to teach the world what he himself had learned. Later, as he made his way into a small village, he was met by the villagers who were all leaving. He stopped them and asked where they were all going. They told him there was a man-eating tiger roaming the streets. The student told the villagers that he would go into the village and calm the tiger, so that they might return to their homes. However, the tiger did not feel like being calmed, and promptly mauled the student. When the student returned to his guru, who had already heard the story of the tiger, the student asked: "If I am Divinely protected, why did I get mauled by the tiger?" His guru replied: "You did not listen to the Voice of God when the villagers warned you about the tiger. They, as well as you, are the Voice of God".

This story brings us to the very point that is the central factor of this entire process. God *is* Individualized in every single person. When someone tells us they think we should alter our behavior, we cannot just ignore what has been said to us, and decide it is merely coming from a "low-life". We must listen to our inner being and respond from its promptings. If we learn to hear other people's voices as the Voice of God, we soon find ourselves being told what we need to hear for our on-going good.

Many years ago the Maharishi, who founded Transcendental Meditation, told us that if we could have ten percent of the world population meditate every day, we would solve fifty percent of the world's problems. Whether these figures are accurate or not, the principle still holds true. We cannot be around enlightened spiritual people without there being some awareness of an indefinable difference in them and their behavior which is not to be found in most of those with whom we have contact in our daily life. Usually, if we happen to be seekers ourselves, we want at least some part of what these enlightened ones have. Without doubt, when we have been around spiritualized people for a considerable period of time, we find that it does provide us with an urge to *do* something about ourselves, instead of just *planning* to do something.

God is Omnipresent and Infinite. Therefore, if that is so, *God has to be you and I*. There is *nothing* else for you and I to be, here or anywhere in the Universe. When we recognize and accept this factor, we begin to move from *belief* to *realization*. So, if there is no room for expression that is not God's, how do we have sin, evil and disease? The only reason that any of these seem to exist is that those involved in these conditions do not accept themselves as the body, mind and Presence of God. It is only by removing God from our Life that we sin – that is the only sin. There is not a single person or religious body to whom this does not apply. Removing God from our Life is the *original sin.*

Nobody who is consciously living the active spiritual life can hurt, harm, steal, injure, lie or perpetrate any act against another being anywhere on the face of this planet or anywhere else in the Universe. We cannot even cheat on our taxes. We cannot be in I AM God Consciousness and manifest anything other than Godliness. The only manner in which we can perpetrate evil or sin is when we actively proclaim: "I am only human". By so doing we are claiming an independence from God, and consequently removing ourselves from the Omniscience of our God-self. When we act in chosen ignorance, we encounter the effects of that ignorance. All those produce their own particular effects. This is the mechanism of free will.

For the most part, having stepped out of our God-self, we do not like what we experience. Having surrendered our responsibility, we go on to blame all those around us for what is happening in our lives. We blame our parents, school teachers, employers, fellow workers, government or anyone other than ourselves. We even go on to ask what we have done to deserve all this, which is not really a question, but rather a statement of complaint against the world because it is not responding as we want it to. Instead, the world is reacting to the level of vibrational consciousness we have projected. We have sent out a Non-God signal, and are receiving Non-God reaction. There is no reason to receive any other signal. Like vibrations attract and unlike vibrations repel.

On this planet, we believe what is called the East to be very spiritual. Yet one of the greatest problems with which the East is confronted is that of poverty. One of the chief reasons for this is that the people are taught to rely on gurus or holy men. In the West, where Christianity abounds side by side with crass materialism, people are taught to rely on Jesus as a personal saviour or on the prowess of scientific intellectualism that is devoid of any spiritual inspiration whatsoever. In each instance, the responsibility is being placed outside of ourselves. There is a recommendation in Holy Scripture that tells us "put not your trust in princes". Like many statements in Scripture, there would appear to be a paradox here, but only because the statement is not clearly understood. It does not refer to princes of national political states alone, but includes princes of denominational theology of every caliber. Whenever we are being told by a person or denominational group that they, and they alone, have the answer to the mystery of God's Presence and Plan, it is time for us to run for the hills. This includes everything that is put forward in this book. Inner guidance from our Divine Self is always paramount. We need to return to our state of beingness which existed before nation states or denominational religion was incepted. We must return to an understanding of our own Divinity. We must remember that Scripture and science have been written by souls like ourselves. All have a Divine role to play.

For example, the five books of Moses were not written by Moses, but were written at a later date. This does not lessen the worth or value of these five books. It allows us to use our innate

God-self to establish for ourselves what it is we need to assist us in our unfolding spiritual awareness. There is a valid reason to proceed along these lines of spiritual development.

It is quite clear to me that there is a fundamental alternative interpretation of the First Commandment to that which is commonly used in orthodox religion. This alternative interpretation places the responsibility firmly on the shoulders of each and every one of us, and not on a guru or personal savior. The characters in bold print make the alternative meaning quite clear – *I AM*, the Lord the God, *I* shall not have strange gods before **ME**. This interpretation fulfills the clearly stated instruction: "Put not your trust in princes".

Not only must we recognize I AM Consciousness, we must also begin to practice it in our daily lives. The orthodox world calls I AM Consciousness God. This is quite valid because this God and this I AM Consciousness is Omniscient, Omnipresent and Omnipotent. There is only One Consciousness, and you and I are part of it, expressing it continuously, aware of it or not. The whole point of Divinity in us is to express it in all phases of our life. Expressed love of our family will do to start.

St. Paul refers to this expression when he states: "By their works ye shall know them". That is how we know spiritual people. It is not enough for us to know about God in secret or in our churches. We must demonstrate God in our lives, and that demonstration must come from within and not from a body of data and doctrine. No dogma or doctrine has a corner on the "God market". People who are God-realized do not talk about kindness, they act kindly to everyone, not just the people they like or admire. They do not talk about compassion, they express compassion toward all and sundry. They are, in effect, expressing omniscience and omnipresence.

Our Godliness must become as real to each other as is our physical presence. We must develop the same strength of feeling about the Godliness of the thought, word, deed or recognition which we are expressing or observing in the presence of another being or in the privacy of our closet. "From the point of Light within the Mind of God, let Light stream forth into the Mind of Man. From the point of Love within the Heart of God let love stream forth into the Heart of Man." These words, taken from the *Great Invocation*, must be the active expression of our *Daily Life*. The Love and the Light must become real to us if we are to express it in our activities. We have been given dominion over the earth, the kingdom below. In order that this lower kingdom may be spiritualized, we must spiritualize ourselves.

It is fair to ask here how we go about becoming God Conscious. The answer is that, like anything worthwhile, we work at it until we get it right. We begin by focusing our attention on the concept of God, then, like an actor rehearsing for a role, we adopt an imaginary (image-in-ary) stance as God. We then repeat the words of the Psalm: "Be still and know I AM God". This command is repeated over as many times a day as is possible within reason. We are now focusing our attention on our God-self and, in so doing, we magnetize our own Individualized Divinity. This begins to raise our basic vibratory rate and opens the channel to I AM Consciousness. Unless we undertake the work of seeking for the connection, we do not enter into the kingdom. "Seek ye first the Kingdom of God, and all other things will be added unto you."

Using this particular mantra out of the many available, will allow us to become actively aware of the I AM Consciousness, which is God. This awareness ennobles our thoughts and words, and permits us to begin living the life that is our destiny. This does not mean that we have to be engaged in world-shaking activity or dramatic events of any kind. It means that we proceed with our daily activities without stress or worry, and achieve what we set out to do with much more cooperation from those around us. That which we do, because of the Source from which we do it, becomes a noble and fruitful act. We have no need to be pious; we simply remain humble.

There are several statements in St. John's Gospel which give us a very clear picture of what spirituality really is, together with the key contact word that takes us into communion with its content and meaning. The first of these statements is "I AM the Way, the Truth and the Life" (John:14.6). Second, "I and my Father are One" (John:10.30). Third, "I can of mine own self do nothing; the Father in me doeth the work" (John:5.30). All three of these statements have a common spine; they all begin with the word "I".

To understand the active meaning of John's words we must realize that he is quoting the Master Jesus. When we look at the life and work of Jesus, we find that the over-riding theme is to direct man's attention to the Father within or, as sometimes expressed, the Kingdom within. If we in the West are to accept the life and work of Jesus as a valid and valuable asset in the spiritual unfoldment process, we must pay close attention to the statements quoted above.

Beginning with the second, we have a clear definitive declaration: "I and my Father are One". This tells us that the word "I" is the Father, not in a particular time frame, but in all eternity. Jesus did *not* say that this applied only to him, at the time and place in which he said it, Israel, circa 30 C.E. Having told his listeners many times that the Kingdom was within them, he could hardly be claiming exclusivity for his persona. He had already shown that he was not unique. He had to be teaching that the "I" of each and every one was never less than the Presence of the Father.

In the first quote – "I AM the Way, the Truth and the Life" – we learn that the Father, I AM Consciousness, is the Way, the process or vehicle of manifestation, and that there is but One Truth, that the Source (Father) is the Life of all Creation. This is again reinforced in the third statement, "I can of mine own self do nothing; the Father in me doeth the work". This tells us quite clearly that in the absence of the Father no-thing can be successfully accomplished.

All these statements are telling us that the carnal mind, when left to itself, is of little avail in achieving successful effects in the material world. Such things as are achieved have a very imperfect aspect and a very temporary life. When we begin to utilize our Divinity, we begin to realize that the human mind is a mere form vehicle of the soul and has no residual power of its own. The soul uses the mind (intellect) as a mold to form the atoms of Consciousness into the atoms of matter to provide the physical vehicle for earthly expression (incarnation). In effect, the carnal mind is no more and no less than a mold or a form shaper, and the energy that pours through it is the substance we call Consciousness (God). The mind is a *broad avenue*, and the breadth of the mind is entirely dependent upon the degree of our own Divine Awareness. This Awareness is the focalized attention of Divine Individualized Consciousness, the essence of mind, and is constantly present and available 'on call', for Consciousness *is* Eternal.

The mind being spoken of here is called the conscious mind by psychologists. This conscious mind is, in fact, *focalized attention*. It is the section of Consciousness that links action, emotion and thought to the I AM. Apparently, we in society have a very reduced measure of power flowing into the carnal mind at this stage of our evolutionary development. Our social, economic and political upheavals are evidence of this fact. This condition will continue as long as we remain in the lower levels of awareness relating to our Divinity Consciousness.

As we realize, accept and become more aware of our Individualized Divinity, we begin to extend our capability to an ever-increasing depth and multiplicity of the factors involving our thoughts, words and actions. We begin to see the connections between our thoughts, words and actions and their effect in the outer world and on ourselves in our daily life. We begin to understand the power of cause and its Source. The power and depth of *focalized attention*, the conscious mind, comes into full capacity, and the entire spectrum of activity then becomes an active expression of our Divinity. The only way we can do this effectively is by consciously practicing our Divinity in personal action. This way we increase the capacity of the conscious mind so that it becomes a broad avenue of expression for Divine Consciousness. With the coming of this extended awareness, we make the recognition that the carnal mind has no power of its own, but is a constant channel of power for Divine Consciousness to express Itself.

The effects that we produce in our life, in terms of objects and relationships, are the effects of the assembly and structure of the sub-atomic particles of spiritual consciousness. The mind is the mold that shapes these particles into the form required for expression in the outer world. This is a Universal Truth that is at work, whether we accept it or not – our consciousness produces conditions of expression.

Once we make the recognition that Divine substance flows through the formulating process which we call the mind, we can become the master of that mind, making it a broad avenue of our expression. The statement "Be still and know I AM God" is a command to the mind to accept its condition as the servant of Consciousness.

A good place to start this mastership is in the domain of our own body. We begin by accepting that every organ and every single cell within our body is an outer expression of our Divine Consciousness. This is taking active command of the structure we put together in the beginning. We have already set up the sympathetic nervous system, an automated system for operating the body we are currently using in furthering creation. If we will remember, each time we move a hand or any limb, that we have given a command to millions of cells, which respond to the command, we will quickly realize our Divine Power.

It requires the *conscious realization* of God in order to have God available in whatever we are doing at any time.

Conscious realization is *POWER*. This is how power is invoked. It is not achieved by pleading, begging or bribing. "Please God help me", when uttered at a level of consciousness where we are not aware of the intimate Presence of God, simply does not work. This plea is made from an accepted condition of separation from God. Unless we are no longer separated from God, we cannot invoke God or the Power of God. In this instance it is the persona, the Mask of God, that is being utilized, not the Presence of God. It is our failure to realize this factor that keeps us from enjoying the fruits of our full Divine Sonship.

When we learn, through on-going and dedicated meditation, the practice of stillness and receptivity, our mind-self becomes a broad avenue for Divine Expression in our daily life.

Chapter 23

Living The Spiritual Life

We hear many concepts about being spiritual, living the spiritual life, or how to become spiritual. They usually involve some form of rejection of the life we are already living. More often than not they advise that we have to give up smoking, drinking, betting on horses or some other so-called sin. Again, we may be advised to do something that we are not yet doing, and this one is the only viable one for us to consider.

It is when we begin listening to the inner voice and studying what it has to tell us that we have begun to live the spiritual life. It has nothing to do with giving up smoking or betting, although that may come as a result of listening to the inner voice, and again it may not. We may very well give up nothing, and still be living the spiritual life. Living the spiritual life means that we do that which we have always done, but now we do it from an entirely different consciousness level, from the level of our Christ Consciousness.

We enter the period of our life wherein we feel within ourselves: "I do not know what infinite truth is; I do not know what yesterday's affirmation was, I am waiting for today's, but I am not waiting impatiently". This is when we begin to rely on and rest in our Divinity. It is then that we begin to accept that where we are is all right. It is when we accept that we do not have to struggle, and realize that what we are experiencing is nothing less than God expressing as us on a daily basis. That is the beginning of spiritual living. It is then we can say to ourselves: "The only truth I really know, for *me*, is what is coming through for me in this very moment".

To rest in our Divinity means to rest in the Lord, which in this instance means to rest and relax within the Will of God, realizing and accepting that what is before us at all times is the expression of God in our lives. We are most familiar with the concept of rest in the designation 'Sabbath Day': "…on the seventh day God rested". Therefore, when we go into a state of stillness, as in meditation, we withdraw from thinking, emoting and acting, and in so doing we open ourselves to receive the inner small voice in our awareness. When in this Sabbath consciousness it is as though we are saying: "Thy Grace is my sufficiency". When we enter this consciousness we become capable of addressing the I AM Consciousness.

It is while in the state of stillness that we most closely resemble God's natural state of being. From the state of stillness the personality gains sufficient focus to establish contact with the I AM Consciousness, its own Soul Being. This is the actual practice of spiritual living. It is a practice whereby we actively focus our attention, our eternal Divine Self. This act of stillness brings all thought, all words and all action into a state of suspended animation. In the early stage of spiritual unfoldment we often require some form of trigger to tune our awareness, so many of us use affirmations. Affirmations do not change Consciousness, they focus attention.

With this focus of attention we are saying: "I am prepared to live in God's Grace. I am prepared not to hustle mentally, emotionally or physically. I am prepared to let it be, as is". This is not easy. It may be simple, but the living of the spiritual life is the most painstaking activity that we can ever undertake. This is so because the carnal mind is always busy, the emotions are volatile and the body restless. There are some people who cannot still the body to begin with. They have all sorts of urgent things to take care of, like taking the car to be washed, putting out the cat and other such momentous doings. There are some of us who actually feel guilty at sitting down and doing nothing, but we have to learn to sit down *doing nothing*. This is the step that clears the way and so allows room for an input of inspiration from our own Indwelling Divine Self.

The next step is translating that stillness into Divine Action. Having become still, really still, not thinking, allowing the voice within to communicate to us, we become a receptive vessel for the Consciousness of the Soul Self. What we hear is not usually a voice in the ordinary sense of the term, and it can take many different forms such as a gentle urging, a feeling, a clear impulse, or even a very definite intuitive input. The one fact that is quite clear is that when we become aware of Its Presence, it cannot be mistaken for anything other than it is. Many people experience a slight difficulty when they first become involved, because they try to make the 'voice' run on just like a tape recorder, and this does not work. We can never control the input with our personality. The I AM or Soul Being dictates the course of the transmissions.

When we enter into the spiritual life and begin to receive our spiritual guidance, we must exercise great care not to go beyond the precise information we receive. Many people make the error of rushing out to implement instructions long before they need to do so. Very often we are advised of information without being given a time frame for implementation, and if we are not given such a time frame, it behooves us to wait for one.

In most cases, when we try to interpret and implement before being told to do so, we produce more difficulties for ourselves. We have to learn to take this slowly, and also not to talk out of turn to everyone who comes along. The purpose of our development is not to look good to outsiders, but to fulfill our part in the Kingdom of God. Unless told otherwise, we resume what we were doing just before the communication. Any activity we are engaged in at any time is always God in action through us. There can be no other Source at work at any time.

If we do not immediately understand the message, we make sure not to go around asking other people to interpret it for us, because the message is always for us alone. If it is not, we will be told to speak with the person concerned. Most of us have a great curiosity and a need to know, but there is one thing we must learn. There is a finite sense of self which we must be prepared to surrender. One aspect of that finite self is the need to know. As long as we are enmeshed in the personality, we have the feeling of being separated from all sorts of God's expressions, but as we overcome the personality and enter into spiritual living which leads to at-one-ment, we gain the sense of all-knowingness.

What we are pursuing in spiritual unfoldment is the death of the old persona and the rebirth of the Soul Being. We must learn not to try to anticipate events. We can know about them, but not try to hasten them. Moses knew of the Promised Land, but he also knew that he, as Moses, would not lead his people into that land. The Promised Land is not territory. It is Christ Consciousness.

When we say that Moses did not plan to lead his people into the Promised Land, we must realize that Moses was limiting himself. We all limit ourselves in all sorts of ways, telling ourselves that we are too young, too old, to ignorant and so on. Whenever we claim limitation we are claiming separation from God. We are saying we do not have the creative essence that is required to manifest what is in question. As we move forward in our development, we become more and more aware of the things we do not really want and become more capable of manifesting those things we need. If we say there are things we need but cannot have, we are saying we do not have the spiritual essence to manifest them, and this is not true, although it is true that we do not have the *awareness* that we *do have* the essence, which is the Love and Power of God. The whole point of focusing our attention on our own Indwelling Divinity is to bring about that awareness in its fullest flowering, right here in this incarnation. This is what is being referred to when we hear the term 'reborn'. Being reborn is not discovering Jesus and placing the responsibility for our spiritual development on his shoulders. He has very clearly told us that the work is up to us – "The Kingdom of God is within you". He further tells us that when we seek this Kingdom and find it, all other things will be added unto us. We must first focus upon our own Indwelling Divinity, and then we will enjoy peace, health, harmony and abundance. But we must first seek the Kingdom.

Understanding what limitation means is one of the major steps in our unfolding process. Because at this time we have a fairly long history of thinking that has been confined in expression to material terms, we have been unable to perceive the Source of that material world. All of us have spent a great deal of our time 'wanting'. This wanting has taken many forms – money, fame, success, companionship and love. Because we believed only in a material world, we thought that the material world would provide these things for us when we asked. Again, many of us even made the God to whom we begged a material God. During all this time we did not realize that all we needed was within our own Consciousness, and that we were not limited. The Kingdom of God is within us, and within that Kingdom is all that we can ever need. Limitation is, in fact, not having the awareness that we have the power within ourselves to manifest all that we need in our life.

There is one other factor of which we need to be aware. The Creation process does not ordinarily work through the miracle method. *The creation or imaging in our mind is instantaneous, but the process of implementation follows a gradualistic path.* Very often things appear to happen miraculously, but that is only because we do not see the invisible world of Creation at work. As we begin to live the spiritual life, we begin to be aware of the outer world as appearance and, at the same time, be conscious of the inner world behind the appearance world.

The entire process of creation and the manifestation of that creation is one that follows a sequence, and is not within time, nor is it controlled by time. Therefore, we must be very cautious when we set out to manifest something we need in our life, and *never* try to set a time limit or a delivery date. Time does not exist in consciousness, but it is a manifestation *of* consciousness. This Consciousness uses our desire to express as a tool of Its manifestation. In effect, we have no desire that is our own; there is only Divinity's wish to express.

Just as soon as we learn to surrender ownership of the various aspects of our personality, and consciously accept that they belong to our Indwelling Soul Being, the sooner will we find ourselves living a life of peace, harmony and abundance. If the Divine aspect of ourselves is not actively involved in that which we do, there is little or no hope of a fully successful outcome. Again, because we have this long history of materialistic living, we tend not to include God, our Divinity, in the more banal activities of our daily living, such as brushing our teeth, filling the gas tank or going to the movies. All of these activities are carried out only through the Presence and Power of Divinity. We *must learn* there is no act, word or thought that is outside the realm of God's Being. It is only when we question our worthiness to be the instrument of God that we separate ourselves from God. We have no life other than the Life of God.

If we are to make progress in our spiritual development, we must get away from the idea that there is spiritual work and there is some other form of work that does not belong to the spiritual world. As soon as we separate God from what we do, we are out of touch with God. "Unless the Lord build the house, they labor in vain that build it." If we are not consciously aware of our Godliness as we work, at whatever we are doing, more than likely we will not do a perfect job. As long as there is only the human element involved, the outcome must be impaired.

It is in the realization of our own Divinity that we can more easily accept the Divinity of others. As we look beyond the appearance we see at a sense level, becoming aware of the inner Soul or Christ Being of those with whom we interact, and our whole life relationships change for the better. At-one-ment does take applied practice, which Joel Goldsmith calls 'Practicing the Presence', and we do need to do exactly that every day of our life.

There are those who will say: "That's all very well, but what do I do when I see someone behaving with less than kindness or civility towards another human being, who is kindness itself?" The answer is simple, but does not come easily to us. When we are faced with situations of this nature or even worse, we must look at what we see and say to ourselves: "I am seeing the Anti-Christ. I am seeing someone who believes in two powers". There is no-one who has accepted the Presence of God in their daily life actions who can hurt or abuse another human being.

Since so many people on the spiritual unfoldment path are constantly confronted by fanatics of all persuasions, it is as well to have an understanding of what exactly the Anti-Christ is in our society. First and foremost, it is not a person or an entity, but can be and frequently is expressed by a person.

The Anti-Christ is the body of opinion that is not enlightened in the knowledge of the One Source. It is composed of such people as those who think there are two forces at work in the world – good and evil, God and Satan, or any of the other dichotomies of theological or philosophical expression. If we believe there are two powers operating or manifesting in the universe, that belief is an expression of the Anti-Christ. To claim that God is not omnipotent, omniscient and omnipresent is an expression of the Anti-Christ. We can never have an All Powerful God and an equally all-powerful opponent. A great number of Western religious people have given themselves endless hours of guilt and anguish because of this simple misunderstanding. It is the not-knowingness of who and what we are that is the Anti-Christ in our daily life. Once we have realized and accepted our own Indwelling Divinity, we are no longer beset with the trauma associated with the Anti-Christ.

There is a secondary confusion in the Western world which arises from the use of the term Christ. A large body of people in our society have been educated into the belief that the term Christ is unique to one Soul Being alone. The term is a descriptive word to describe a particular state of Consciousness, the Consciousness which realizes and accepts that the Presence of God is in each and every one. It further means that all who have this understanding are the anointed ones, Sons of God. It is our *recognition* and *acceptance* of our Divine state of being that is our Christ Consciousness. It is this Consciousness that lightens our understanding and raises us from spiritual death.

It is also well for us to know that Christ Consciousness is not and never has been unique to Christian society. As long ago as the middle years in Ancient Egypt, there was widespread understanding in Egyptian religious practices in relation to this level of Consciousness. Much of the study, ritual and initiation practices were intimately connected with the process of adherents achieving the level of Consciousness that we in the modern Western world call Christ Consciousness. The teachings of Moses, an Egyptian, were also along these very same lines. He taught that the I AM is present in all of us These esoteric teachings have always been available to any who are prepared to seek.

Concurrently with the Egyptian religious practices, there were also the Hindus in India who were following similar teachings with the same goals, reaching similar levels of Consciousness to those spoken of in this book. Unfortunately, they all too frequently tried to confine the practicing of the Presence to their Holy Men. We are not offering anything new in these pages, only the Eternal Truth.

Having made all the recognitions that go along with spiritual unfoldment, how do we know that we are making progress? The first thing we have to do in relation to ourselves is *not judge by present appearances*. Much of what we are currently experiencing is an outcome of our thinking in the past. What we projected for ourselves and others in the past, is happening to and for us today. We must remember that when we project a thought-form, we are the most likely recipients of that projection. Like vibrations attract, unlike vibrations repel. Therefore, if we are fairly new to the domain of spiritual living, we most likely have quite a few debts to pay to ourselves. Unless we have been through our own forgiving and redemption process, we have some outstanding Karma.

We can be assured that spiritual progress has already begun, even while we are paying for the past. In fact, it is the effect of this spiritual progress that provides the spiritual strength and nutriment to deal with our difficulties. When, in the here and now, we can take the effects of the past and transmute them into present achievement, we are making progress. Every obstacle that is set before us is an opportunity to develop new spiritual stamina. We also must realize that problems do not leave the very day we become spiritually aware. Remember, it is an evolutionary process.

If we are not too sure that we still want some of the things we asked for and also projected for others, we can cancel the order. All of the things and conditions that we have contracted for in the past can be nullified. All of these that are as yet unfulfilled, are still centered in the thought realm, and therefore respond to the thought process. We simply proclaim: "I bless and release you", knowing that since we had the power to create, we retain the power to relinquish. As for those things and conditions we set up a long time ago, maybe several incarnations past, in our reborn consciousness we can now release and forgive ourselves the resultant debt. Because we are eternal beings, with all the spiritual power we choose to grant ourselves, we are capable of releasing the form of the energy which we shaped, and thereby returning it to the general body of Universal Consciousness.

There are ways to measure our spiritual progress, and not just how good we feel, although feeling more calm, healthy and benign are valid indications. Our first real sign of growth is our response to that which is presented to our senses. If, for example, we are exposed to data of a very cruel and brutal nature or the horrors of war somewhere in the world, and discover that our fear about such matters is lessening due to our new awareness, we know that we are making progress. We make the recognition that all this horror is brought about because the people involved believe in two powers, temporal and otherwise. And we know this cannot produce either well-being or harmony. The Anti-Christ is always the provider of the imperfect in our lives.

There is another aspect to which we need to give our attention. Even after we find our sense of fear lessening in our life, we find ourselves going through experiences that we do not wish to endure. We can be going through an unsavory experience that we initiated some time in the past, but we have not fulfilled in outer expression. We have to take that situation and transmute it, working our way through to the other side. This does not mean that we are not making spiritual progress, nor does it mean we are not one with God. It shows a temporary occlusion of our awareness of God's Presence. Even if these conditions should appear to continue for some time, a week or a month, the outcome is close at hand. We must always remember that we are not dealing in time, but in Eternity.

We have become culturized, through our own creation of the culture, into the condition of instant gratification, coffee, tea and instant success. It is very difficult for us to accept the fact that, although we are reborn spiritually, we are still having problems. The problems do not leave the day that we are reborn. We may think they should have done, but they do not, because their expression path is already well established and set long ago in the past. The process of spiritual change is, like all manifestation, evolutionary.

The question is frequently asked as to what to do with all the things we no longer wish to deal with – all these ideas set in motion a long time ago which we no longer wish to come to fruition. As stated earlier, we send in a cancellation order, declaring that we surrender all claim upon all such thoughts, all desires and all words and actions, and retain only those which enable us to express the Conscious Divinity within us, now and henceforth. Again, we have to bear in mind that we are not dealing with things we just initiated in this incarnation. We may have had desires two incarnations ago which we were not capable of expressing then, and it is only now that we have gained that capability, but now we realize that is not what we want to express.

When using a declaration such as the one outlined above, we must remember that it is not our words themselves that contain the *power* of cancellation, but the present active awareness of our own Individual Divine Consciousness. No words are ever causative, they are the effects of existing consciousness. If that consciousness is not focused on Divinity, then Divinity is not in operation at that time. This is the reason many people do not gain any benefit from using affirmations. They are sterile.

In this area of self-development we are dealing with a belief system that is not only individual but collective and social. Our individual belief in matters of evolution, religion and philosophy are group related, and have been for many generations. We are constantly immersed in the surroundings of these collective beliefs, and must therefore continuously restate and reinforce the Presence of our own Individualized Divinity. The sense of separation from our own Divinity (Soul) has been in effect for many generations. This is particularly true of the Western Christian world, which has attempted to restrict God to special locations and to unique personalities. We must continually reaffirm the Presence of God within ourselves. We do not have to proclaim this to anyone; we simply have to remind ourselves that we are Divine Creative Mind in action.

One of the most difficult experiences we undergo in our spiritual awakening is the condition of scarcity in our life – lack of money, opportunity and even perhaps love. At any given moment of our life we have to allow Divinity to manifest in the manner needed at the time and place in which it is manifesting. Otherwise, we are trying to interfere with Divine Will. Since Divinity is already omniscient, it does not require advice from our personality, which is far from omniscient. When we attempt to do this, we are trying to place our will, ideas and emotions in the Mind of God. We have two things to take note of at this stage of our development. Firstly, not reacting to the conditions before us, but remaining passive. Secondly, to add the positive aspect of making the recognition that this condition only exists because of a belief in material supply being the source of our well-being.

When we achieve this outlook, we can be sure that we have taken a step forward in our spiritual development. We have, in effect, a distinct sign of our active spiritual awareness. When we add the concept that all supply is spiritual in essence, and therefore omnipresent, we have taken a profound step towards helping the bereft and hungry on the earth plane. We are saying they can be fed, they can be helped, they can be supplied, they can be nurtured. Through this Consciousness we begin to help the needy, to help them awaken spiritually. The poet John Donne expresses this concept in the words: "No man is an island".

Every time we raise the level of our consciousness we have participated in raising the level of the consciousness of all Mankind, because there is only One Consciousness in the Universe, Divine Universal Consciousness. An example of this process in action is the times when we have been in the presence of certain people, maybe just sitting having coffee together. We feel terrific, and when we leave those people we feel a sense of lightness and enhancement. Our consciousness has been raised, even if we have only talked about the most banal things. These people are the saints of our society. They bring us joy, happiness and peace and, because of our upliftment, we go forth to spread the same good feeling to many others. This is the manner in which spiritual evolution takes place. In this way we gain the ambition to seek out for ourselves the Kingdom of God. When we ourselves are the giver of this bounty, we do not have to lecture the receiver.

Another sign of our spiritual growth is the degree and frequency with which we forgive our enemies. These enemies are not necessarily some great political force somewhere in the world, unless we are thinking of them as such. Much more often our enemies are those people with whom we have daily or frequent contact. They are usually people we know very well – brothers, sisters, relatives of all kinds, neighbors and other nationalities. All of these, at one time or another, play their part as our enemies. For a great number of people, their enemies are those with whom they disagree about religion, politics or social behavior. Whatever and whoever the enemy may be, there is only one way for us to deal with the situation. We cease to see the enemy as merely human and begin to see that they, like ourselves, are Divine Presence, even though they do not as yet know this. They not being aware of their Divinity does not absolve us from the obligation of treating them with the grace and sanctity they warrant as Divine Expression.

This condition of our relationships is exactly the place where we can do more in the way of growing than any other situation. "Forgive your enemy, bless them that persecute you." This is no idle recommendation. It is imbued with the highest Spiritual Law. When we recognize the Divinity in another, we recognize it in self.

It is during our life on this earth that we have the opportunity to gain our spiritual advancement most quickly. All of our relationships, whether of marriage, family, work, neighborhood or the community of nations, will provide us with endless opportunities for the growth of our spiritual awareness. It is where we do our homework, and begin to see the outcome of that work.

Until we learn to live the Spiritual Life here on earth, we cannot hope to enjoy it later in another dimension. There is no special place to start, nor is there an ideal time, *other than now*.

Chapter 24

Creating Our Tomorrow Today

At some time or other we have all asked ourselves the question: "How come I keep losing control of my life and reacting to what other people want of me all the time?" We could put that question in even more precise terms. "How soon after waking up to the day did I lose control of myself and the events of which I am a part?" Even if we remember when it happened, do we know how it happened?

Many people who are on the path of unfoldment start out each day with good intentions. For a great number of people the road to 'hell' is paved with good intentions. Somehow or other well-intentioned people, who are following the spiritual path, find themselves lost or frustrated by their own apparent inability to maintain their spiritual dominion as the day goes on.

It is all too easy for someone to tell us that all we have to do is remember we are the I AM. This is nice, but it is also glib. It is not quite so easy to do this when we have to go out into Caesar's world, where we function in our daily life. What really happens is that there is an apparent inability to maintain an even keel while sailing on the ocean of life. The more aware we seem to become, the harder it is to deal with many of the events in daily life. So, first and foremost, let us look at what does happen when we start to become aware.

The very first thing that is likely to come to our attention is that before we became spiritually aware, we were so unaware we did not know much of what was going on around us anyway. This is literally true for many of us when we first begin our journey. As soon as we start to spiritually unfold, we begin to be aware of things that were always there in the past, but we were not aware of their existence. The good news is that instead of becoming frustrated by what we are newly experiencing, we can congratulate ourselves for having become aware of obstacles that we had not formerly seen at all. We have been standing right by them, but we never knew they were there. The reason for this is quite simple. Our Divine Self never presents anything to the personality until it has grown and been prepared to handle it to our benefit.

There are many people who are not aware. They are so insensitive to what is happening around them that they do not even realize their effect on those with whom they interact. They live in an enclosed environment, which is what they need at this stage of their development.

The first thing we *have* to do is look at the obstacles of which we are becoming aware. The first obstacle that shows up in the morning may be nothing more than the coffee pot malfunctioning. It can be as simple as that or it may be our thirteen-year-old son telling us that he is leaving home and going to live in a free lifestyle commune. The magnitude or the complexity of the situation has no bearing at all on the opportunity for self-growth that is presented to us by the obstacles in our daily life. In the case of our son's statement, we may just not have been aware of where his interests in life were aiming. We were too busy caring for his material needs, like any other 'good parent'.

When we encounter an obstacle in our day, we must always first look at the obstacle and seek in it for the opportunity for our own growth. *Every obstacle is an opportunity for a new level of awareness*. It is also an opportunity for a new level of expression of that awareness. The opportunity to talk to our son about his desire and aim may also give us time to remember all the occasions we wished to be somewhere that would provide us with an area of peace and quiet in our life. Now we have an opportunity to share our inner feelings with our son, and get acquainted with his inner feeling. In this particular example a new relationship is established that is a benefit factor for both parties.

When we meet an ornery person in the course of our working day or social time, the thing we need to do is ask what we have to learn from this situation, from this particular encounter, and ask ourselves to whom has our behavior been unpleasant or nasty. This brings us to the kernel of the matter. If, in the course of our day, we come in contact with someone who is expressing hostility towards us, there can be only one reason – that we have not as yet eliminated hostility from our own personality. Since it is in our Consciousness, we continue to attract it to ourselves. Like vibrations attract, unlike vibrations repel.

Maybe our hostility is very lightweight in character, and is only expressed on a very general and abstract level, but it still draws to us those who have hostility towards us. It may simply be a hostility towards an unidentified tax official or postal worker who has not yet delivered our tax rebate. Civil service personnel are frequent objects of our hostility. More particularly there is the hostility we feel towards our own past, that we now blame for our current situation. All of these are fertile grounds for drawing hostility to ourselves.

As we become more aware, we become more magnetic and must, therefore, pay greater attention to our own inner feelings and mind-sets. It is within our thoughts and feelings that the true power of our creation resides. It is for this reason that hostility towards ourselves is so inimical to our own spiritual growth and awareness. We must constantly remember that all that we are and all that we have ever been is the Expression of God in the Universe.

Just as soon as we appear to resolve any situation – and here is the hardest part of spiritual unfoldment – we find ourselves facing a test. As soon as we think we have the situation nailed down, we are presented with a set of circumstances that test our new level of awareness and resolve. It is at this point that we discover whether or not we have achieved a newer and higher level of spiritual being-ness. If we find that we are still having difficulty dealing with the situation, we know that we have more work to do in this regard. If we can face the situation in the full recognition of seeing what is before us as the Expression of God in our life, then we know we have gained a step in expanded awareness, in which case we will find ourselves no longer reacting with our own hostility or the frustration we formerly felt in such situations.

The fundamental thing we must come to understand is that there is no outside experience we ever encounter, for which we do not have a residual magnetic quality of attraction. The only reason we can ever have a 'bad' experience is because we have the very same essence of that expression within ourselves. It may be only a micro-particle, but it is sufficient to act as a magnet and thereby attract the situation to us once more. A typical example of this is the person who at one time would cheat in any way they could, but now would return an undercharge of a penny to the cashier in a store. This same person would then return to their home and fill out their income tax return, deliberately not recording five percent of spare income. It probably would not even seem like stealing, as it is the government that is involved. Cheating is cheating and hostility is hostility.

The whole process of spiritual development is a cleansing mechanism. It is a way of doing home-repair, cleaning house so that we can function more efficiently in our lives. If we were to make a note of all the things and activities which we would define as non-optimum in our day, we would have a list of the things we need to work on in our life. We would not need to go to a lecture, read a book or visit a psychologist to discover the solutions to our problems. There is a cardinal rule for changing our lives and gaining spiritual upliftment. Each time we become aware of and focus on a condition, emotion or thought, in ourselves or in others, which causes us distress, we immediately bless it, recognizing that the energy of which it is made is none other than Universal Divine Substance, of which all of manifested creation is made. The reason it has come to our attention is precisely so that we can do just that. In this circumstance, as in all others, we will very soon have the opportunity to test our new-found understanding.

The *whole purpose of any incarnation is to derive the necessary experiences that are food for the soul.* The experiences we have in any one day are the nourishment for our soul growth that day. Just as soon as we digest the experience, transmuting the non-optimum concept energy into the positive, thus allowing the soul to absorb the nutriment from the experience, we never have to undergo that same or a similar experience again. This is what spiritual growth actually is for us on the earth plane. Many people will not accept that it is so simple, but it is. It is simple, but not simplistic. It is only when processes belong to the intellect that they become cumbersome and complex. But when the processes are part of the Soul Consciousness, they belong to the Divine realm of creation, and do not require complexity for their fulfillment. As we overcome our various obstacles – hostility, anger, jealousy, envy, hatred, gluttony, sloth and lust, to mention the more common failings – and gain freedom from them, we find ourselves ever more peaceful and at ease. Having overcome the first obstacle, we find we have much more energy to tackle the second. And again, having dealt with the second, we have even greater energy to handle the third, and so on until we have overcome all our difficulties. The reason for this is that there is a vast amount of energy used in non-optimum behavior which remains unavailable to us as long as we retain that pattern in our life. Once we release the particular behavior pattern, we have the prime energy restored to us for use in further work on our spiritual development. This allows us to have and to use greater power on what we still need to resolve in our daily life. As each obstacle is overcome, we become more capable in all our daily activities.

Let us look at some of the obstacles by which we can be confronted in the course of our unfoldment. One of those that can carry a seriously retarding effect in our life is that of promises we have failed to keep. The breaking of commitments is one of the most common spiritual mistakes all of us can make. We do so because we fail to realize that when we promise something to another person, we are making that commitment through the medium of our own Divinity. In addition, we are making that commitment to another part of Divinity, called another human being. The next time somebody promises to do something for us or with us, and fails to carry out their promise, we had better look carefully at our own promise-making record.

Having tuned into that record, we will find that we have not been too careful in keeping our promises to other people, starting with our own family. Many people go through life with a careless and slap-dash attitude towards the members of their own family. This cavalier attitude completely discards the need to recognize the Divinity within the members of the family. We also carry this conduct into the wide world of friends and business activity. This germ of consciousness becomes contagious to many others with whom we interact. When we become aware of this factor in our life, our best remedy is to cease making promises. As soon as we begin to learn about what is involved in making promises, we begin to develop the strength of character to say no to those who would try to have us make promises to them. We reply to these requests with such phrases as: "I will have to think about it and get back to you later" or "No, I am not prepared to loan you my car, but I would be happy to drive you where you want to go". It is better to say no than to say yes just so we can hope to 'cop-out' later. We use this with such excuses as "He is such a nice person, I wanted to let him down lightly". We do not owe a person an explanation for our conduct; all we do owe to anyone is the truth, a simple yes or no to any request. We do not even have to provide information when asked, unless it is of direct concern and the business of the questioner.

The other aspect of commitment is volunteering to do something for someone else. We then have second thoughts about the whole thing, but fail to tell the person in question that we have changed our mind. We can be sure we will have the same thing happen to us, but in all likelihood it will be of a more serious nature. If we *do not wish to be a victim in life, we must make absolutely sure that we are not making victims out of the people with whom we function in that life*. When we project an aura of dishonesty, callousness or disregard for other people, that is what we are creating, and that is what we will receive in due course. "As a man thinketh, so he is". This is not just an empty cliché; it is an accurate denominator of *Divine human power.*

The greatest obstacle by which we are faced in our daily life is the one which we create constantly and with little thought for its power and effect. We fail to *obey* our intuition. It is our besetting 'sin'. Because we do not recognize the Source of our intuition in normal societal living, we penalize ourselves as a result of this lack of awareness. Intuition does not come from the carnal mind, the personality or even the Higher Mind; it comes directly from the Divine Mind. This Mind is known in our society as Cosmic Mind or Universal Mind. It is the I AM Consciousness, and as such it is the Consciousness that spoke to Moses on Sinai, to Paul on the road to Damascus and to Jesus on several occasions. We *must* come to realize and accept that there is but one Consciousness.

In creating a tomorrow of harmony and effectiveness, we *must* begin to recognize and accept the true meaning of the First Commandment spoken through Moses on Sinai: "I AM the Lord the God, I shall have no strange gods before Me". The "I" that spoke then is the "I" that was before Abraham, and is the "I" that is ever present in each and every human throughout all eternity. There is only one "I"; there is no separate "I" for any one of us, no matter how lowly or exalted. It is sheer spiritual arrogance to assume that we have a consciousness apart from God. This is the only sin we can commit, to think that we can have an existence or an individual power apart from God.

To the degree that we refuse to accept our Divinity, to that same degree do we become ineffective in our daily activity. As we refuse to accept that we are God in expression, we limit the quantity and quality of our individualized omnipotence. This means that we spend our time merely responding to the stimuli of the external world, and ignore the promptings of the inner world. We cannot possibly create a life of harmonious effect if we are using only a small proportion of our inheritance. Only as Sons of God can we exploit our full potential. Only by accepting the uniqueness and totality of our Divinity can we come into the fullness of our capability. Our entire purpose on this planet is to co-create, so that the "Will may be done on earth, as it is in Heaven".

When we fail to respond to the input of our intuition (God Consciousness), we begin to produce a spiritual abortion in our carnal mind that later reflects itself in a malfunctioning and painful physical body. When Divine Consciousness is stymied, it begins to withdraw the focus of its attention. The final outcome of this withdrawal process is the death of the physical organism. That which society calls death is the withdrawal and the refocusing of consciousness to an alternative state. When we stymie our Divine Consciousness we begin to restrict omniscience and omnipresence, with the consequent result that we can no longer express perfectly that which we have conceived in mind.

It is quite true that in the beginning responding to our intuition may seem to be wholly irrational or impractical, but that is because we are habituated to thinking laterally. We can be quite sure that when we first begin to respond to our intuition we will not be directed into either foolish or harmful areas of activity. It is sometimes true that we do experience difficulties, but that is always because we have not given full and proper attention to what has been conveyed to us. The most common difficulty is one of timing. We learn through our intuition that we have to make a journey to the big city, or overseas, or somewhere that takes us away from home. Because we are keen to respond to our message, we immediately rush out to obey it. If we stop and examine our message carefully, we will find that an important factor is missing – there is no time element given. We have 'jumped the gun'. The first message is merely to alert us to the fact that we shall be undertaking a journey to a particular place. First of all we must accept that we will be making this journey, and learn to wait with patience for the message that will tell us when and how. We do not become adepts overnight. We have to practice slowly and gently being a channel of Divine Expression. The input is always precise. It is our personality that alters, adulterates or accelerates that which we have received. Accepting the gifts of the Kingdom is accepting that which is given, no more and no less. We cannot hustle God.

There are many among us who have a burning desire to be cosmic conscious or to be super-persons. Some wish to achieve this so they may appear to be superior to all others around them. Others desire simply to be the best they can be in themselves. Whatever the motive, to be super-conscious or cosmic conscious, we first must become fully aware of the totality of our moment. We must become aware of all that we are before we can become capable of fulfilling our potential. Any efforts that are aimed at super-person goals or activities without the recognition of our primary power Source are doomed to failure. We must be prepared to surrender the limitation of separation, and see each other as the multiple expression of the Single Source. This is the straight and narrow path that leads to the resurrection of omnipotence and omniscience.

In order that we may place our feet on this path, we *must* learn to be fully perceptive in the moment to the *outer appearance* and the *inner reality* of this earthly kingdom. So that we may grow spiritually, we cannot afford to ignore our intuition, the voice of the Soul. This is a voice we do not hear with our ear, but feel with our heart. It is the heart that is sacred. It always brings us the true message of our sacred being. If we listen, we will know where to put our energies, we will know where to serve. We *must* actively proclaim that we will respond to the heart's urgings, ignoring the temptations of the mind's bickering.

The second greatest obstacle we have in our pursuit of personal development is our unwillingness or failure to give service to those around us in our daily life. Many will say that they are too busy or do not have the opportunity to provide service to other people, that they have enough to do taking care of themselves. Doing aerobics and reading several features weekly on the latest methods of psychological self-development will not suffice. All this will do is help us to become a more efficient human in handling the external world. It will not assist us to become an active consciously creating being. It is a good starting point, but that is all it is.

How then does the busy person find the time to serve? It is quite simple and takes neither additional time nor effort. All of us are involved in some form of daily activity – lawyer, bus driver, homemaker, teacher or social worker. Most of us do these jobs because this is what we do to earn a living. All we need to do to begin with, is change our viewpoint on our activity. Instead of seeing it as something we do so that we may get something – money – in return, let us begin to see it as God providing a way for us to express our Divine capability. By our work we continue the process of creation, and by being aware of this fact we share in the bounty of this creation kingdom. Now we are consciously creating in every single and simple task we undertake at work, home or in our community. By raising the conscious quality of that which we do through this awareness we enhance the quality of the days of our life that are yet to come. When we do that which we do for immediate gratification, there is nothing left to receive in the future, tomorrow or the next incarnation.

We may still hear the argument that in serving we will find ourselves being taken advantage of by free-loaders. That is an unsound posture, because our purpose is not invalidated by the actions or attitudes of those we serve. Just because the free-loaders see only the outer appearance, it does not mean that the Presence of God is absent. It only needs *our awareness* to admit God to the scene of operations. We are the point in the physical universe where the invisible God becomes consciously visible. This is a spiritual truth which is imparted in all of the world's great scriptures. We must remember that the truths in the scriptures do not belong to any one religious denomination. As stated earlier, the scriptures are work manuals written and designed by enlightened beings to assist us in our spiritual development. They are not and never were intended to be books of worship owned by some religious fraternity.

Like all other levels of consciousness in the creation process, that of serving is no different. It needs to be actively practiced. In order that we may develop a clear channel of intuition, we must begin to accept ourselves as an active tool of creation. There is nothing wrong with seeing ourselves as God in action. There is nothing wrong with seeing ourselves as serving the needs of our fellow beings or any other expression of the earthly kingdom. It is necessary for us to seek and actively express our Divinity in order that the fullness of our Divinity may come into manifestation. "Seek ye first the Kingdom of God, and all other things will be added unto you." This simple instruction is *adamant* and cannot be by-passed if we are to enter into our spiritual inheritance. We are the heirs to the creative success of the Kingdom of God. We have been given dominion over the earth. Knowing this, we still need to have some specific process by which we can trigger our awareness of our Divinity in action.

The selection of such a trigger is simple and easy. We select an aspect of our daily life which is highly repetitive, and use it as a reminder. The most common activity for all of us is eating. We can, therefore, use our mealtimes as our trigger time. In our role as servers, during meals we can recognize that we are bringing the gifts of the Kingdom to our dining table. We can do this in very simple words: "I bless and pronounce good this bounty of *my* kingdom, which I have brought forth in this hour, as it was from the beginning". In so doing we remember that we are the I AM that planted the seed in the ground, harvested the mature product, transported it to the marketplace, dispensed it in the food store and prepared and served it at the dining table. There is but One I AM, and we are that I AM. This process is an active understanding of "I and the Father are One".

The concept 'the Kingdom of God' has been discussed and debated for generations, by religionists and philosophers, together with many thousands of seekers of truth. It would seem that the time has come for us to postulate an answer that will serve as a working vehicle in our path of unfoldment. We already know that it has been established for eons of time that God is Omnipresent, Omniscient and Omnipotent. We can, therefore, ask ourselves where these qualities of God are most apparent in our lives. There is a very satisfying answer to this question that can be comprehended by all. Everything that exists, that is seen, heard, touched, smelled or tasted, becomes a reality for us through the medium of our consciousness. It is Consciousness that is Omnipresent, Omniscient and Omnipotent. It is the one Universal quality of life – it is never absent from expression in some manner or other throughout the entire range of Cosmic Manifestation. *Consciousness is God.* Consciousness is I AM, the inner being of us all.

Because of the sacredness of the word "I", we must never use this word in vain – we must be constantly aware of the sublime and exalted essence of this word as we use it in our daily life. This is what is meant by "You shall not take the name of the Lord

(God) in vain". This is why every sentence we utter in our speech is a creative process. "In the beginning is the Word, and the Word is with God." If we will remember that every word we speak and every act we commit is a creative event, we will only say and do that which we are prepared to see manifest as an experience in our life. This path, and this path alone, is the one that allows us to create today the tomorrow we want.

Chapter 25

The Future of Man

In order that we may look at this concept with a degree of perception and pragmatical clarity, there are essential factors that must be examined. The first clarification is what the words psyche or psychic actually mean. This is spoken of earlier in this book, but warrants reiteration.

The word psyche, which comes from the Greek, means soul. Its associative, psychic, refers to the action and function of that soul. To coin a phrase, to be psychic is to be 'soulic'. When we are in the presence of psychic phenomena, we are being exposed to soul action of one kind or another. It is well we note at this point that soul action is always the result of Consciousness expressing. It is also as well to realize that Consciousness expresses independently of soul action, as in the successions of the seasons.

Most importantly, we must never allow ourselves to be enticed into the belief that psychic action is unique to select people, nor is it a form of aberrant behavior. All activity initiated by Mankind is psychic behavior. It is the activity of a functioning soul operating in the earth plane. The most sublime activity of the soul/psyche is the building of the physical body within the womb, the body it will utilize during its sojourn on this earth plane.

Many people in our society are already in a hurry to get rid of their bodies. They tell us that they intend to go on to better things. If we look around us we will see that we have not yet managed to build the perfect body. We are surrounded on all sides by people with imperfect limbs and malfunctioning organs. Until we learn to build the perfected body, not marred by any form of dis-ease, we will have to go on reincarnating until we get it right. Some of us are walking around with what we were born with, while many of us are operating with seventy percent or less, some even with artificial replacements. Is this a condemnation? No, it is not, but it is a reality we must accept if we are to prepare ourselves for the development we all desire. It is a recognition of the degree of capability we have reached in our ability to implement the design we have set for ourselves.

There is another factor that must come into the focus of our attention. It is necessary that we learn to make the best possible use of the bodily vehicle we have already built. We cannot abuse the violin we have and expect someone to provide us with a Stradivarius to replace it. Many people in our society spend a great deal of time condemning their bodies and, even worse, condemning the bodies of others. We must learn to accept and bless what we and others have, with the understanding that these bodies are the expression of the soul being. The original design is always perfect; it is the implementation that falls short of perfect replication. We have to learn to take that clay (spiritual substance) we already have in our spiritual hand, and mold it into that which will be an improvement on what we have now. This is why so many people, perhaps unknown to themselves, are involved in so much body work in health clubs and gyms. They are setting up the blueprint for the body they will use in their next incarnation.

We must begin to accept that the bodies we currently use have been designed by ourselves. They have also been built by ourselves, however poor and ineffective the resultant body may be at this time. We have been successful so far; we have built better and better bodies with each succeeding incarnation. Remember that there was a time when the Soul that we are did not yet have a body (see *Atlantis, The Creation Process – Page 71*). Despite the socially-induced diseases we have now, we are nonetheless on a success path of physical growth balance and perfection. At this time we have devoted a tremendous amount of earth living time to the eradication of malfunctioning in the bodies we use. Like cars, they are improving.

We must remember how long we have been developing our capability; not a mere one thousand years, but more like at least twenty million years, to get from the non-physical state to where we are today. The semi-dense state took place and was developing for millions of years before that. Evolution *is* a fact, but it is not limited to what many of our scientists would have us believe. Such scientists are severely limited in their education and understanding, limited to their carnal mind.

Let us understand this condition as it was known on Lemuria. Long before we reached the level of existence pertaining to Lemuria, we had already gone through many other chains of manifestation, above and beyond the physical expression. The atoms of our Soul being were far less dense and consequently we appeared much taller by today's standards. This race memory is why we have a mythological image of a race of giants in our past. It has taken several millions of earth years to traverse from Godhead to manifesting physically as Man. We have descended from a rarified high frequency vibration to the atomic physical rate at which we now express. This is as low as we ever get to descend. We shall never be members of the lower animal kingdom, nor were we ever members in the past. We have *not descended from the animal kingdom*. This is why there is still no trace of the missing link, even at this late date. There is no such link. When the creationists and the evolutionists cease combating each other, they will be able to turn their attention to the actual truth of evolution. Consciousness is the prime Source of all manifestation, and is still developing its capability of expression.

Long before we arrived on Lemuria, we had been in existence as Individualized Consciousness Beings. These levels are known by many names, such as Polarian, Hyperborean and Edenic (as in the Garden of Eden). This Eden was never a place on Earth, it was a condition that preceded our Earth sojourn. Our first body was not built on Earth, but was an Astral body, and we built it on the Moon. This is the reason why so many people are still affected by the phases of the Moon. Consult any Police Authority, and we will learn of their problems with people at the time of the Full Moon.

It is a little sobering when we come to realize just how long we have been on this job of building a perfect body. It gives cause for a little more patience with the situations in life. We cannot really expect to tell our children something at breakfast, and have them doing it perfectly by dinnertime. We certainly cannot expect such rapid results if we are truly spiritually open.

We must begin to be patient with ourselves, and with those around us, in growing physically, mentally and spiritually. We *must* accept the on-going rate at which evolution moves. We are doing a splendid job of building the Universe as already designed. Let us bless and dedicate our work each day before we begin and bless and give thanks each night before we go to sleep, and also bless our body each night before we go to sleep. Let us begin by focusing our attention on the crown of our head, and then moving our attention all the way down through the body to the soles of the feet, recognizing as we do so that every part of this body has been brought into expression by ourselves. The Soul-Consciousness doing this activity is the self-same being that will alter the condition of our bodily expression in order to manifest the newer and better body-life in the future.

The focalization of our attention on our own Individualized Consciousness is the process by which we make contact with the substance, or the raw material, from which the Universe is constructed. It is our only substance, and has been so for several millions of years, and it will remain the substance for the entire period of our physical manifestation on this planetary chain. *There is no other source or substance for us to draw upon.*

When we focus our attention on the material kingdom, we are focusing on spirit made matter, for matter is simply spirit vibrating at a slower rate. I, Father and Spirit are all one and the same. Mother and matter are one and the same. Therefore, when we read "The Word became flesh", we are being told that Spirit has reduced its vibratory rate and has entered into material expression.

We must begin to relinquish the concept that our bodily expression is a mistaken state or condition. We must also release the idea that living in the bodily state is some form of punitive condition for some wrongful activity in the distant past. Consequently, we can no longer entertain the idea that we must dispose of this body as soon as possible in order to get on to the next stage of our spiritual growth. We shall not pass on to any other level until we learn to accept our responsibility for the body we have, which we ourselves have built.

We cannot make spiritual advancement by throwing out or ignoring a large segment of manifesting Spirit. We cannot develop our spiritual emotions nor our spiritual mind by reneging on the area of spiritual matter over which we have dominion. We are unable to transmute physical energy into emotional (astral) or mental (manas) energy until we learn to deal with it at a spiritual cellular level. Each of us, every day of our lives, has the opportunity to deal with life at the cellular level. Every time we get a little twinge, a little pain or a little ache, we are being reminded that we have dominion over matter. Pain is our warning bell to alert us to the need to bring our attention to the dominion we possess over the body (temple) we have built. Our body is the Temple of the Holy Spirit, and it is built without the sound of hammer. It is the Temple where Divine Consciousness chooses to dwell.

For all those of us who have been working for years to achieve Christ Consciousness, there is good news. It is not, nor ever has been, confined only to selected people. We can become Christ Conscious in the twinkling of an eye – all we have to do is accept that we ourselves and alone can do no-thing. Instead, we accept that the Father does the work at all times and that the Father is our own Individualized Consciousness. It is to this that St. Paul refers when he says: "I live; yet not I, but Christ liveth in me" (Galatians 2.20). The Christ always dwells in the 'me', we need but to become aware of this fact.

No human can finally and totally depart from the Earth Plane and sojourn in another spiritual dimension until having learned about and accepted dominion of this earth life and its place in the Creation Plan. We must also realize that the Earth Plane includes all of the Solar System. In effect, it includes all that exists within the visible spectrum. In our process of descent and ascent through our incarnations, we dwell on other cosmic bodies, in varying states of vibration. Our sojourn on the Planet Earth is the period of our most dense expression in three dimensional form. This aspect of our development is extensively covered in the works of Rudolf Steiner.

When we ascend in Consciousness to full dominion of the Earth plane, the planet as we know it will also have ascended to the condition of perfection in conformity with Cosmic Consciousness. This Earth is our vineyard.

This ascension has already begun. As already stated, Christ Consciousness *cannot be limited to* a single Divine Human, and therefore ascension cannot be limited to a single Divine Human. If it were, the entire Christian message becomes non-workable. Jesus has commanded His followers to follow Him, through crucifixion, resurrection and ascension. "Take up your cross and follow me." This is not and cannot be an empty directive. Jesus does not speak loosely, and we cannot take it loosely. To many, this expanded understanding of spiritual growth through Bible use may not come easily, but it will come, for we are all destined to return to the Father's House.

In terms of spiritual evolution, the ascension began a little over two thousand years ago. The true significance of the Master Jesus is that *He is* the forerunner of the Way, the Truth and the Life for Mankind. He taught that the Father is within us, and that *HE* (the Father) does the work that we do in thought, word and action. Many people have failed to understand the true significance of the teaching, and have deified Jesus singularly, and consequently have not as yet followed His directive to seek their own Divinity within their own Being.

Jesus is the prime inspiration for the Western world. There are a great many who cannot see this because they have only been exposed to the canonically altered teachings, which stem from

St. Augustine for reasons that are not our concern in this book. It is these altered teachings that so many spiritual seekers cannot accept today. This is quite understandable, since most seekers are now pursuing development within themselves, and looking towards the outside less and less. At the lower end of the scale it is called 'doing your own thing'.

As of this time, the main focus is on the physical, the body, and this is as it should be, since we have not yet perfected our bodily expression. But in that focusing we are in the process of assuming responsibility for our body, and in so doing we are beginning to exercise dominion of the Earth Plane. Since our body is an expression of our Soul, we are fulfilling our destined undertaking. We are at work in our vineyard.

With the focus we have today on the physical body, many people are experiencing what may be called entombment. This means that the Spirit which we are is enclosed in a limited awareness that does not as yet allow for the enlightenment of resurrection, an inevitable event for all of us. As already stated, neither resurrection nor ascension can be restricted to a single person or even a specialized group. We all go through the process of crucifixion, resurrection and ascension in the course of our spiritual development. Jesus has shown the way to self-redemption for humanity. It is for this reason that He invited us to follow Him. At the time this invitation was issued, Mankind had reached the deepest level of physical and spiritual density, which is experienced on the Earth sojourn. The process of return to total spiritual awareness began two thousand years ago and is still going on today, and will continue to go forward.

If we were to take the average person today, matched for weight and height, we would find that they are lighter and taller than those two thousand years ago. We have only to examine the door heights of existing buildings of the time to become aware of this fact. People are now taller and lighter because the density of the individual physical cell has begun to lessen. Again, this means that there is a change in the rhythm of the physical atom which itself has been altered by the non-physical atom of Consciousness.

As we are losing weight, so is the planet and the entire Cosmic system. This process has been accelerating since 1899, the dawn of the Aquarian Age. This Age, like other Zodiacal Ages, will last for two thousand, one hundred and sixty years.

What does all this mean for us as individuals? It means that when we make the recognition of our own resurrection from unawareness, we must fully accept our recognition and decide to live our life accordingly.

It is not enough to recognize that we are Divine. We must implement that recognition in our daily life. This is the big holdout that our society has at this time. We have thousands and thousands of development groups all over the world, who are still pussyfooting around in the shallow water. They are refusing to let go, trying to hold on to the land they have decided to leave. Many of us do not as yet really trust our own Consciousness to take care of us. We are still looking to the outside and the familiar. We are looking backwards to the shore we are departing.

Spiritual development requires a deliberate, conscious implementation of our acceptance of our Divinity. We *must accept our Divinity as we are right now*. We must come to realize that we do not have to change anything to become Divine, but simply accept that we are that and nothing else. We do not have to change wives, husbands, secretaries or lovers. We do not have to become Divine – we are Divine.

That which we decide and intentionalize today becomes our expression in the days to come. Because there is only One

Consciousness in the entire Universe, what we set out before us will come to pass. We cannot think and feel as God and not express God. We are not separated. We are One. What is written here by the writer and read by the reader is expressed by the One Consciousness.

As we live in the physical world at this time, and will do so for quite a long time yet, we must make our decision to implement our recognition as soon as possible. The sooner we do so, the quicker will we change our life to what we wish it to be. We have been working in the physical domain for over eighteen million years, and it is time to move on to the next stage of our development. We have had three phases of development before the present one, all of them of a non-physical character, namely Polarian, Hyperborean and Lemurian, the present one being Atlantean. Our next two phases are also non-physical. These phases are known as the Root Races.

This Atlantean phase has several sub-groupings, the present one being the Aryan group, which peaked during the reign of the Nazi regime. We are now in the process of eradicating the last remnants of this totally physically focused vibration of Consciousness. We must realize that Aryan is more than a national racial group. It is a vibrational period of Consciousness.

This Consciousness is already dissolving, and as it fades and merges into the expression of the Fifth Root Race level of existence, we now begin the act of ascension. When we move totally out of fourth root race Consciousness we, at that time, relinquish our need to express our presence in physical form. We see a preview of this when we see the form of someone who has passed from the Earth Plane through the process society calls death. There is no death, only the change of a vibratory expression.

In the beginning of the movement from the Fourth to the Fifth Root Race Consciousness, we start to exercise more and more responsibility for the body we currently have. Already many have come to realize that the body they have is the body they themselves built within the womb of their mother. We not only build the body, but we also design it before we enter into the womb. Our behavior towards our body in this incarnation will, to a very large extent, dictate what kind of body we will have next time we incarnate. Our thoughts and actions of today set up our future conditions.

One of the things we need to do is pay attention to the language of our body. It is not an inert mass operating by chance. It is a living Soul Expression operating in the Earth Kingdom. Pain is the alert signal to give attention to our body. Without this signal system we would fail to do maintenance.

A doctor in a hospital will ask where it hurts. Why does he want to know this, why does he not just diagnose without knowing where it hurts? He wants to know where it hurts because that is the indicator light that functions as a locator of the area that requires attention. The attention that is focused is the attention of Divinity. Attention is a vibration of Consciousness, and all Consciousness is Divinity.

Our attention is our Divinity in action. There is never a moment during the day when our attention is not present and in action. It may be focused in the past, on happy days at school, or it may be focused in the future, when we might receive a large inheritance, but it is focused. As we proceed through our day, our attention is constantly focused, on the smell of the flowers, the neighbor's new car, the lay of the clouds, the song of the birds and a hundred other things.

If we really want the key to the secret of success in spiritual development, it is to remember that our attention is our Divinity in action. As we become more and more aware, consciously aware, and deliberately function with the concept of *Divinity as attention in action*, we will advance and increase our spiritual unfoldment. If we are truly dedicated to this purpose, we will also add meditation to our program of spiritual exercises, and this of itself will hasten our progress. The existence of yoga and meditation is an active sign of spiritual unfoldment in our society.

What is immediately ahead for us, when we consciously and deliberately move into this Consciousness? We can start to eliminate all the unwanted characteristics of our personality which have produced unpleasant experiences in the past. When we know what they are, we become capable of releasing them forever. We do this by simply blessing and releasing them, in the full knowledge and understanding that by this attention practice we are functioning in our Divinity. It is not the words, but the conscious awareness behind the words of our own ever present Divinity acting as our attention that creates the new condition of freedom and peace.

We can, in time, remedy poor sight, impaired hearing and many of the other imperfections we do not enjoy. We will begin to have the sort of relationships in our life that we have always known we needed, because we have become that quality of vibration. Like vibrations attract, unlike vibrations repel. All of this will not take place overnight; there are no miracles involved in our unfoldment. The miracle is the unfoldment and the fact that we can change the outer world around us through the mechanism of an inner adjustment of our own Individual Consciousness.

If we add to the release process the act of blessing all the things in our life that we do want and enjoy, we again enhance the capability of our unfoldment. By giving recognition and blessing to those things which our Divinity has already provided, we allow ourselves the awareness of our creative ability. We do this with the simple words: "I bless and pronounce you good". These words have an exalted and hallowed history in the domain of spiritual creation. This is following through the principle established in first chapter of Genesis, where God (Consciousness) looks upon His Creation and sees that it is good. When did we last look at our creation and pronounce it good? It is now time for us to start doing so if we are to change ourselves and the world we live in at this time.

Let us note our imperfections, but let us note also that they are the imperfections of an Individual Consciousness that until now has been occluded as to its own Divinity. Having taken this responsibility for our creation of the past, we ready ourselves for a more *enlightened* responsibility for the future. This is Soul growth and development in pursuit of its destiny.

As we note all the things and conditions we wish to express in the future, we are being consciously aware of the Divinity we are. If we were not, we would not be noting down these things or conditions in the first place. Writing down what we would like to happen without developing our awareness of our Divinity, will produce little if any concrete results. Again, it is not the words but the Consciousness behind the words. The intention in Consciousness is the initiator of the process. It is for this reason that when a doubting materialist attempts to test these procedures, they will not work for them and so allow them to scoff.

This process of self-development is not a theory, it is a spiritual working system. When we actively *focus our attention* on our Individualized Divinity we make the connection with Universal Divinity, and thereby become a participating power in the creative world. In consequence, we become capable of altering our spiritual genetic code, and in so doing change our mental, emotional and physical pattern of conduct. In effect this is Spiritual Psychology. It is the only psychology that can ever be relied upon to work one hundred percent.

If we wish to advance our own individual development, we use spiritual tools. Hugging, kissing and telling each other how much we love each other is excellent spiritual playtime, but we need to do more than just be nice to one another. Now is the time to practice being Divine – we must consciously focus on the within of our being. Only by using our Conscious Divinity will we become capable of replacing our self-known imperfections with the perfections we desire to express in our advancing awareness.

That which we wish to express, but are not as yet expressing, is already a reality in the Kingdom of God, awaiting expression by us as individuals. The Kingdom is Consciousness, and that which is in Consciousness will manifest in the Earth Plane.

If we only realized the tremendous power that is carried by our mind, we would be even more ready to undertake our own spiritual development. We can tap into and conduct enough power to light a whole city's street lighting system.

Despite all of the unwholesome aspects currently to be seen in our neighborhoods and in the world as a whole, this is growth. Mankind has been advancing along a quickening path of spiritual evolution. It is true that not all people are advancing co-equally in the outer material world, but the overall condition of society is one of upward spiritual mobility. The mechanism of desirable and effective growth is becoming more widely known with each passing day. Many thousands of people from all walks of life are already seeking a meaning to life, and they are doing so through the medium of an inner search. Many who read this book will find in it the spur that will set them on the road to self-discovery and spiritual enlightenment. This is not the only book available that deals with self-development from the standpoint of Spiritual Psychology; there are many such, together with numerous well-conceived and effective audio and video tapes and DVDs.

We are rapidly approaching the time when there will be a greater number of people working consciously on their own and society's well-being. This work is already being done on an inner level of Consciousness by a great many people, but may not yet be apparent to those who do not as yet vibrate to that frequency. We have now passed beyond the stage of the dawn of the Aquarian Age. The ground is ploughed, the soil is primed, and all we have to do is spread the spiritual seeds of Consciousness.

In the foreseeable future we will develop the capability to overcome our personal faults and begin to reduce the effects of our Piscean/Aryan Consciousness. This has been the era of the cult of personality. In the new era, the personality will no longer dominate our individual and social activity. We will be much more socially oriented, seeing ourselves as an integral part of an ongoing world creation team. We will have surrendered our very limited goals and merged into a commonly shared goal in the Cosmic Divine Plan of Creation.

This is not a very long way ahead of us. We are already moving into this realm of Consciousness, and through it the planetary problems we currently experience will fade from our awareness. This Age of Aquarius will also bring an increasing capability for out-of-body experiences, and this condition will enhance our capability of working directly on the Etheric Body, and resolving several of our bodily ailments and disorders. Part of the assets of entering into Christ Consciousness is the capability of moving the main focus of Consciousness beyond the parameters of physical limitation. Together with this will be an increasing capability of communicating with each other over long distances without the use of electro-mechanical instruments. Teleconferencing and fax machines will then be museum artifacts. As we move even further into the Fifth Root Race domains, we shall spend less and less time in physical manifestations, until such time as all our activity will be centered in beyond-earth applications.

It is very difficult for us, while immersed in the carnal world, to grasp a true understanding of what life will be like when we have moved beyond our present level of functioning. This is so because, until we begin to see with our spiritual eyes, we are unable to relate to non-material manifestation. At the level of human physicality the carnal mind vibrates far too slowly to be able to even form the appropriate questions that would give the answers we seek. Life in the Fifth Root Race realm does not receive its stimulus from the Earth Plane, but from an even higher vibratory plane than itself. Only on the intuitive level, or sometimes in the dream state, can we even come anywhere near an approximation of what Life beyond Earth level can provide.

Our current spaceology/science fiction is still locked into a very low frequency vibration in terms of hardware for life beyond Earth. Most of the people involved in space thinking are limited to three dimensional functioning. Uplifted humanity, when fully developed, will not require to travel throughout the Cosmos. Spaceships will be Stone Age tools, when compared with the technology of the Fifth Root Race. All current space technology is the work of a low level vibratory carnal mind. This mind is imprisoned in physicality. It is a mind that barely monitors the biology of humanity, let alone control the functioning of the carnal mind. As long as humans continue to see causation in physicality, they are prevented from perceiving the Primary Cause, for it resides in the realm beyond measurement by machine.

In order that we may understand the true reality of physical life, we must take a brief look at its origins. While evolution may be a fact, its beginning does not rest in some single cell life form nor even in a big bang. The so-called single cell is preceded by a period of great extent in which there is no physical form, even gas, as we normally understand form. That to which the earth sciences direct their attention is a very late comer on the scene.

By the same token, the time frame of orthodox religious creationists is also wide of the mark by millions of years.

The whole story of the descent from the Garden of Eden is an exposition of the process of Divine Being (Consciousness) descending from a level of non-physical manifestation to a level of physical manifestation. Adam and Eve are not two physical first parents, but represent the two poles of Divine Being when in expression. We call them positive and negative vibrations in energy. They are, in fact, that which creates energy. Within Divine Being, which is Consciousness, yours and mine, is the polarity of power which creates *all that is created* in the physical world.

This polarity-power of Being has been in manifestation in the physical world for upwards of 1,350 million earth years. Even before physical manifestation, Consciousness *is in existence*. This is what is meant by the words that God is eternal and immortal. Consciousness is eternal and immortal. This lengthy sojourn of Consciousness in the non-physical and physical states is divided for convenience into four divisions for the purpose of definitive study. As already stated, they are known as Adamic (Polarian), Hyperborean, Lemurian and Atlantean, and we belong to the latter group, the one to which earth science directs its attention. In the course of this Atlantean sojourn we, as Individualized Consciousness, enter into several physical expressions over the course of many thousands of earth years. With each newer expression we improve the physical vehicle we build and occupy. It is this latter process that is referred to when most people speak of evolution.

As we improve our biological engineering ability, we also improve our bi-location capability. This means that we develop the ability of being able to move into and out of the physical vehicle with greater ease and facility. We learn to monitor the body from beyond its physical limits. This is what many people are already doing, and some can even project the image of their being to others, and are seen to bi-locate.

Those who have not yet developed to the extent and capability of being aware of the unified energy field, of which Einstein spoke, tend to wish to discredit the existence of that field. We must be careful not to judge or condemn such people for their current state of awareness, because it will change all in good time.

Another of the things we need to understand, and will begin to do so in the next two or three decades, is that we cannot confine our growth and development to ourselves alone. We are going to have to become more involved, at an awareness level, regarding our societal responsibilities and functioning. We are about to step out of isolation and the uniqueness of self, into the realization of At-one-ment of all nations, all mankind and all things under the sun.

Although it may have taken twenty or more million years to reach the stage of sophistication we have attained in the building of physical matter, it is not going to take anything like that length of time for us to attain full dominion over the entire process. The most likely time lapse is about twenty-one hundred years. In the next decade we cannot but be aware of the acceleration of the overall development process throughout the activities of Mankind. Even our machines and communicating processes are getting faster all the time.

We have been doing a good job of learning to manifest our Consciousness through the building of a material universe. We have also done a good job in getting to know and use the mind we developed a long time ago as the connecting link and monitoring device needed to operate the day-to-day workings of this Earth

Plane. It is not easy to formulate and operate the mechanism of a physical body, an aircraft or space vehicle, but we do this very effectively most of the time. Due to tissue failure and metal fatigue we have to provide replacements, but the system works very well. We have done all this without being aware, most of the time, that we are always more than just human.

Already there are many people operating on this planet who are aware that they are not just mere humans, and are undertaking the job of assisting many others reach the same understanding. It is not an easy task, for they are beset by both materialists and religionists to disavow their awareness of their own ever present Individualized Divinity. However, there are events, which are already foreshadowed, that will help bring a rapid extension of the awareness of the actual process of Creation. Neither the ultra-religious nor scientific materialism can now prevent the evolution of Consciousness Expression.

Conscious Awareness is inevitable. For many thousands of years we 'humans' have been living quite happily within a parenthesis, mostly side by side with ultra-religious superstition and/or a scientific materialism. These but represent two degrees of a circle that has another three hundred and fifty-eight degrees, of which most of the members of these two groups appear to be ignorant.

Why limit ourselves to two parentheses, however wide the arc on the circle. When we focus on just one degree of the Circle of Life, we are focusing on being merely human. Let us increase it by making a decision here and now that from this day on we will remember, each day, to focus *our attention* on our own ever present Individualized Divinity, and thereby expand the range of our awareness of who we really are *at all times*. When we remember who we are, we find ourselves becoming more effective in our chosen activity. This activity may be small or it may be large; it may be of great import or it may be very, very ordinary, but it never becomes meaningless, because it is always an action of Creative Consciousness.

All of us have spent endless hours seeking our Soul-mate, but in actual fact, the Soul-mate we have sought is none other than our own Divine-Self. Every time we look out towards our environment and see another person, we are looking at a Soul-mate, because they too share the same Divinity in Expression. All actions are an Expression of Divinity. All words are an Expression of Divinity. All thoughts are an Expression of Divinity.

No matter how often we forget about our Individualized Divinity, it does not limit or affect the final outcome of our spiritual unfoldment. We never fall back, we simply delay our forward movement.

We are always in the folds of Divine Consciousness. Let us climb the mountain together, since we know we can get there from here.

OMEGA

Christopher Phelan, M.A., D.D.

Born in Dublin, Eire, Christopher Phelan was a lecturer, counselor and spiritual pathfinder in England for many years, where he established a reputation as an authority on all aspects of metaphysics. He came to America in 1962, where he conducted classes, workshops and seminars on all aspects of metaphysics in many major cities, as well as appearing on television and radio. He later became associated with the Universal Mind Science Church and was ordained as a minister there in the early 1970s. Until his death in 2004, as well as continuing his classes in many facets of mind expansion and unfoldment, and in the spiritual and metaphysical interpretation of the Bible (which he regarded as a "work manual"), he went on helping all those who sought his counsel.

www.ingramcontent.com/pod-product-compliance
Lightning Source LLC
Chambersburg PA
CBHW020737160426
43192CB00006B/224